The Graded School.

A GRADED

COURSE OF INSTRUCTION

FOR PUBLIC SCHOOLS:

WITH

COPIOUS PRACTICAL DIRECTIONS TO TEACHERS,

AND

OBSERVATIONS ON PRIMARY SCHOOLS, SCHOOL DISCIPLINE, SCHOOL RECORDS, ETC.

BY W. H. WELLS, A.M.,

SUPERINTENDENT OF PUBLIC SCHOOLS, CHICAGO, AND LATE PRINCIPAL OF THE STATE NORMAL SCHOOL, WESTFIELD, MASS.

A. S. BARNES & COMPANY,

NEW YORK AND CHICAGO.

1877.

PREFACE.

THE Graded Course of study here presented, is substantially the Course adopted in the Public Schools of Chicago. It is believed to combine the best elements of the different systems adopted in Boston, New York, Philadelphia, Cincinnati, St. Louis, and other cities.

Most of the Directions which accompany the Course have been suggested by the author's diary of visits to the schools of Chicago and other cities; and they are designed to supply the deficiencies most frequently observed in schools, and to correct the most common faults.

The kind reception of the author's Seventh Annual Report, which embraced a large portion of the Course here presented, and the success of the system in the schools of Chicago, have induced the belief that the same Graded Course and accompanying Directions may prove acceptable to teachers in the present revised form.

For a more full elucidation of the special features of the Course, the reader is referred to the Introduction.

Several brief articles on Discipline, Records, and other topics, are appended to the Course, in the hope that they may add somewhat to its value.

W. H. W.

CHICAGO, July, 1862.

CONTENTS.

INTRODUCTION.

A GRADED SCHOOL is a school in which the pupils are divided into classes according to their attainments, and in which all the pupils of each class attend to the same branches of study at the same time.*

Number and Division of Grades.—In all cities and large towns, there are numerous transfers from one public school to another. As pupils from different schools are thus brought together, it is often found that those who are equally advanced in one

---

* "All the pupils in any one class attend to precisely the same studies and use the same books. In each room there will be a first and a second class, and it is important that the identical pupils which constitute the first class in one branch should constitute the first class in every branch pursued by the class. By this arrangement, while one class is reciting, the other is preparing for recitation, and an alternating process is kept up through the day, affording the pupils ample time to study their lessons, and the teacher ample time to instruct each class. . . . . This is what is meant by a graded and classified school."—*Ira Divoll, Superintendent of Schools, St. Louis.*

"The due classification and grading of the schools is but the application to the educational cause of the same division of labor that prevails in all well-regulated business establishments, whether mechanical, commercial, or otherwise. It is not only the most economical, but without it there can be little progress or prosperity."—*H. C. Hickok, late Superintendent of Public Instruction of Pennsylvania.*

branch of study are very unequally advanced in other branches. This creates constant confusion and inconvenience in the classification. Hence the importance of some uniform system of gradation in all the schools of a city or town.

It is obviously unreasonable to expect one school to make the same progress, in all cases, as another more favorably situated; but it is not impracticable so to arrange the course of study, that there may be certain stand-points in it, at which the pupils shall be required to reach a given standard of attainment in all the parallel branches, and from which no one shall be allowed to advance in one branch before all the other branches are brought up to the same standard. At these particular points, it is plain that the pupils will be together in all the branches in all the schools; and if these points are made sufficiently numerous in the course, a pupil may pass from one school to any other in the city or town, at any time, and he will find some class equally advanced with himself in all the studies.

In classifying the pupils of cities and large towns, it has been found convenient to divide all that belong to the Grammar and Primary Schools into *ten grades*—four Grammar Grades and six Primary. In smaller towns a less number of grades will be found more convenient.

In order to give efficiency and value to a graded course of study, it is important that the divisions between the successive grades should be plainly and sharply defined. Special cases may sometimes occur, in which it will be necessary for a time to relax the stringency of this rule; but these cases should be made as few and brief as possible.*

In the course herewith presented, the number of pages or chapters belonging appropriately to each grade, can not be given with exactness, since the text-books adopted in different cities and towns do not always correspond, either in the number of volumes or in the extent to which the subjects are carried. The divisions of the several branches in the present course, are made as definite as the circumstances will allow. They are the result of systematic experiments extending over a period of several years, together with a careful study of the classification adopted in a large number of cities and towns.

No pupil should be advanced from one grade to another, till he has first sustained a thorough and satisfactory test-examination on all the branches of the grade from which he is to be transferred. These examinations by the Superintendent or Principal, at frequent and regular periods, comparing the attainments of each grade with a fixed and known standard, will try every teacher's work, and award to the most deserving the credit which justly belongs to them.

General Directions accompanying the Graded

---

* "Other things being equal, the closer the classification the better the school system."—*H. F. Cowdery, Superintendent of Schools, Sandusky, Ohio.*

"The advantages of the union school arise chiefly from the grading. The more perfect, therefore, the grading, the more certain and marked will be the success of these schools."—*J. M. Gregory, State Superintendent of Schools, Michigan.*

Course.—Of the large body of teachers engaged in public schools, many of whom are inexperienced, and all of whom are controlled, in a greater or less degree, by habits formed under a variety of different influences, it is not to be expected that all will reach the same standard of excellence, nor is it desirable that all should attempt to reach this standard in precisely the same way. The individuality of each teacher must be preserved, and his originality and invention should be constantly tasked. There are, however, certain principles which belong to every good system of instruction, and the teacher who claims the privilege of rejecting these because he thinks he can teach better in some other way, is an unworthy member of the profession.

Public-school teachers are as faithful and progressive as any class of persons in the community, and yet cases will constantly occur in every city and town, in which suggestions repeatedly given by School Directors and Superintendents, are repeatedly forgotten. The power of habit is strong, and will, in many cases, reassert its claims even against the best intentions to resist it; and there are always some whose sympathies are not fully enlisted in their work, and who need to be admonished by a uniform standard of duty, kept always before them.

In preparing these directions and observations, the mere correction of errors has not been my highest object. I would fain hope that they may be the means of aiding all classes of teachers in their efforts to introduce improvements and advance the standard of excellence in their modes of instruction. I have taken special care to give no directions that will check the enterprise of progressive teachers, and I believe that no one will be found to act *against* any thing except positive errors and inferior methods of instruction.

On the various and somewhat numerous points to which these suggestions relate, they are offered as a substitute for a constant visit from Superintendents and School Directors.

Practicalness in Teaching—Oral Instruction.—The regular course of school studies, in most cities and towns, is already sufficiently extended, and yet it is notorious that pupils leave the public schools lamentably deficient on a great variety of subjects connected with a sound practical education.

It is found impracticable to introduce the study of physiology in the Grammar Divisions, with an additional text-book and a course of daily recitations; and so most of the pupils complete their course without any knowledge of the important functions of the lungs and heart, and the general laws of health. We can not add the study of mineralogy and geology to the course; and pupils go out from the schools without any satisfactory knowledge of the materials employed in constructing the flag-stones on which they walk. We can not introduce natural philosophy; and most pupils leave without any definite knowledge of the principle involved in rowing a boat, or even in floating it. We can not add chemistry; and pupils leave without being able to explain the rising of a loaf of bread, or the burning of a common fire.

And yet, a careful study of the philosophy of education will show, that the schools are all this time suffering for the want of the relaxation which would be afforded by a systematic course of oral instruction, exactly suited to supply these important deficiencies.*

A series of oral lessons, occupying fifteen minutes a day, and continued through the entire course of the Grammar Department, would be sufficient to embrace a wide range of practical exercises in common philosophy, and common things. Such a course of lessons would introduce an agreeable variety, without interfering with the successful prosecution of the other branches. If called up at the right

* "Nor need any one fear that the use of object lessons will diminish the amount of book-learning that will be acquired by the pupils. On the contrary, experience proves that the little child will learn to read faster and better, under a course of instruction such as proposed, while the older pupils will go forward with more intelligence and ease, when the theoretical statements of the text-books are prepared for and illustrated by the plain facts of sense. All teaching in our schools would gain both in vividness and value if a more frequent appeal were made from the facts as stated in books to the facts as they are exhibited in the world without. . . . . Our knowledge of the nature and uses of common things and our skill in common affairs—that knowledge and skill which constitute the implements of our daily work and influence—are obtained not from books, but from the action of our senses and the exercise of our individual powers."—*J. M. Gregory, Superintendent of Public Instruction, Michigan.*

"Oral training lessons, in natural science and the arts, are found to be not merely a highly intellectual exercise, but are valuable to persons in every rank of society. . . . . Children of both sexes should be exercised daily on some point of science or the arts, particularly in relation to ordinary life and common things."—*David Stow, Founder of Glasgow Normal Training Seminary.*

time, it would infuse new life and vigor in the classes, and prepare them to do more in the time that remains, than they would otherwise accomplish even with the additional fifteen minutes.

In many cities and towns, considerable attention is already given to *object lessons* and other conversational exercises, *in the Primary Divisions.* In some schools these elementary object lessons are admirable, and could hardly be improved;* but it is probably true that in a majority of cases, where object teaching is introduced, the teachers do not attempt any thing like a systematic and progressive course of lessons, while many teachers conduct these exercises without any definite object in view.

Instruction by *object lessons* is a method comparatively new in this country, and many teachers do not know how to set themselves at work. The subjects are often selected in the upper grades without any regard to the topics already discussed in the grades below; and some teachers seem to think that they have given a satisfactory *object lesson*, when they have conducted a free conversation on some common subject, even though the children may not have gained one new idea of the properties and relations of objects, nor learned the use of a single new word.

In the course of instruction herewith presented, I

* In Oswego, N. Y., the Pestalozzian system of object teaching is fully and successfully introduced in all the Primary Schools. The system herewith presented was adopted in the Chicago schools in March, 1861. Many of the principal features of the course were adopted as early as 1857.

have endeavored to digest a pretty full outline of a systematic and progressive oral course, embracing object teaching, moral lessons, and other conversational exercises, and extending through all the Grammar and Primary Grades.* It has been a leading object with me to supply in this oral course the lack of *practicalness* to which I have already alluded Though necessarily confined to the limits of a mere syllabus, and not designed to relieve teachers from the labor of making special preparation for the daily lessons,† I trust it will be found sufficiently full to guide even inexperienced teachers in the selection and arrangement of topics, and in the general method of treating them. References are made to some of the principal sources of information on the various subjects introduced, and other sources will occur to teachers as they have occasion to employ them.

---

* "Object lessons should not only be carried on after quite a different fashion from that commonly pursued, but should be extended to a range of things far wider, and continued to a period far later than now. They should be so kept up during youth, as insensibly to merge into the investigations of the naturalist and the man of science."—*Herbert Spencer*.

† "It will always be found true that whatever method saves the teacher from the burden of thinking, prevents the pupils from realizing the most valuable results of education,—correct habits of thought, and a well-disciplined mind."—*New York School Report.*

COURSE OF INSTRUCTION

FOR A GRADED SCHOOL,

EMBRACING THE

GRAMMAR AND PRIMARY DEPARTMENTS;

WITH

ACCOMPANYING DIRECTIONS TO TEACHERS.

NOTE.—The *Regular Course of Instruction* and the *Directions to Teachers* are preserved distinct from each other, in different sizes of type, and each is complete in itself. For convenience of reference, the directions are numbered consecutively through the course.

All the directions designed to be consulted with any grade, are either found in connection with the *regular course* for that grade, or they are referred to directly by numbers.

GENERAL DIRECTIONS FOR ALL THE GRADES.

§ 1. *Reading.*—Teachers should adhere rigidly to the rule, that no reading lesson is to be left till the pupils understand the meaning of every word contained in it, and are able to express that meaning in their own language. When definitions are given by the author, in connection with the lesson, the pupils should be required to give other definitions of their own, or modify those of the author, so as to satisfy the teacher that the real meaning is comprehended. It is highly important that pupils should not only understand the meaning of words when taken by themselves, but that they should also understand their meaning and use in connection with other words. For this purpose, they should often be required, after giving the definition of a word, to embody it in a short sentence. Even this exercise falls short of the highest end of intellectual reading. Pupils should often be called on to explain the import of phrases, and sentences, and even of whole paragraphs.* Explanations and illustrations should also be added by the teacher; but let it ever be borne in mind, that an explanation drawn from the scholar is of far more value to him than the same explanation furnished by others.

While examples are constantly occurring in which pupils do not read "with the understanding," there is also an opposite fault that is equally to be shunned. Some teachers seem to suppose that the principal object of a school exercise in reading, is to understand the meaning of the piece read. This is a mistake. The principal object is to read the piece so as to *express* that meaning. The sense of the piece must be studied then, not in this case as an *end*, but as a *means* to enable the pupil to execute the read-

* "From the moment that a child knows the powers of the letters, and readily associates with the written form the pronunciation which it represents, his attention should be directed to the ideas. His progress in the art of reading should be regulated by his intellectual progress. The power of reading different words should not anticipate his power of understanding them. The habit, early acquired, of associating the ideas with their written signs, will secure his acquisition of the art of reading, and make it a delightful occupation."—*Marcel.*

ing successfully. This being the case, it is obviously a great fault to spend half or three-fourths of the hour allotted to a reading lesson, in discussing the meaning of words and the general sense of the passages read.

While a class is engaged in reading, it should receive the undivided attention of the teacher. If the teacher is necessarily called away, by all means suspend the exercise. It is far better to omit a lesson altogether, than to leave the pupils to read by themselves.

The voice of the teacher should be frequently heard in every reading exercise, as an example for the scholars to imitate. It is by imitation that children learn to talk, and their skill and accuracy in reading will depend mainly upon the character of the models which are brought before them. A child may make a dozen trials in reading a sentence, and not only fail every time, but read it worse and worse, if he does not hear it read correctly by the teacher or by some member of the class.

The use of capitals and italics, marks of punctuation, quotation points, and all other marks employed in the reading lessons, should be learned as fast as examples present themselves.

Teachers should be particularly on their guard against adopting unsatisfactory modes of teaching this important branch, and allowing them to be confirmed into habit. In conducting classes over the same ground from term to term, and from year to year, some teachers lose their interest in the exercise, and fall unconsciously below their own previous standard. A good method must be secured by effort and retained by effort. Effort relaxed always leads to retrogression.

§ 2. *Spelling.*—In conducting oral exercises in spelling, pupils should pronounce each word distinctly before spelling it, and they should never be allowed to try twice on a word.* Whenever a pupil misses a word, let him afterward be required to spell it correctly. This may be done as soon as the correction is made in the class, or deferred till the close of the recitation.

In giving out the words to a class, teachers sometimes commit the error of departing from the ordinary pronunciation, for the sake of indicating the orthography. Thus in the word *variance*, the vowel in the second syllable is given very distinctly as long *i*, to show that the letter is *i* and not *e*. The words should in all cases be pronounced exactly as they are pronounced by a correct reader.†

As pupils are constantly liable to misunderstand the pronunciation of words, it is a very useful practice, in all written exercises, to call on some pupil in the class to repronounce each word distinctly, as soon as it is pronounced by the teacher.

* "One trial is better than a score of guesses, both to decide whether the pupil has mastered the lesson, and to insure its study in future."—*B. G. Northrop, Agent Massachusetts Board of Education.*

† "An undue emphasis, or prolongation of the utterance of a syllable, may enable the scholar to spell the word as pronounced, but will never make him an expert speller of words as properly spoken."—*Northend.*

Special attention should be given to syllabication, in connection with both written and oral spelling. In oral spelling, pupils should syllabicate in all cases, as in the following example: *a-m am*, *p-l-i pli*, *ampli*, *f-y fy*, *amplify*. In written spelling, it may not be necessary to syllabicate at every recitation; but in a portion of the exercises, even in written spelling, pupils should be required to divide the syllables, and failures should be marked as errors.*

Teachers should bear constantly in mind, that unless habits of correct spelling are formed early, there is very little probability that they will ever be acquired.

However thorough the drill in spelling may be, from the lessons of the speller and reader, every teacher should have frequent and copious exercises in spelling words from other sources. These should be words in common use, chosen as far as possible from the range of the pupil's observation, including the new words that arise in object lessons, and in geography, arithmetic, grammar, etc. The more difficult of these words should be written in columns on the blackboard, and studied and reviewed with the same care as lessons from the speller and reader. Failures in spelling these words should be marked with errors, the same as failures in any other lessons.

Teachers should put forth their best efforts, especially in primary classes, to secure the attention of

* "If this division of words into their proper syllables is to be learned by itself, it will be found an enormous labor; but if learned while spelling, it will hardly add any thing to that task."—*Mann.*

the pupils, and render the lessons as interesting as possible. Occasional exercises in "choosing sides," when properly conducted, may be made highly useful. The exercise of "spelling down" a class may also be resorted to occasionally with good effect.

If a teacher finds at any time, while conducting an oral exercise in spelling, that a portion of his class are becoming listless, he can easily recall their attention by the following simple measure: The whole class pronounce distinctly the word given by the teacher, as *notation;* then one scholar says *n;* the next *o;* the next pronounces the syllable *no;* the next says *t;* the next *a;* the next *ta;* the next *nota;* the next *t;* the next *i;* the next *o;* the next *n;* the next *tion;* then the whole class pronounce the word *notation.*

Another useful method is to read a sentence of reasonable length, and require the members of a class to spell the words in order; the first scholar spelling the first word, the next scholar the second, and so on to the end.*

§ 3. *Writing.*—Writing should be taught as a simultaneous class exercise, all the members of the class attending to the same thing at the same time.†

In conducting exercises in writing, teachers should

* For other directions respecting exercises in spelling, both written and oral, teachers are referred to Northend's Teacher's Assistant.

† The advantages of this system of teaching, over that in which different pupils of a class are allowed to write from different copies or in different books, at the same time, have been fully demonstrated in the schools of Boston, Chicago, and other cities

make constant use of the blackboard. Important letters and principles of the copy should be written on the board, both correctly and incorrectly, illustrating the excellences to be attained and the errors to be avoided. Teachers who are not accustomed to this mode of illustrating, will find that they can easily qualify themselves to introduce it.*

Many teachers who excel in imparting a knowledge of other branches, teach penmanship only indifferently well. Teachers who have little taste for this exercise should discipline themselves to increased effort. Even a poor writer may make a good teacher of penmanship; and no one who attempts to teach writing is excusable for not teaching it successfully.†

Exercises of special excellence should receive marks of special credit; and deficiencies resulting from carelessness or indifference, should in all cases receive marks of error and affect the scholarship averages as much as failures in any other lessons.

§ 4. *Concert Exercises.*—In all the lower grades of

Reference.—§ 4. Barnard's Object Teaching, Art. 13.

* "Where the best results were produced, the blackboard was in constant use, and a whole section of pupils wrote the same copy at the same time. In some divisions, the blackboard did not seem to be used at all in teaching this branch. Such a neglect shows a want of competency, or a want of faithfulness on the part of the teacher."—*Report of Boston School Committee.*

† "A bad handwriting ought never to be forgiven; it is shameful indolence; indeed, sending a badly-written letter to a fellow-creature is as impudent an act as I know of."—*Niebuhr.*

the Primary Department, brief concert exercises should be introduced, as often as once a day, in connection with reading, spelling by letters, spelling by sounds, arithmetical tables, etc.; but they should in no case occupy more time than the individual exercises. They are only means to an end; not the end itself. Their proper use is to aid in securing the success of individual efforts. Frequent concert exercises should also be introduced in connection with reading, in the upper divisions of the Primary Department, and in all the divisions of the Grammar Department.

Great care should be taken, in all concert exercises, to secure free and natural tones of voice. It is always better to dispense with exercises in concert, than to have them become a means of forming bad habits in modulation and inflection.

§ 5. *Rapid Combinations in Arithmetic.*—Classes in Arithmetic should have frequent extemporaneous exercises in combining series of numbers, involving the principles which they have gone over. These numbers should be given by the teacher, slowly at first, and afterward with more and more rapidity, as the pupils are able to carry forward the computations. The following is an example: Take 5, add 3, add 10, subtract 9, multiply by 8, add 20, add 8, subtract 40, divide by 10,—result? Those who are prepared to answer raise the hand, and the teacher calls on one or more of them individually, for the answer, or on all together. Exercises of this kind should be commenced as soon as pupils are able to add simple numbers together, and continued through the entire course. Similar examples may occasionally be carried rapidly round a class, each pupil giving in turn the result for one step of the process, with as little delay as possible.

§ 6. *Good Language. Composition.*—Teachers should be watchful on all occasions, and especially during recitations, to secure habits of readiness and precision in the use of language. Every question should receive a complete and grammatical answer. Teachers should be clear and accurate in their own expressions, and impress upon their pupils the importance of selecting at all times the best words and phrases, and forming the *habit* of using good language in early life. As fast as new words are learned in the various oral exercises, the children should be required to embody them in spoken or written sentences, and thus fasten their meaning and uses securely in the memory.*

Reference.—§ 6. Manual of Elementary Instruction, vol. 2, article, *Language.*

* "Great attention should be given to the language used in the school-room, both by teachers and pupils. It should be pure English, free from all provincialisms; and the construction of the sentences should be grammatical. It is of the utmost importance that the teachers of our Primary scholars should be accurate in the use of language; quick to notice, and prompt to correct all "bad grammar" heard in their school-rooms. No *slang*, no useless expletives, no unnecessary repetitions, no obsolete words, no violations of orthography or syntax, should, at *any time*, or under any circumstances, be allowed to pass without careful correction. The power of expression may be cultivated by "Object Lessons" and

Exercises in composition may be introduced in such a manner, that pupils will never regard them as irksome tasks. With proper care and skill on the part of the teacher, they may be made as interesting and attractive as any of the exercises of the school. The following are some of the first steps that may be taken to secure this object:

(1.) Let the pupil take his slate to a window during a recess, and write down any thing that he hears from the children in the play-ground. At the close of the recess, let him read before his class what he has written, and he will be interested to learn that the

---

conversation. Pupils should also be advised and required to write much. Recitations may sometimes be conducted by writing, and will be found mutually profitable. Questions should be pointed and precise; answers should be concise and exact. Every answer should embrace a complete proposition. Frequently the pupil gives the answer only in part. Every exercise, and every recitation should be so conducted as to habituate the scholars to correct, terse, and elegant modes of expression. All indistinctness of utterance, all clipping of words, all hesitancy of speech, should at once be noticed and the proper remedies faithfully applied."—*J. G. McMynn.*

"*Conversational Lessons.*—One great object in early education should be to awaken the mind of children to activity, and to furnish them with language. Conversational lessons are well calculated to effect these objects, inasmuch as they accustom children to speak of things they daily see and use; leading them to make their own observations upon such things, and in their turn to ask for further information.

"These lessons are of course conducted without any formality, and do not require any particular hints. The subjects chosen are very simple, and the teacher ought to be quite easy and familiar, letting the children take the lead; merely stimulating them by judicious questioning."—*Manual of Elementary Instruction.*

sentences from the different scholars are so many little compositions. He will then understand, that every time he speaks a sentence, he makes a composition, and if he will only write it on his slate or on paper, it will be a written composition.

(2.) Select a common and familiar subject, as a horse, and ask the pupil various questions respecting it. As he gives his answers, let him write them down on his slate. He will soon find that he has written an original composition, almost without effort.

(3.) At the close of an object lesson on any familiar subject, let the pupils write or print on their slates every thing they can remember of the description that has been given, and read their exercises in turn before the class.

These different exercises should be examined carefully by the teacher, and the errors that occur in language, orthography, punctuation, etc., should be kindly pointed out and corrected before the class. The pupils should then be required to rewrite their exercises correctly.

The establishment of a school paper, sustained by the pupils, under the general direction of the teacher, is one of the best means of cultivating this important art.

§ 7. *Morals and Manners.*—Love to parents and others, friendship, kindness, gentleness, obedience,

---

References.—§ 7. Calkins's Object Lessons; Cowdery's Moral Lessons, and Cowdery's Primary Moral Lessons; Barnard's Object Teaching, arts. 7, 9, and 12; Hooker's Natural History, chap. 36; Willson's Third Reader; Barnard's Journal of Edu-

honesty, truthfulness, generosity, self-denial, neatness, diligence, etc., are cultivated in children, not so much by direct exhortation and formal precept, as by resorting to expedients that will call these affections and qualities into active exercise. Lead a child to do a kind act, and you will increase his kindness of heart; and this is the best of all lessons on kindness. Let teachers ever remember that the *exercise of virtuous principles, confirmed into habit*, is the true means of establishing a virtuous character.

Little anecdotes and familiar examples, illustrating the love of brothers and sisters, the respect due to the aged, kindness to animals, mutual love of companions and associates, benevolence, etc., are among the best means of cultivating these virtues. Such a work as "Cowdery's Moral Lessons," teaching mainly by examples, will accomplish far more than the same principles when abstracted from the narratives in which they are found, and embodied in a formal catechism of moral instruction.*

Teachers should frequently read to their divisions short, entertaining narratives, and make them the subjects of familiar and instructive conversations with their pupils. So also in lessons on animals, trees, and all the works of nature, opportunities should be constantly improved to show the wisdom,

cation, vol. 1, art. 10; Dwight's Higher Christian Education Hall's Manual of Morals; Mayhew's Popular Education, chap. 8

* "Nature, reason, and experience proclaim this order, *example before precept*."—*Marcel*.

power, and goodness of the Creator, and to inculcate the reverence that is due to Him, and a sense of dependence upon Him.

Every case of quarreling, cruelty, fraud, profanity, and vulgarity, should be made to appear in its true light. The selfishness of children is the greatest obstacle to moral training. To moderate this strong instinct, to teach self-denial and self-control, must be the constant care of the teacher.

There is no time when the watchfulness of the teacher is more necessary than during the recesses and other hours of relaxation at school. This is the time when little differences are most likely to spring up, and bad passions to gain the ascendency. No parent's eye is upon the children, and yet they should constantly feel that some kind guardian is near—not to check their cheerful sports, but to encourage every kind and noble act, and to rebuke every departure from the path of virtue and honor.*

* "Let the play-grounds never be left without the supervision of a teacher when the pupils are there. To accomplish this, they should not be opened to pupils till a fixed hour, when the teacher should be present. If the recesses, also, be given to both sexes at once, the teacher may go with his pupils on to the play-ground, and while he encourages the cheerful hilarity of the games, his presence will hold in awe the quarrelsome spirits or profane lips, which will otherwise work so much evil. It is the unwatched and unrestrained association of the pupils, good and bad, upon the play-ground, that forms one of the most fruitful sources of moral corruption. Remove this, and we have abated, at one blow, more than one half of the dangers that attend our schools."—*J. M. Gregory, State Superintendent of Public Instruction, Michigan.*

See also Young's Teachers' Manual.

Good morals are intimately connected with *good manners*, and teachers should improve every opportunity to inculcate lessons of civility and courtesy. In the Primary divisions, especially, the teachers should give frequent and somewhat minute directions respecting the ordinary rules of politeness. Let the pupils be taught that when a question is asked them, it shows a lack of good breeding to remain silent or shake the head, even if they are not able to answer it. They should receive some general directions respecting the manners of younger persons in the presence of those who are older. They should be taught that well-bred persons seldom laugh at mistakes, etc. The manners of the children in their intercourse with each other before and after school, and at the recesses, and in going to and from school, should receive the constant and watchful care of the teacher.

§ 8. *Oral Exercises.*—The oral lessons of the course are not intended to be exhaustive and complete; but they present a pretty full outline of most of the exercises that should be introduced. This outline should be filled out, and, in most cases, extended by the teachers; but none of the subjects introduced should be omitted.

"In every exercise, it is of the highest importance that there should be some definite aim and purpose,

---

References.—§ 8. Calkins's Object Lessons, pp. 291–348; Barnard's Object Teaching, arts. 2 and 12; Hailman's Object Teaching.

and that the teacher should work with reference to obtaining certain results."*

The oral lessons of the Grammar divisions are designed to occupy an amount of time equal to about fifteen minutes a day. This will be found more than sufficient to present all the topics introduced.

An outline of each oral exercise should be written out and preserved for review. This may be done by the teacher on the blackboard, or by the pupils on slates or paper, as the exercise progresses; or the pupils may be required to write it out from memory immediately after the close of the lesson.

§ 9. *Reviews and Abstracts.*—The time devoted to reviews, both oral and written, should be very much increased.†

Each lesson should be made, to some extent, a review of the previous lesson, without, however, consuming very much time, except in cases in which the previous recitation has been unsatisfactory. Pupils should understand that they are liable to be called on to recite any portion of the previous lesson,

---

* "Oswego Report."

"The order in which the various impressions of objects and other facts connected with them should be considered, depends, to a great extent, on the knowledge which the pupil has already of the object.

"The following are the principal facts to be considered, though not always in the order given, in the various objects: 1. *Name;* 2. *Place;* 3. *Touch, Sound, Odor, Taste;* 4. *Color;* 5. *Shape;* 6. *Size;* 7. *Material, Uses,* etc."—*Hailman's Object Teaching.*

† "The great secret of being successful and accurate as a student, next to perseverance, is the constant habit of reviewing."—*Todd's Student's Manual.*

and questions enough should be asked in review to make it necessary for them to read over the last lesson before coming to the recitation, unless their previous preparation has been sufficient to fasten it in the memory.

The oral lessons should, in most cases, be reviewed more than once, and in all cases till they are thoroughly learned and remembered.

In most of the studies in which the recitations occur daily, one lesson of each week should be a review of the four preceding lessons. Classes reciting only two or three times a week may have a review every second week; and there may be a few exceptional cases in which it will be best to have these reviews only once a month.*

In the Primary divisions, the reviews will necessarily be oral; but in the Grammar divisions they should be both oral and written. In the 1st, 2d, and 3d grades, most of the classes should have at least one written review in a month, besides the oral reviews.

It may be well, occasionally, to devote an hour to a written review of all the different branches, in one exercise, selecting ten or more questions promiscuously from all the studies of the class.

In the five upper grades, all the classes should have occasional exercises in writing a few lines of

* "The regulation recently adopted by the Board, requiring a weekly review of every class by its teacher, without the use of books, can not fail to accomplish much good, and encourage a more intelligent system of teaching."—*New York Report.*

prose or verse, dictated orally by the teacher, as a test of their proficiency in spelling, punctuation, use of capitals, penmanship, etc. In the 4th and 5th grades, the pupils may use either pen or pencil, at the discretion of the teacher; but in the 1st, 2d, and 3d grades they should be required in all cases to use a pen. These exercises should be strictly extemporaneous, and every paper should be passed to the desk at the close of a specified time.

In conducting written reviews, great care should be taken to remove from the pupils, so far as possible, all temptation to seek assistance from books, or papers, or classmates. When two pupils of the class are seated at the same desk, it is often desirable to have two sets of questions of about equal difficulty —one set for all the pupils sitting at one end of the desks, and one for those sitting at the other end.

Written reviews are among the most successful means that can be employed for securing thoroughness and accuracy of scholarship. They afford a reliable test of the pupil's knowledge of the subject, cultivate habits of freedom and accuracy in the use of language, and afford a valuable discipline to the mind, by throwing the pupil entirely upon his own resources.

In addition to the written reviews, teachers of the higher divisions should require frequent written exercises in connection with the daily recitations in history, grammar, arithmetic, etc.

All written reviews, abstracts, etc., should pass under the critical examination of the teacher; the important errors should be corrected; and pupils presenting papers carelessly written, should be required to rewrite them.

§ 10. *Number of Classes in a Division.*—As a general rule, the pupils assigned to each teacher in the Grammar Department, should be divided into two classes; in the 5th, 6th, 7th, and 8th grades, into three classes; and in the 9th and 10th grades, into four.

The number of pupils in a division, or other circumstances, may make it desirable, in certain cases, to depart from this arrangement.

It is desirable that each class in the Grammar Department should not number more than 20 or 25 pupils, and each class in the lower grades not more than 10 or 15 pupils; but this arrangement is impracticable where a division numbers more than 40 or 50 pupils.*

§ 11. *Number of Branches to be pursued at a time.*—It requires the constant watchfulness of teachers to prevent pupils from undertaking too many branches of study at a time. Pupils should rarely be allowed to study more than three branches at once, besides reading, spelling, and writing; and it is generally better to have some of the lessons come only on alternate days than to have even the six exercises in one day.

* "In a large class, each of whom seldom, and at best only for a short time, receives individually any attention from the teacher, the progress is slow, the faculties little developed, and the education altogether very imperfect."—*Reid's Principles of Education.*

§ 12. *Order of Exercises and Length of Recitations.*—Every teacher should have posted up in the room an established order of exercises for each day in the week, assigning a definite time for the beginning and ending of every exercise, and of every interval between the exercises.

It is impracticable to establish a uniform rule respecting the frequency and length of recitations. The following scale will serve as a general guide to teachers in this matter:

Recitations in the Grammar Department from twenty-five to forty minutes in length, except exercises in spelling, which may usually be completed in fifteen to twenty-five minutes; in the 5th, 6th, and 7th grades, from twenty to twenty-five minutes; in the 8th and 9th grades, from fifteen to twenty minutes; and in the 10th grade, from ten to fifteen minutes.*

* "From four to five lessons a day for a Primary school, is better than six, even for mental proficiency. A Primary school that has even five hours of session per day should have an hour or more of interval at midday. Besides, there should be one or two recesses during each session. The exercises of the school should be so arranged as to give a change of position and subject as often as every fifteen or twenty minutes. No child will give sufficient attention to derive much benefit from a lesson that continues more than twenty minutes. Five and ten minute lessons, on some subjects, are better than longer ones. Lessons occupying different senses should follow each other, as the change affords relief to the mind." —*N. A. Calkins.*

The following is the programme of exercises for two days of the week, in one of the Primary schools of Oswego, N. Y. It includes only the pupils of a single teacher, in the upper Primary grades,

§ 13. *Frequency of Recitations.*—The following arrangement will serve as a general guide, but cases may sometimes arise in which it will be necessary to depart from it: Reading Classes in the 1st grade, two or three times a week; in the 2d and 3d grades, three

---

and is introduced here to show the minuteness of detail, the range of topics, and the arrangement and distribution of time and subjects, that have been adopted in a city that is distinguished for the excellence of its school system:

MONDAY.

8.30 to 8.45—Opening Exercises.
8.45 to 8.55—Moral Instruction.
8.55 to 9.15—Reading, B, subd. 1.
9.15 to 9.20—Gymnastics.
9.20 to 9.35—Lessons on Number, B, subd. 2.
9.35 to 9.45—Recess.
9.45 to 10.00—Lesson on Place, A class.
10.00 to 10.25—Reading, B, subd. 2.
10.25 to 10.30—Gymnastics.
10.30 to 10.50—Lesson on Number, B, subd. 1.
10.50 to 11.00—Recess.
11.00 to 11.20—Reading, A class.
11.20 to 11.40—Writing on slates, B, subd. 1.
11.40 to 12.00—Lesson on Number, A class.
12.00 to 2.00—Intermission.
2.00 to 2.20—Lesson on Number, A class.
2.20 to 2.30—Lesson on Animals, A and B.
2.30 to 2.35—Gymnastics.
2.35 to 2.55—Reading, B, subd. 2.
2.55 to 3.10—Lesson on Number, B, subd. 1.
3.10 to 3.15—Calling Roll.
3.15 to 3.30—Recess.
3.30 to 3.45—Spelling, A class.
3.45 to 4.10—Reading, B, subd. 1.
4.10 to 4.30—Reading, A class.
4.30—Dismission.

or four times; 4th grade, four or five times; 5th and 6th grades, five to eight times; 7th and 8th grades, eight to ten times.

Slate arithmetic, three or four times a week; mental arithmetic, in 4th and 5th grades, four or five times a week; in 3d grade, three or four times; in 2d grade, two or three times. Numbers, in five lowest grades, five times a week.

TUESDAY.

8.30 to 8.45—Opening Exercises.

8.45 to 9.00—Lesson on Form, B, subd. 2.

9.00 to 9.15—Lesson on Weight, B, subd. 1.

9.15 to 9.20—Gymnastics.

9.20 to 9.35—Spelling, A class.

9.35 to 9.45—Recess.

9.45 to 10.10—Reading, B, subd. 2.

10.10 to 10.20—Drawing, B, subd. 1.

10.20 to 10.25—Gymnastics.

10.25 to 10.50—Lesson on Number, B, subd. 1.

10.50 to 11.00—Recess.

11.00 to 11.15—Lesson on Objects, A class.

11.15 to 11.35—Reading, B, subd. 1.

11.35 to 12.00—Lesson on Number, A class.

12.00 to 2.00—Intermission.

2.00 to 2.15—Lesson on Number, B, subd. 2.

2.15 to 2.30—Drawing, A class.

2.30 to 2.35—Gymnastics.

2.35 to 2.55—Reading, B, subd. 1.

2.55 to 3.10—Lesson on Weight, B, subd. 2.

3.10 to 3.15—Calling Roll.

3.15 to 3.30—Recess.

3.30 to 3.45—Lesson on Number, A class.

3.45 to 4.00—Lesson on Form, B, subd. 1.

4.00 to 4.10—Spelling, A class.

4.10 to 4.30—Lesson on Number, B, subd. 1.

4.30—Dismission.

Geography, from three to five times a week.

History, three or four times a week.

Grammar from three to five times a week.

Spelling, in 1st grade, two or three times a week; 2d and 3d grades, three or four times; 4th grade, four or five times; all grades below the 4th, eight to ten times.

Writing, in the Grammar divisions, two or three times a week; in the 5th and 6th grades, four or five times. See § 14.

§ 14. *Division of Time and Labor.*—In deciding what proportion of time should be given to spelling by letters, what to spelling by sounds, to reading, to numbers, to geography, etc., the rule should be this: whenever a class is less advanced in one branch assigned to the division than in other branches, let that particular branch receive special attention till it is as familiar as the others. It is very common to find a class more advanced in reading than in numbers, and still devoting less attention to arithmetic than to reading; the observance of this rule will correct all such errors.

§ 15. *Rhetorical Exercises.*—The first five grades should devote about one hour every Friday afternoon, to exercises in composition, declamation and recitation, and reading select pieces. The same course may be adopted in the other divisions, when the convenience of rooms and other circumstances permit.

In the 1st and 2d grades, every pupil should be required to take a part in both the elocutionary and the composition exercises, as often as once a month. When pupils have important written abstracts or other similar exercises to prepare, these may in certain cases be accepted as equivalents for the regular compositions. There may also be instances in which it will be best to accept the reading of a piece of poetry or other selection, as an equivalent for a declamation or recitation; but in all ordinary cases it is better even for the girls to commit to memory the pieces which they recite.*

* "*The Recital.*—Akin to the debate, we have introduced another exercise which, for want of a better name, is termed the RECITAL. The primary object is to cultivate the power of clothing thought in appropriate language, and of presenting it in an easy, colloquial style, to a company of listeners. The pupil may select for a topic any thing that will require a description. It may be an event in history, a brief biographical sketch, the relation of current events, or a good story. The subject-matter for a *Recital* may be obtained, after reading a book, by forming a synoptical outline of the same, detailing the more interesting portions with a proper degree of minuteness. Among the topics which have been thus presented, are the following: 'SIR JOHN FRANKLIN,' in which was given a brief sketch of his life, explorations, loss, expeditions sent in search of him, and the discovery of his remains; 'Account of Lady Esther Stanhope,' 'Grace Darling,' 'The Sack of Rome,' 'Aaron Burr,' etc.

"The exercise is equally adapted to both sexes. While it furnishes many of the advantages of the debate, it affords others of equal value. It accustoms the pupil to comprehend, with promptness and ease, the substance of a volume or subject; induces concentration of thought; cultivates memory; encourages the habit of investigation; affords practice in the use of language; stores the mind with useful information; forms the habit of noticing important facts and events, and imparts the power of presenting information to others with facility and in an agreeable manner.

"The exercise greatly increases the interest of our 'general ex-

§ 16. *Mental Discipline.*—The highest ultimate object of intellectual education, is mental discipline, and this discipline can only be acquired by mental labor. Cases are constantly occurring in which pupils require explanation and assistance, and unless they receive this aid they will be greatly retarded in their progress. But examples are also frequently arising in which teachers give assistance that is not required, and thus rob the pupils of the discipline which they would gain by overcoming the difficulties themselves. Teachers should study carefully the capabilities of their pupils, and never do for them what they are able to do without assistance. Pupils should also be guarded against the dangerous habit of assisting one another, without the knowledge and approval of the teacher.

It is one of the most important duties of the teacher, to exercise a watchful care over the pupils' hours and habits of study. Some pupils never learn to study a lesson abstractedly and with the whole mind; and some teachers have heretofore been so unfortunate as not to know that they have any special responsibility in this matter.

The power of attention is essential to the successful prosecution of study at every stage of prog-

Reference.—§ 16. Watts on the Mind.

ercises,' stimulates the minds of the school to more elevated modes of thought and conversation, and induces a higher and more profitable course of reading."—*A. Parish, Principal of High School, Springfield, Mass.*

ress, and the best efforts of teachers should be directed to the cultivation of this great educational power.*

TENTH GRADE.

[PRIMARY DEPARTMENT.]

REGULAR COURSE.

Oral instruction, embracing lessons on common things; on form, color, flowers, animals, morals and manners. Two or more lessons a day, each from five to eight minutes long.

Repeating verses and maxims, singly and in concert.

Reading from blackboard and from charts, with exercises in spelling, both by letters and by sounds. Two or more lessons a day.

Counting, from one to sixty. Simple exercises in adding, with use of numeral frame, pebbles, beans, etc.

Drawing on the slate, imitating letters, figures, and other objects from blackboard sketches by the teacher, tablets, cards, and other copies. Printing the reading and spelling lessons, and the numerals as far as learned. Two or more exercises a day. [All the pupils should be provided with slates and pencils.]

Physical exercises as often as once every half hour; each exercise from three to five minutes. See § 105.

The recitations in this grade should never exceed twenty minutes in length. In ordinary lessons, fifteen minutes will be time enough, and in some lessons ten minutes.

* "The surest way to succeed in cultivating and improving the other intellectual powers, is to acquire a command over attention, and to give it a useful direction."—*Marcel.*

"I was told by the Queen's Inspector of the Schools in Scotland, that the first test of a teacher's qualification is, his power to excite and to sustain the attention of his class. If a teacher can not do this, he is pronounced, without further inquiry, incompetent to teach."—*Mann.*

DIRECTIONS.

§ 17. *Oral Instruction.*—The period embraced in the tenth grade should be regarded as a bridge from the freedom of home-life to the more regular discipline of the school-room.* The first lessons should be simple conversational exercises upon home objects, with which the children are already familiar, and in which they feel the greatest interest,—their toys, their plays, their friends, etc.

In all the object lessons given in the 9th and 10th grades, the teacher should bear in mind that the prominent objects to be accomplished are, to cultivate habits of observation, improve the perceptive faculties, and secure habits of accuracy in the use of language. See § 8.

§ 18. In conducting conversational exercises in all the grades, teachers should be careful not to aid the pupils so much as to check their curiosity and deprive them of the opportunity to discover and investigate the properties of objects for themselves.†

References.—§ 17. Calkins's Object Lessons, pp. 11–40; Welch's Object Lessons, first 90 pages.

* "As in the transplanting of the tree from the nursery to the orchard, its continued life and unchecked growth demand that there should be as little change of circumstances, as to climate, soil, and position, as possible, so in the transfer of the child from the nursery to the school-room, he should be led to feel the change as little as possible."—*Report of Board of Education, Oswego, N. Y.*

† "The process of self-development should be encouraged to the fullest extent. Children should be led to make their own investi-

§ 19. *Form.*—The first exercises may be devoted to straight lines, comparing short lines with long ones, and selecting the straight lines from the letters of the alphabet and other figures. Illustrate with slate and blackboard exercises. Adopt a similar course with curved lines, and continue the slate exercises. Simple plane figures may also be introduced, as the square, the circle, the triangle.

§ 20. *Color.*—With the help of a box of paints, the teacher can easily prepare a set of cards, each bearing a separate shade of color. Let the children be exercised in selecting particular shades of color. Next let them distinguish the colors in articles of dress, books, furniture of the room, etc. After this, they can exercise their memory in naming a variety of colors and shades of color that belong to objects not present. This will cultivate accuracy and precision in the use of language, and prepare them for

References.—§ 19. Welch's Object Lessons; Calkins's Object Lessons; Barnard's Object Teaching, arts. 9 and 12; Hill's First Lessons in Geometry.

§ 20. Manual of Elementary Instruction, vol. 1; Calkins's Object Lessons; Welch's Object Lessons; Barnard's Object Teaching, arts. 9 and 12; Parker & Watson's Second Reader, lesson 65; Science of Common Things, index; Reason Why, index.

gations, and to draw their own inferences. They should be *told* as little as possible, and induced to *discover* as much as possible. Humanity has progressed solely by self-instruction; and that to achieve the best results each mind must progress somewhat after the same fashion, is continually proved by the marked success of self-made men."—*Herbert Spencer*.

useful exercises in describing objects. · Children should also be encouraged to bring to the school various articles representing as many different shades of color as they can find.

§ 21. *Flowers.*—Flowers are among the first ob jects that attract the special attention of children and they furnish desirable subjects for some of the earliest object lessons of the school-room. The pupils should be encouraged to bring flowers to school, and exercised in distinguishing their names, colors, forms, etc., but all the lessons in this grade should be strictly rudimental. Flowers afford some of the best illustrations of the different shades of color, and may be studied profitably in connection with the study of color.

§ 22. *Animals.*—Lessons on common domestic animals, as the horse, the cow, the dog, and the cat, are among the most entertaining and suitable exercises for pupils in this division. These lessons should be made very simple, extending only to the most familiar and obvious points, as form, color, size, speed, strength, food, covering, habits, uses, etc. The prominent object of these lessons should be to excite observation and cultivate feelings of humanity. Short anecdotes respecting the different

---

References.—§ 21. Child's Book of Nature, part 1; Manual of Elementary Instruction, vol. 2.

§ 22. Barnard's Object Teaching, art. 9; Willson's Third Reader; Carll's Child's Book of Natural History; Manual of Elementary Instruction, vol. 1. Also selected articles from the different school Readers.

animals should be presented by the teacher, and, when practicable, drawn from the pupils. Pictorial illustrations and outline sketches should be employed in connection with these exercises as far as practicable;* and the animals themselves should in some cases be brought to the school-room, if it can be done without materially interrupting the exercises.

Morals and Manners.—See § 7.

§ 23. *Verses, Maxims, etc.*—A few simple, easy verses, embodying moral sentiments or useful information, will help to furnish an agreeable variety in the exercises. The children may also be taught to repeat a few brief maxims and sentiments, as, "What is worth doing at all is worth doing well;" "It is better to suffer wrong than to do wrong;" "A place for every thing, and every thing in its place;" "Never leave till to-morrow what should be done to-day."

§ 24. *Reading and Spelling.*—The first lessons in reading and spelling should be taught from the blackboard. First, present an object to the class, as a hat, and have the pupils pronounce the word *hat.* They already understand that the word which they *hear* represents the object which they *see.* Other illustrations of *seeing* and *hearing*, as applied to the same object, may be introduced by the teacher, or drawn from the class.

References.—§ 23. Sanders's Third Reader, lesson 50; Parker & Watson's Third Reader, lesson 30; Chambers's Information for the People.

---

* See Manual of Elementary Instruction, vol. 1.

Next, print the name *hat* neatly on the black-board, and teach the class that the word which they *see* represents the same thing as the word which they *hear;* and that both represent the object which they see before them. The word should now be pronounced by the class individually and in concert, with their attention directed to the board, till each member is able to call the word at sight. Similar exercises, with other words, may be continued for several days; but no word should be introduced which the pupils can not be made to understand. Each new word placed upon the board, should be made the subject of familiar conversation, and, if practicable, of illustration, so that it may convey to the mind of the child a clear idea of the object represented.

As the spoken language consists of *sounds*, the teacher should now commence teaching the pupils to analyze these sounds and utter them separately. The words already learned should be employed for this purpose, so that the child may be required to learn only one new thing at a time.

As soon as the pupils have learned to analyze all the words they have gone over, they may next learn the *names of the letters*, using the same words as before.

After the class have learned in this way from five to ten words, so that all the children are able to call each word at sight, and spell it correctly, both by letters and by sounds, the teacher may introduce Primary Cards containing simple monosyllabic words and sentences. The teacher should continue to print simple exercises on the blackboard, as before, and use them in connection with the lessons on the cards. See also §§ 1 and 2.

§ 25. The pupils should now be required, at stated hours, to print every lesson neatly on their slates; and they should receive a mark of credit for every satisfactory effort. As often as once a day, they should be called on at recitation to read or spell a lesson from their slates.

§ 26. From this time forward, let it be regarded as essential to the completeness of every lesson that each scholar shall be able to define all the words introduced, and spell them both by letters and by sounds.* Teachers too often accept definitions that are exceedingly vague and defective, not to say erroneous. The construction of a simple sentence embodying a word, is often the most satisfactory definition of it that can be given by the young learner.† Let it also be regarded as a rule of paramount importance, that every lesson learned shall afterward be made the subject of frequent and thorough *reviews*, so that the pupils may not fail to retain what they have once acquired.

* "Each difficult word should be uttered clearly, first by its elements, and then by their combination."—*Wm. H. McGuffy.*

† "More attention should be given to defining than it now receives. The knowledge of the meaning of words possessed by most pupils in our schools, is exceedingly limited. It is by *using* words that we best learn their meaning; hence one of the first exercises in a well-conducted Primary school is forming sentences which shall embrace the words of the reading lesson."—*John G. McMynn.*

§ 27. An important direction to be observed from the commencement, is to give constant and special attention to *articulation*. There can be no good reading without correctness of articulation, and it is far easier to form good habits at first, than to correct bad ones at a later period.*

§ 28. *Numbers.*—It is highly important that the first exercises in counting and adding should be illustrated by the use of the numeral frame and various convenient objects, such as pebbles, beans, kernels of corn, etc. Let each number or addition named be illustrated by a corresponding number or addition of objects. Let the children count around the class, each giving a number for himself in turn; let them count the number of children in the room; the lights of glass, the seats and desks, etc.

See, also, §§ 4, 6, 10, 12.

References.—§ 28. Calkins's Object Lessons; Barnard's Object Teaching, art. 12; Manual of Elementary Instruction, vol. 2.

* "Every faculty of the mind, as well as of the body, with regard to its mode of action, has a strong tendency to take a *set*, according to the first impressions made upon it, or the character of its first observations. It becomes, as it were, preoccupied by the first impressions, to the exclusion or diminished force of succeeding impressions."—*Reid's Principles of Education.*

NINTH GRADE.

[PRIMARY DEPARTMENT.]

REGULAR COURSE.

Oral Instruction, embracing lessons on parts, form, and color, illustrated by common objects; on plants; on animals, mostly those with which the children are already familiar; morals and manners; miscellaneous topics. Two or more lessons a day, each from five to ten minutes long.

Verses and maxims.

Reading and Spelling.—Blackboard exercises continued. Cards reviewed. Primer completed. Spelling both by letters and by sounds. The exercises in both reading and spelling to be heard twice a day.

Counting from one to a hundred, forward and backward. Reading and writing Arabic numbers to 100. Addition tables from blackboard, to 4 + 10, forward and backward, in course; also, by taking any of the numbers irregularly; with use of numeral frame. Extemporaneous exercises in adding series of small numbers. See § 5. Roman numerals to L, both in course and out of course.

Exercises, at least twice a day, with slate and pencil, using elementary drawing-cards, plain figures, pictures placed on the blackboard, and other copies; and printing lessons in spelling, numerals, etc.

Physical exercises from two to five minutes at a time, not less than five times a day. See § 99.

DIRECTIONS.

Oral Instruction.—See §§ 8 and 18.

§ 29. *Parts.*—Pupils in this division should have frequent exercises in distinguishing and naming the different *parts* of which objects are composed.

References.—§ 29. Mayo's Object Lessons; Manual of Elementary Instruction.

Thus, the parts of the human frame, as the head, arms, shoulders, elbows, hands, wrists, fingers, nails, forehead, eyes, eyelids, teeth, etc.; the parts of a house, as sides, ends, doors, windows, floors, roof, stairs, etc.; the parts of a table, book, chair, tree, field, road, carriage, coat, knife, etc.*

Form.—See § 19.

Color.—See § 20.

§ 30. *Plants.*—Common and obvious properties and uses. Distinguish the parts, as roots, stem, leaves, buds, flowers, fruit, and seeds. See § 21.

---

* "*Object.*—To concentrate observation on actions done in the sight of the children; to call upon them to imitate those actions; and to teach them to describe them in accurate language.

"1. The teacher to perform some action,—such as placing the palm of the right hand on that of the left; and, without requiring the children to describe the act, call upon them to imitate it; or placing the right hand on the left shoulder; the left hand on the right shoulder; extending the right arm, and bending the wrist; holding up the extended right arm, while the left is held downward; folding the arms, etc., requiring the children to imitate each action exactly.

"2. The teacher may then *describe* an action, in place of performing it, requiring the children to carry it out: Put the right hand on the right shoulder, the left hand on the left shoulder; put one arm behind, the other across the chest, extend the left arm, and bend the wrist, etc., etc.

"3. The teacher to perform the action, and the children to describe it: for example, the teacher may touch the upper eyelid of the right eye with the forefinger of the left hand; or touch the inner corner of the left eye with the thumb of the left hand; or fold the arms; or hold up both arms extended, etc., the children describing each successive action: if in doing this they express themselves inaccurately, the teacher should correct them."—*Manual of Elementary Instruction.*

Animals.—See § 22.

Morals and Manners.—See § 7.

§ 31. *Miscellaneous Topics.*—Meaning and use of the terms *hard*, *soft*, *dozen*, *score*, *right*, *left*. Time by clock or watch. Name ten articles of table furniture; six articles made of glass; eight different kinds of fruit; four things that please the teacher; four things that displease the teacher, etc. The teacher will vary and expand these exercises at pleasure.

Verses and Maxims.—See § 23.

Oral Instruction.—See §§ 8 and 18.

§ 32. *Reading and Spelling.*—The following method will be found highly useful in securing the attention of Primer classes, and giving to each pupil the benefit of reading the whole lesson, or such portion of it as may be desired: Let one scholar read the first sentence; then let the class follow, reading the same in concert, and pointing to all the words as they read. Let the next scholar read the second sentence, and the class follow in concert as before, and so on.

The practice of mental reading should also be frequently introduced; all the members of the class pointing carefully to the words of a paragraph or lesson, as they are read by the teacher. If these exercises are properly conducted, they will advance

---

References.—§ 31. Fireside Philosophy; Graded Course of Instruction, by Home and Colonial School Society; Calkins's Object Lessons.

a class much faster than the method of hearing each pupil read a sentence in turn, without the concert practice in oral and mental reading.

The pupils should be able to point out and explain the *title-page*, *table of contents*, *leaves*, *pages*, *margins* *frontispiece*, and the *headings* or the *titles* of the lessons. They should also be able to spell all these words before leaving the 9th grade.

Let them be taught to hold a book in a proper manner, in the left hand, with the thumb and little finger on the pages in front, and three fingers on the cover behind.

In preparing an exercise in spelling, it is highly important that young pupils should hear the words pronounced by the teacher. A very useful method is, for the teacher first to pronounce all the words of the lesson distinctly, while the pupils listen attentively and point to the words in the books, as they are pronounced. Next, the teacher pronounces one word, which is repeated by the first scholar in the class; then another word, which is repeated by the second scholar, and so on. After this, if time permits, the teacher and class may pronounce in concert, and then the class pronounce in concert without the teacher.

All the spelling lessons should be neatly printed by the pupils on their slates, and the classes should be required to read the words from their slates in connection with the spelling exercises. See, also, §§ 1, 2, 26, and 27.

Numbers.—See § 28.

§ 33. *Drawing, Printing, etc.*—The teachers of the several Primary grades should assign definite lessons in drawing, printing, etc., to be prepared by all the pupils, with the same regularity and care as any other exercise.* The teacher should spend at least ten minutes each day in assisting the pupils and giving such directions as they may need. When the exercises are completed, they should in all cases be examined by the teacher. Lessons of special excellence should receive marks of credit, and failures resulting from carelessness or indifference, should receive marks of error.

See, also, §§ 4, 6, 10, 12, 14, 15.

EIGHTH GRADE.

[PRIMARY DEPARTMENT.]

REGULAR COURSE.

Oral Instruction.—Parts; size; general qualities; color; animals; plants; trades and professions; morals and manners; miscellaneous topics. Two or more oral exercises a day, each from five to twelve minutes long.

Verses and Maxims. See § 23.

First half of First Reader read and reviewed, with punctuation, definitions, and illustrations. Short daily drill in enunciating the

References.—§ 33. Welch's Object Lessons; Calkins's Object Lessons; Barnard's Object Teaching; Philbrick's Primary School Tablets; Manual of Elementary Instruction.

* "The spreading recognition of drawing as an element of education, is one among the many signs of the more rational views on mental culture now beginning to prevail." —*Herbert Spencer.*

vowels and consonants, and their combinations.* Spelling the columns of words, and words selected from the reading lessons, both by letters and by sounds.

Drawing and Printing.—Two or more exercises a day with slate and pencil, or paper and pencil, using blackboard sketches prepared by the teacher when practicable, drawing-cards when they can be obtained, pictures and various figures from books and cards, etc. Printing lessons in spelling and arithmetic. See § 33.

Addition table completed; thoroughly and constantly illustrated and applied. Extemporaneous exercises in adding series of numbers. See § 5. Reading and writing Roman numerals to one hundred, forward and backward in course; also irregularly.

Physical exercises, from two to five minutes at a time, not less than five times a day. See § 105.

DIRECTIONS.

Oral Instruction.—See §§ 8 and 18.

Parts.—See § 29.

§ 34. *Size.*—Let the children receive their first ideas of a foot, a yard, an inch, etc., by the actual measurement of these different lengths in their presence. Place lines of known lengths on the blackboard as standards of comparison. Let the pupils estimate the length of the room, the hight of one of their own number, the width of the street, etc., and then test their different estimates by measuring the objects. Now let the pupils draw lines of speci-

---

References.—§ 34. Calkins's Object Lessons; Welch's Object Lessons; Barnard's Object Teaching; Manual of Elementary Instruction, vol. 1; Mayo's Lessons on Objects.

---

* See Watson's National Phonetic Tablets, Philbrick's Primary School Tablets, Sanders's Elocutionary Chart, and Page's Normal Chart of Elementary Sounds.

fied lengths on their slates or on the blackboard, as a foot, half a yard, two inches, etc.; after which their lines should be subjected to the test of measurement. The same measures may next be applied to width, and illustrate as before.*

§ 35. *General Qualities.*—After completing the special exercises on each of the qualities of *form*, *color*, etc., a large number of lessons should be devoted to the *general qualities* of objects, including those that have already been taken up separately.

---

§ 35. Barnard's Object Teaching, particularly art. 12, by James Currie, of Edinburgh; Welch's Object Lessons; Calkins's Object Lessons; Mayo's Lessons on Objects; Manual of Elementary Instruction.

---

* The following is a report of one of the exercises before an Educational Convention recently held at Oswego, N. Y., to examine into a system of Primary Instruction by Object Lessons:

"Ages of children, five to seven.

"The children were requested to hold their forefingers one inch apart while the teacher measured the space between them.

"Then the children were required to draw lines on the blackboard an inch in length, and others to measure them, stating whether too long, too short, or correct.

"Next they were required to tear papers an inch in length; then to tear them two inches in length; then to fold them three inches in length, and so on, the teacher measuring them meanwhile. At east two out of each three tore and folded their papers of the exact length named.

"Then the children were requested to draw lines on the blackboard one foot in length; then to divide them into twelve inches.

"They readily measured inches, and feet, and yards, both with the rule and with the eye, and drew lines representing them, showing that they understood the relations of these to each other as well as the length of each,"

Thus, the following qualities will be discovered in a *quill.* It is *long*, *light*, *stiff*, *useful*, *natural*, *inanimate*, *animal production*. The barrel is *transparent*, or *semi-transparent*, *hard*, *elastic*, *bright*, *light-colored* or *yellowish*, *cylindrical*, *hollow*. The shaft is *feathered*, *white*, *stiff* or *limber*, *opaque*, *solid*, *grooved*. Let each of these qualities be illustrated by comparing it with a similar quality in some other object, and let the meaning of each term be clearly fixed in the mind by an actual examination of the object in which it exists. The principal topics introduced and the names of qualities should be written very plainly on the blackboard, to aid in impressing the lesson on the minds of the pupils. Before closing the exercise, let the pupils be called on to explain the meaning of the terms used, in their own words, and to construct short sentences or phrases embracing them.

This is the best class of lessons that can be given to aid the pupils in enlarging their vocabulary of useful words; and the teacher should be careful to select such subjects as will introduce one or more new words at each exercise.*

§ 36. *Color.*—More extended exercises in discrim-

References.—§ 36. See the references of § 20.

* If properly conducted, these lessons will be found the most efficient means of improving the children's powers of observation, discrimination, and description, and of increasing their stock of useful information. They will also do much to prevent the confusion and misunderstanding of terms which we so often witness in ordinary conversation.—*See Marcel on Language*

inating the shades and tints of color. Primary and secondary colors.

§ 37. *Animals.*—These lessons should be gradually extended to include animals less common and familiar, as the squirrel, the fox, the deer, the owl; with a few foreign animals, as the lion, the camel, the ostrich. As far as practicable, the lessons should be illustrated by pictures in books and on the blackboard, to be copied by the pupils.

Let the characteristics of different animals be pointed out; as, the fidelity and sagacity of the dog, the docility of the horse, the intelligence of the elephant, and the cunning of the fox. Let examples be selected from each of the different classes of animals, for object lessons. Attention should frequently be directed to the wisdom and goodness of the Creator, as shown in adapting the form, covering, etc., of the different animals to their peculiar modes of life, and the climate in which they are found.

Plants.—See § 30.

§ 38. *Trades, Professions, etc.*—Object lessons relating to different employments—the farmer, the blacksmith, the shoemaker, the carpenter, the teacher, the lawyer, etc.; including a particular description of the tools used by the mechanic, farmer, etc., and illustrated, when practicable, by presenting the instruments themselves, and by drawings on the slate and blackboard.

References.—§ 37. See the references of § 22.

§ 38. Hazen's Trades and Professions, in Harpers' Family Lib.

Morals and Manners.—See § 7.

§ 39. *Miscellaneous Topics.*—Relative position oi objects, as the direction of a pupil from the teacher, or from another pupil, or from the door. Let the children name the city they live in; the county; the State; the country; capital of the State; of the country; mayor of the city; governor of the State; President of the United States, etc. Day of the week; of the month. Short table, embracing the common divisions of time. Estimate by pupils of the length of a minute, of five minutes, fifteen minutes, etc., without the aid of a clock or watch; submitted to the test at the close of the trial. Five duties to parents; five to brothers and sisters; five to companions at school; six different modes of conveyance; six things made of wood; six made of leather; six streets, with their relative location; six different kinds of food, etc. Meaning and use of terms *natural*, *artificial; animal*, *vegetable*, *mineral; metal; simple*, *compound; native*, *foreign; indigenous*, *exotic; century*, etc.

Reading.—See §§ 1, 26, 27, and 32.

§ 40. *Spelling.*—Let the children spell their own names; the name of the city or town; State; days of the week; months of the year. These exercises should be repeated till the pupils are able to perform them well. See, also, § 2.

§ 41. *Analysis of Sounds.*—"Articulation should be taught and practiced by a thorough analysis of

References.—§ 39. Barnard's Object Teaching, art. 9.

the elementary sounds of the language, and their separate and powerful execution by the organs of speech; then, sentences and short passages that require unusual command of the articulate powers may be made the subject of diligent practice."* It will also be found a highly useful exercise to give the elementary sounds occasionally, in a clear and forcible whisper. The analysis of sounds relates chiefly to reading, and should, therefore, be studied and practiced more in connection with the lessons in reading than with those in spelling.†

---

* Zachos's Analytic Elocution.

† "After all the elements and their combinations have been made so familiar by practice as to be readily recognized, proceed to analyze, and then to spell the words in the following exercises, in this manner: 1. Pronounce deliberately and firmly.

"2. Divide the word into its syllables, speaking each one separately, and as fully as if it were a word by itself.

"3. Articulate, in proper order, every element separately and very fully.

"4. Enunciate every syllable as it is completed, preserving the distinctness of its elements.

"5. Pronounce the word with due proportion of force and time on each syllable, taking care that the elements, as before articulated, be distinctly preserved in the pronunciation.

"The mode of spelling here proposed is the only proper way of assisting a child that is learning to talk. It can not reasonably be expected that a distinct and organically correct articulation can be acquired by the common custom of learning merely to pronounce words. There can be no doubt that nearly all the stammering, blundering, and indistinct articulation which we so continually hear, while few are conscious of it in themselves, have come very naturally, if not of mere necessity, from the folly of those who expect or allow children to execute words without mastering the simplest elements of which they are composed."—*Hillard's Third Class Reader.*

Drawing.—See § 33.

§ 42. *Numbers.*—Counting to 100 by twos, using the even numbers, 2, 4, 6, etc.; also using the odd numbers, 1, 3, 5, etc.; forward and backward.

See, also, §§ 4, 6, 10, 12, 13, 14, 15, 16.

SEVENTH GRADE.

[PRIMARY DEPARTMENT.]

REGULAR COURSE.

Oral Instruction.—Form ; size ; general qualities ; weight ; color ; animals ; the five senses ; common things ; miscellaneous topics ; morals and manners. Two or more oral exercises a day, each from seven to fifteen minutes long.

Last half of First Reader completed and reviewed, with punctuation, and definitions and illustrations. Short daily drill in enunciating the vowels and consonants, and their combinations.*

Spelling, both by letters and by sounds, from Speller, and from reading lessons.

Drawing and Printing.—Two or more lessons a day ; same as in eighth grade.

Subtraction table completed, and multiplication table to 5×10 or 5×12, constantly illustrated by use of beans, etc., and applied. Extemporaneous exercises in adding and subtracting series of numbers. See § 5. Reading and writing Arabic and Roman numerals to five hundred, forward and backward in course ; also out of course.

Physical exercises, from two to five minutes at a time, not less than four times a day. See § 105.

References.—§ 42. Barnard's Object Teaching, art. 12; Calkins's Object Lessons; Davies' Grammar of Arithmetic.

---

* See Philbrick's Primary School Tablets, Page's Normal Chart of Elementary Sounds, Sanders's Elocutionary Chart, and Watson's National Phonetic Tablets.

DIRECTIONS.

Oral Instruction.—See §§ 8 and 18.

§ 43. *Form.*—Lessons on the various relations and conditions of *lines*, as horizontal, vertical, perpendicular, oblique, parallel, diverging, converging, curved waving, spiral, etc.; on *angles*—right, acute, obtuse, on the different kinds of *triangles;* and on *parallelograms*, *quadrangles*, the *square*, *rectangle*, *rhombus*, *oblong*, *rhomboid*, *trapezoid*, *trapezium;* use of the term *diagonal.*

Copious slate and blackboard exercises, illustrating all the above lines and figures.

§ 44. *Size.*—It is now time to introduce measures of surfaces and solids. Actual measures, as the gill, the quart, the gallon, the peck, should be brought to the school-room and used in illustrating these lessons, till the children become familiar with them. Let the pupils estimate the measure of a cup, bowl, bottle, pail, basket, etc., and then correct their errors by measuring. Similar exercises should be introduced in relation to surfaces. First, place a square inch, foot, yard, etc., on the board, as standards of comparison. Next, illustrate the division of a square yard or foot into square inches, etc. Let the pupils estimate the number of square yards, feet, inches, etc., in various objects, as the floor, the teacher's

---

References.—§ 43. Calkins's Object Lessons; Barnard's Object Teaching, arts. 9 and 12; Hill's First Lessons in Geometry.

§ 44. Calkins's Object Lessons; Barnard's Object Teaching, arts. 9 and 12.

desk, a slate, blackboard, window, etc. Test their accuracy by calling on them to measure the objects. Accompany with copious slate and blackboard exercises.

General qualities.—See § 35.

§ 45. *Weight.*—First call the attention of the pupils to the attraction of the earth, as shown in falling bodies, the tendency of water to run down hill, the effort required to lift a heavy body, etc. Give them different articles of the same size, but made of different substances, as cork, wood, iron, lead, a vial of water and a vial of quicksilver, a bag of shot and a bag of beans. Let them handle and compare them. Distinguish bodies heavier than water from those which are lighter, by actual experiment. Now introduce various standard weights. Let the pupils handle a pound of lead, a pound of wood, a pound of cotton; a body weighing 5 lbs., 10 lbs., 20 lbs., etc. Next let them handle a variety of bodies, and estimate the weight of each; after which their judgment should be tested by the scales.* In this way they will cultivate accuracy of judgment in respect to the weight of different objects presented, an attainment which very few persons ever make.†

Color.—See § 36.

References.—§ 45. Science of Common Things, index; Barnard's Object Teaching, art. 9; Welch's Object Lessons.

---

* A pair of scales, or some other instrument for weighing, can easily be obtained for this purpose, through some of the pupils.

† See Young's School Teacher's Manual.

Animals.—See § 37.

§ 46. *The Five Senses.*—General description of the eye, the ear, and other organs of sense. Exercises illustrating the cultivation and use of these organs. Let the children name ten things discovered by the eye; five discovered by the ear; five by touch, etc. Name different qualities, etc., and let the children tell the sense by which they are discovered.

§ 47. *Common Things.*—Object lessons on a clock, watch, nail, carriage, pin, needle, rope, pitch, tar, etc.

§ 48. *Miscellaneous Topics.*—Name six public buildings in the city or town; six different kinds of carriages; ten different foreign fruits; six birds of prey; six different kinds of stores.

The names of the young of different animals. The flesh of different animals used for food,—what called? The voice or natural call of different animals. The largest fish, quadruped, bird, insect, reptile. A collection of men, birds, cattle, fishes, insects,—what called?

Meaning and use of the terms *density*, *attraction of gravitation*, *quadruped*, *biped*, *insect*, *reptile.*

§ 49. *Sentence-making, etc.*—At the close of every object lesson, let each pupil make up one or more

---

References.—§ 46. Child's Book of Nature, part 2; Calkins's Object Lessons; Mayo's Lessons on Objects; Mayhew's Popular Education, chap. 6.

§ 47. Fireside Philosophy, index; Mayo's Lessons on Objects, *passim;* Brande's Cyclopædia, words *Horology*, *Pin.*

§ 48. Hooker's Natural History, chap. 13.

§ 49. Barnard's Object Teaching, art. 12

sentences embodying certain points of the lesson, or containing new words that have been learned. The pupils may ordinarily be called on to repeat these sentences in course, extemporaneously; but they should occasionally be required to print or write them with care on their slates, for the inspection or the teacher. Exercises specially meritorious should receive marks of credit; and defective exercises should receive marks of error.

Reading.—See §§ 1, 26, 27, and 41.

§ 50.—*Analysis of Sounds.*—Besides the ordinary exercises in analyzing, by *uttering* the different sounds, pupils should frequently be called on to analyze by *describing* the sounds. Other explanations respecting the forms of words, uses of letters, etc., may be given at the same time.

Examples.—*Fate:* sound of *f*, atonic; first sound of *a;* sound of *t*, atonic; *e* silent. *Garnish:* hard sound of *g*, subtonic; second sound of *a;* sound of *r*, subtonic; sound of *n*, subtonic; second sound of *i;* sound of *sh*, atonic.—How many sounds has *g?* What are they? Give a word containing the soft sound of *g;* one containing the first sound of *a*. How many syllables in *garnish?* Which syllable is accented? What is accent? Which of the letters in *garnish* are vowels? Which consonants? What letter or letters represent the last sound in *garnish?* Can you name any other elementary sound that is represented by two letters united?

Reference.—§ 50. Wright's Analytical Orthography.

The description and utterance of the sounds should generally be united in the same exercise; first analyze by uttering the sounds; then by describing them.*

§ 51. *Spelling.*—Spell and review the new terms introduced under "Miscellaneous Topics." Spell the names of all the objects that can be *seen* in the school-room. Let the scholars bring objects to the school to furnish names for spelling. Spell twenty or more names of visible objects not in the school-room; twenty or more names of invisible objects; twenty or more words denoting motion. The more difficult of these words should be written on the blackboard, and reviewed several times. See, also, § 2.

Drawing.—See § 33.

---

* The following is a very complete form of analysis, copied from Watson's National Phonetic Tablets:

"ANALYSIS.—1st. The word SALVE, *in pronunciation*, is formed by the union of three oral elements: s ä v—salve. (Here let the pupil utter the three oral elements separately, and then pronounce the word.) The *first* is a modified breathing; hence, it is an atonic. The *second* is a pure tone; hence, it is a tonic. The *third* is a modified tone; hence, it is a subtonic. 2d. The word SALVE, *in writing*, is represented by five letters; s a l v e—salve. *S* represents an atonic; hence, it is a consonant. Its oral element is chiefly formed by the teeth; hence, it is a dental. Its oral element is produced by the same organs and in a similar manner as that of *z*; hence, it is a cognate of *z*. *A* represents a tonic; hence, it is a vowel. *L* is silent. *V* represents a subtonic; hence, it is a consonant. Its oral element is chiefly formed by the lower lip and the upper teeth; hence, it is a labia-dental. Its oral element is formed by the same organs and in a similar manner as that of *f*; hence, it is a cognate of *f*. *E* is silent.

See, also, Holbrook's Normal Methods of Teaching.

§ 52. *Numbers.*—Counting to 100 by two's and by three's, forward and backward: 2, 4, 6, etc., 1, 3, 5, etc., 3, 6, 9, etc., 2, 5, 8, etc., 1, 4, 7, etc.* Adding single columns of figures on the slate and blackboard.

See, also, §§ 4, 6, 9, 10, 12, 13, 14, 15, 16.

SIXTH GRADE.

[PRIMARY DEPARTMENT.]

REGULAR COURSE.

Oral Instruction.—Form; animals; trees and plants; foreign productions; miscellaneous topics; common things; manners and morals. Two or more oral exercises a day, each from eight to fifteen minutes long.

Reading and Spelling.—First half of Second Reader completed and reviewed, with punctuation, definitions, and illustrations. Frequent exercises in enunciating the elementary sounds separately and in their principal combinations.† Spelling, both by letters and by sounds, with definitions, from speller, and from reading lessons.

Drawing, writing, etc., with slate and pencil or paper and pencil, using drawing cards when obtainable, cuts from books, and other copies; writing the large and small letters of the alphabet in plain script hand.

References.—§ 52. Barnard's Object Teaching, art. 12; Manual of Elementary Instruction; Davies' Grammar of Arithmetic.

---

* See a valuable article on Oral Lessons in Arithmetic, by Daniel Hough, of Cincinnati, in Ohio Educational Monthly for February, 1862. Also *Course of Studies for a True Graded School*, in Report of Hon. J. M. Gregory, for 1861.

† See Sanders's Elocutionary Chart; Watson's National Phonetic Tablets; and Philbrick's Primary School Tablets.

Elementary arithmetic. Multiplication and division tables completed, with constant illustrations and applications. Extemporaneous exercises in combining series of numbers. See § 5. Reading and writing Arabic and Roman numerals to 1,000.

Abbreviations.

Physical exercises, from two to five minutes at a time, not les than four times a day. See § 105.

DIRECTIONS.

Oral Instruction.—See §§ 8, 18, and 49.

§ 53. *Form.*—Copious explanations and illustrations on the *circle*, and on the terms connected with it, as *diameter*, *radius*, *chord*, *segment*, *sector*, *tangent*, *semicircle*, *quadrant*. Also, terms *oval*, *ellipse*, *parabola*; *pentagon*, *hexagon*, *heptagon*, *octagon*, *nonagon*, *decagon*, *polygon*; line of beauty. Measurement of angles.

§ 54. *Animals.*—Twenty or more lessons on the following topics, with pretty full descriptions and copious illustrations by engravings, and cuts, and slate and blackboard sketches. Division into classes—beasts, birds, fishes, insects, reptiles; quadrupeds, bipeds; domestic, wild; useful; amphibious; poisonous; beasts and birds of prey, etc., with illustrative examples of each class. Instinct of animals, care of their young. Tools of animals, their cover-

---

References.—§ 53. See references of § 43.

§ 54. Child's Book of Nature, part 2; Reason Why, index; Barnard's Object Teaching, art. 17; F. A. Allen's Primary Geography; Hooker's Natural History; Willson's 4th and 5th Readers; Carll's Child's Book of Nature; Webster's and Worcester's Quarto Dictionaries; Hailman's Object Teaching; Chambers's Elements of Zoölogy.

ing, food, habitations, motions. Plumage of birds, nest-building, migratory habits, etc. Contrasts and resemblances of different classes of animals.

§ 55. *Trees and Plants.*—Similar lessons to those given in the 8th and 9th grades, but more extended Compare the leaves of different plants and trees; the flowers; the seeds; the fruit. Compare flowers with leaves; branches with roots. Specimens should be brought to the school, and the children should have exercises, in naming and distinguishing them.

§ 56. *Foreign Productions.*—Object lessons on foreign productions in general use, including ginger, pepper, cloves, cinnamon, nutmegs, oranges, lemons, olives, dates, almonds, tamarinds, prunes, pineapples, tea, coffee, cocoa, chocolate, figs, bananas, raisins, sago, india-rubber, ivory, pearls, camphor, sponge, whalebone, gum arabic.

§ 57. *Miscellaneous Topics.*—Description and value of the different coins in common use, with exercises in distinguishing them. The names of thirty differ-

---

References.—§ 55. Child's Book of Nature, part 1; Fireside Philosophy, index; Willson's 4th and 5th Readers; Carll's Child's Book of Natural History; Manual of Elementary Instruction, vol. 2; Hailman's Object Teaching; Reason Why, index; Brande's Cyclopædia; Allen's Primary Geography; Webster's and Worcester's Quarto Dictionaries.

§ 56. Fireside Philosophy, index; Reason Why, index; Calkins's Object Lessons; Mayo's Lessons on Objects; Barnard's Object Teaching, arts. 9 and 12.

§ 57. Barnard's Object Teaching, arts. 9 and 12; Willson' Third Reader; Brande's Cyclopædia, words *Coinage*, *Numismatics*, *Money*.

ent kinds of vessels to contain liquids and solids, and the use of each. Object lessons on spring, summer, autumn, winter.

§ 58. *Common Things.*—Object lessons on common articles, including leather, sugar, honey, glass, porcelain, starch, hemp, flax, cotton, wool, ink.

Manners and Morals.—See § 7.

§ 59. *Reading.*—Pupils should now be required to devote a portion of each day to the preparation of their reading lessons. They will need the special assistance of the teacher in learning how to set themselves at work, and the reading exercises should be conducted in such a manner, as to test the fidelity of the pupils in making the necessary preparation.* See, also, §§ 1, 26, and 27.

Spelling.—See § 2.

References.—§ 58. Fireside Philosophy, index; Reason Why, index; Mayo's Lessons on Objects; Norton & Porter's First Book of Science, part 2.

§ 59. Davies' Logic of Mathematics.

---

* "It is in connection with the reading lessons that the peculiar work of the intermediate grade—the work of *learning how to get lessons*—begins. The first step will be to secure the careful attention of the pupils to the meaning of their lessons, by questioning them on the sense. This should be kept up from day to day, till the pupils acquire the habit of reading attentively, and become able to close their books immediately and give the substance, first of a single sentence, then of a paragraph, and finally of a page or an entire lesson. The inflections and emphasis should be carefully studied, to bring out the true sense of the lesson."—*Course of Studies for a True Graded School, in Report of J. M. Gregory, Superintendent of Public Instruction, Michigan.*

Drawing.—See § 33.

§ 60. *Numbers.*—Counting by three's, four's, and five's, forward and backward.

Special pains should be taken to explain and illustrate the operation of multiplying one number by another, and of dividing one number by another; the relation of multiplication to addition, division to subtraction, multiplication to division, etc. Let the pupils also repeat these explanations and illustrations till the relations are thoroughly understood.*

§ 60½. *Writing.*—Pupils must be provided with long pencils, and hold them as they would hold a pen.

See, also, §§ 4, 6, 9, 10, 12, 13, 14, 15, 16.

References.—§ 60. Barnard's Object Teaching, art. 12; Manual of Elementary Instruction, vol. 2.

---

* "Age of children eight to nine years.

"The design of the lesson was to show the relations between addition, multiplication, and division.

"The teacher wrote on the blackboard, and the children repeated the following:

3+3=6, 6+3=9, 9+3=12, 12+3=15, etc., up to 99.

"Then the teacher wrote 99−3=96, 96−3=93, and so on down to 6−3=3.

Then 6+6=12,	12÷6=2,
6+6+6=18,	18÷6=3,
6+6+6+6=24,	24÷6=4, and so on.

"The children read 6+6=12, two times 6 are 12, etc.

7+7=14,	14÷7=2,
7+7+7=21,	21÷7=3,
7+7+7+7=28,	28÷7=4, and so on to 100.

"Children read 7+7=14, two times 7 are 14. 14 divided by 7=2. 7+7+7=21, three times 7 are 21. 21 divided by 7=3."—*Report of Examination; Oswego Primary Schools.*

FIFTH GRADE.

[PRIMARY DEPARTMENT.]

REGULAR COURSE.

Oral Instruction.—Form; color; common things; trees, plants, etc.; animals; shells; geography; miscellaneous topics; morals and manners. Two or more oral exercises a day, each from ten to twenty minutes long.

Reading and Spelling.—Last half of Second Reader completed and reviewed, with punctuation, definitions, and illustrations. Frequent exercises in enunciating the elementary sounds and their combinations, using charts and tablets of sounds, etc. Spelling both by letters and by sounds, with definitions from speller and from reading lessons.

Primary Geography from text-book, gradually introduced in connection with Oral Geography.

Sentence-making, written abstracts, etc. See §§ 6, 9, and 49.

Drawing, writing, etc., with slate or lead pencil; writing with ink in script hand.

Mental Arithmetic.—Multiplication table to 12×12, and Division table to 144÷12, thoroughly reviewed, in course and out of course. Extemporaneous exercises in combining series of numbers. See § 5. Reading and writing Arabic and Roman numerals to 10,000. Slate and blackboard exercises in adding numbers—examples of three or four columns each.

Abbreviations reviewed.

Declamations and recitations.

Physical exercises, from two to five minutes at a time, not less than four times a day. See § 105.

DIRECTIONS.

Oral Instruction.—See §§ 8, 18, and 49.*

§ 61. *Form.*—Brief lessons on the five regular

* "The pupils, it should be remembered, are to observe and tell what they have observed, rather than to learn what the teacher

solids—cube, tertrahedron, octahedron, dodecahedron, icosahedron; and on the pyramid, prism, parallelopiped, cylinder, cone, sphere, hemisphere, spheroid, etc. Terms, *spherical*, *cylindrical*, *conical*, *spheroidal*.

§ 62. *Color.*—A few lessons in mixing colors. How to produce secondary colors. Harmony of colors.*

References.—§ 61. Davies' Elementary Geometry and Trigonometry, which contains full directions for making the five regular solids from pasteboard; Welch's Object Lessons; Calkins's Object Lessons; Barnard's Object Teaching, art. 9; Brande's Cyclopædia.

knows. Knowledge lying much beyond their power of observation and discovery is of but little use to them yet."—*J. M. Gregory.*

* The following is a report of one of the exercises before an Educational Convention held at Oswego, N. Y., to examine into a system of Primary instruction by Object Lessons:

"Children from nine to ten years of age.

"The children were led to distinguish primary, secondary, and tertiary colors from mixing colors. The teacher held up vials containing liquids of red, yellow, and blue. She then mixed some of each of the *red* and *yellow* liquids, and the children said the color produced by the mixture is *orange.* She then mixed *yellow* and *blue*, and the children said *green* had been produced. Then she mixed *blue* and *red*, and *purple* was the result.

"The teacher printed the result of each mixture on the blackboard thus:

First Colors or Primaries.		*Second Colors or Secondaries.*
Red + Yellow	=	Orange.
Blue + Yellow	=	Green.
Blue + Red	=	Purple.

"Next she proceeded to show how the idea and term *tertiary* is derived from the secondaries by mixing the secondaries, and printing the result on the board, as before:

§ 63. *Common Things.*—Object lessons on common objects, including vinegar, alcohol, wine, yeast, bread, paper, glue, soap, putty, silk, linen, spermaceti, wax, indigo, butter, cheese.

§ 64. *Trees, Plants, etc.*—Ten or more oral exercises. Qualities, structure, and office of roots, leaves, buds, stem, flowers, seeds, etc. Growth of the differ-

---

References.—§ 63. Fireside Philosophy, index; Mayo's Lessons on Objects; Barnard's Object Teaching, arts. 5 and 9; Norton & Porter's First Book of Science, part 2; Brande's Cyclopædia.

§ 64. Willson's Fifth Reader; Child's Book of Nature, part 1; Fireside Philosophy, index; Reason Why, index: Worcester's and Webster's Quarto Dictionaries.

Secondaries.				*Third Colors, or Tertiaries.*
Green	+	Orange	=	Citrine.
Orange	+	Purple	=	Russet.
Purple	+	Green	=	Olive.

"After the children had read over in concert what had been printed on the board, it was erased, and the pupils were required to state from memory what colors are produced by mixing primaries, with the name of each secondary; also, what by mixing the secondaries, and the name of each tertiary.

An exercise on *Harmony of Colors* was then given to the same class of children. They were requested to select two colors that would look well together, and place them side by side; then two were placed together that do not harmonize. During these exercises, the teacher printed on the board—

Primary *yellow* harmonizes with *secondary purple.*
" *red* " " " *green.*
" *blue* " " " *orange.*

This was read by the pupils, then erased, and the individuals were called upon to state what color will harmonize with these several colors, as their names were respectively given."

ent parts. The teacher should bring as many specimens as practicable to the class, and encourage the children to bring them also. Let the pupils examine several different kinds of wood, and exercise their skill in naming them. Some attention to the classification of trees, plants, etc., in families—the oak family, the pod-bearing family, the rose family, the grasses, etc., with specimens and illustrations when practicable. The innumerable uses to which vegetable substances are applied, in food, medicine, clothing, building, etc., furnish an ample field for extending these exercises as far as time permits.

Name five different evergreen trees; ten fruit trees; five ornamental trees; five used for fuel, etc. Lessons on cork, mahogany, logwood, rosewood.*

§ 65. *Animals.*—Transformations of certain insects. Animalculæ.

§ 66. *Shells.*—Five or more lessons on shells, illustrating some of the principal classes.

§ 67. *Geography.*—This branch should be introduced by familiar lessons on the geography of the city or town; its rivers or small streams, direction in which they flow, their width and depth; bridges;

References.—§ 65. See references of § 54.

§ 66. Hooker's Natural History; Brande's Cyclopædia, word *Conchology;* Mayo's Lessons on Shells; Worcester's and Webster's Quarto Dictionaries.

§ 67. Primary Geography on the basis of the Object Method of Instruction, by F. A. Allen; Barnard's Object Teaching, art. 12; Calkins's Object Lessons.

---

* See Hailman's System of Object Teaching.

location and direction of the principal streets, their width and length; public buildings, their location and use; public and private schools; manufactories; boundaries; date of settlement; early history; present population; population twenty years ago; town or city officers, etc.

Let these exercises be illustrated by the use of an outline map of the city or town, drawn on the blackboard.

Next, extend the exercise so as to embrace the county, and illustrate by map on the board as before. Then extend to the State; boundaries of the State; rivers; cities; capital; railroads; canals; length and width of the State; surface; soil; climate; productions; Governor; Legislature; population, etc.

§ 68. *Miscellaneous Topics.*—Origin and meaning of the names of the months. Traveling by land; by water.

§ 69. *Metals.*—Which are the precious metals? Which the most useful of the metals? Which are the heaviest? Which is a fluid?

Object lessons on iron, zinc, tin, copper, lead, mercury, silver, gold; on steel, wire, brass, pewter, etc. Terms *ductile*, *malleable*.

References.—§ 68. Fireside Philosophy, word *Month*, in index; Sargent's Third Reader, lesson 139.

§ 69. Carll's Child's Book of Natural History; Fireside Philosophy, index; Mayo's Lessons on Objects; Calkins's Object Lessons; Norton & Porter's First Book of Science, part 2; Brande's Cyclopædia.

Morals and Manners.—See § 7.

Reading.—See §§ 1, 26, 27, 41, 50.

§ 70. *Spelling.*—Spell the names of the different books of the Bible; of the different studies pursued in school; of a hundred different articles, selected from the "Prices Current" of the newspapers; of the principal streets of the city or town; of the numerals, both ordinal and cardinal, from one to twenty. Dictation exercises.

The spelling exercises of this grade should be mostly oral; but the classes may occasionally be called on to spell by printing the words with a pen or pencil, on their slates or on paper. See, also, § 2.

§ 71. *Arithmetic.*—Pupils should receive special assistance from the teacher, in *learning how to prepare their lessons* in mental arithmetic. Counting by sixes, sevens, eights, nines, and tens, forward and backward: 1, 7, 13, etc., 2, 8, 14, etc., 3, 9, 15, etc.; 1, 8, 15, etc., 2, 9, 16, etc., 3, 10, 17, etc.; 1, 9, 17, etc., 2, 10, 18, etc., 3, 11, 19, etc.; 1, 10, 19, etc., 2, 11, 20, etc., 3, 12, 21, etc.; 1, 11, 21, etc., 2, 12, 22, etc., 3, 13, 23, etc.

Slate arithmetic should be gradually introduced, on the blackboard and on slates, preparatory to the use of a text-book in the next grade. Elementary exercises in notation, numeration, and addition.

Adding columns of numbers; short columns grad-

References.—§ 70. Northend's Dictation Exercises; Parker & Watson's Speller; Worcester's Speller; Sanders's Speller, etc.

§ 71. Barnard's Object Teaching, art. 12; Manual of Elementary Instruction, vol. 2.

ually extended to long ones; slowly at first, but more and more rapidly as the pupils acquire facility in the operations. Dictate columns of twenty or more figures; then let all the pupils commence at the same moment and note the time required by each to complete the addition. All the pupils should learn to add by giving the sum at each step, without naming the number to be added: thus, in adding the numbers 5, 8, 6, 9, etc., say 5, 13, 19, 28, etc., and not 5 and 8 are 13, and 6 are 19, and 9 are 28, etc.

§ 71½. *Drawing.*—The study and application of the principles of drawing should be gradually extended till the pupils are able to produce representations of objects with facility and accuracy. Let the classes use cuts from books, drawing-cards, when obtainable, and other copies. They should also have frequent exercises in sketching directly from the objects represented.* See, also, § 33.

Writing.—See § 3.

See, also, §§ 4, 6, 9, 10, 12, 13, 14, 15, 16, 49.

* "This beautiful art should certainly be placed among the *necessaries* of education, to be begun early, and imparted to all. There is no one who has not, on some occasion, found that it would have been extremely serviceable to him to have been able to *draw* his ideas, as well as to speak or to write them; a slight sketch will often show in a moment, and with great precision, what many words would fail to make clear; and a very little time in early youth devoted to lessons in drawing, including mechanical as well as other branches of drawing, would impart to every one a power which, in after life, could not fail to be useful in a variety of ways; that is, real practical lessons in drawing, carried out on the principles of the art—not mere copying, nor getting the master to patch up for

FOURTH GRADE.

[GRAMMAR DEPARTMENT.]

REGULAR COURSE.

Oral Instruction.—Sound; light; water; meteorology; miscellaneous topics; geography; morals and manners. The time devoted to oral instruction each week to be equal in amount to fifteen minutes a day.

Geography from text-book.

Construction of sentences, etc.

First half of Third Reader (or corresponding number of the series), with punctuation, definitions, and illustrations, and spelling by sounds.

Written and oral spelling, with definitions from speller and from reading lessons.

Drawing.

Writing.

Mental arithmetic continued. Slate arithmetic to long division, and reviewed. Extemporaneous exercises in combining series of numbers. See § 5.

Declamations and recitations.

Physical exercises, from two to four minutes at a time, not less than three times a day. See § 105.

DIRECTIONS.

Oral Instruction.—See §§ 8 and 18.*

§ 72. *Sound.*—How produced. Illustrate by stretched cord, or some other vibrating body. Ac-

---

the pupil something presentable at home, but real training to the power of making good representations of a variety of objects on a flat surface."—*Reid's Principles of Education.*

* "*Lessons on objects* are most valuable; especially lessons on the various familiar objects around us, when the learner is required to notice, or himself to suggest, every thing that can be remarked

tion on the ear. High and low sounds—how produced. Relation of the air to sound. Velocity of sound. The human voice. Varieties of the human voice. Name twenty different kinds of sounds. Echoes; whispering gallery; ear-trumpet. Musical instruments; bells.

§ 73. *Light.*—Luminous bodies. Velocity of light. Difference between the light of the sun and that of the moon. Laws of reflection; mirrors. Refraction; experiment with piece of money in a bowl of water. Action of the microscope and telescope. Solar spectrum; rainbow. Structure and action of the eye. Danger of injuring the eyes from excessive use; from imprudent exposure to light; from

---

References.—§ 72. Science of Common Things, index; Reason Why, index; Calkins's Object Lessons; Barnard's Object Teaching, arts. 4 and 9; Norton & Porter's First Book of Science, part 1; Brande's Cyclopædia.

§ 73. Child's Book of Nature, parts 2 and 3; Fireside Philosophy; Science of Common Things, index; Reason Why, index; Barnard's Object Teaching, art. 4; Calkins's Object Lessons; Norton & Porter's First Book of Science, part 1; Beechers's Physiology and Calisthenics; Brande's Cyclopædia.

---

about them. Such lessons should be begun early, but not stopped soon, as is too often the case. It is a mistake to suppose that they are useful only to young children; they should be continued, of course with more detail and with greater exactness, and with a greater variety of objects, up to a late period. Nor should they be confined to the pupil suggesting the qualities with the object before him; he should be made to describe it again minutely, from recollection, and then write down an account of its qualities."—*Reid's Principles of Education.*

reading in twilight; from reading fine print. Danger of allowing young children to look steadily at a light. Average distance at which a book should be held from the eye; effect of holding a book too near the eye. How cats and other animals see in the night. Cause of color. Twilight.

Terms, *iridescent*, *spectrum*, *solar*.

§ 74. *Water.*—Four or more lessons on the common properties and uses of water. Hard and soft water; water of the ocean, etc.

§ 75. *Meteorology.*—Six or more oral lessons on winds, clouds, fogs, dew, frost, moisture settling on a vessel of cold water in a warm room, rain, snow, hail, ice.

§ 76. *Miscellaneous Topics.* Oral lessons on printing, parchment, Julian calendar, copyright, patents, jail of the county, prison or prisons of the State.

§ 77. *Geography.*—After the introductory exercises of the previous grade, introduce a map of the United States, showing the situation and relative size of the State in which the pupils reside; the principal rivers of the country, mountains, capital, largest cities, etc. Divisions of the United States;

References.—§ 74. Science of Common Things, index; Reason Why, index; Brande's Cyclopædia; Calkins's Object Lessons.

§ 75. Barnard's Object Teaching, art. 2; Child's Book of Nature, part 3; Norton & Porter's First Book of Science, part 2; Science of Common Things, index; Fireside Philosophy word *Winds;* Reason Why, index; Hailman's Object Teaching; Brande's Cyclopædia.

§ 76. Brande's Cyclopædia.

compare the climate of the Northern and Southern States; principal productions of each division; commerce; compare productions with those of other countries; President, etc.

The use of the globe should be introduced in this connection, showing the rotundity of the earth, rotation on its axis, day and night, poles, equator, parallels of latitude, meridians of longitude, tropics, polar circles, zones, points of the compass at any given place, the continents, oceans, and relative position of places, situation of the United States, and of the State and city or town in which the pupils live; relative size of each.

Similar illustration should be constantly given with the globe in connection with the recitations from the text-book, and no definition should be passed by till the teacher has satisfactory evidence that the pupils understand clearly the object described.

Lessons in geography should be accompanied by brief historical sketches of important events connected with the different countries, and by some allusions to ancient geography, and the changes through which the countries have passed in their governments, boundaries, etc.

One of the most common faults in teaching geography is the practice of requiring pupils to learn the names of a large number of unimportant places, the exact population of unimportant cities, etc.* It is

* "Great improvements have been made, especially of late, in teaching geography. Higher views of the whole subject have been

not desirable that pupils should be required to "give the names of thirteen towns on the Tocantins river," nor even the number of square miles in every State of the Union. They may be able to learn these things so as to recite them, but they will not be likely to remember them; nor is the knowledge thus gained an equivalent for the labor required, even if it could be retained.

Construction of Sentences.—See §§ 6, 9, and 49.

Reading.—See §§ 1, 41, and 50.

§ 78. *Analysis of Sounds.*—The pupils of the Grammar divisions should have frequent exercises in spelling by sounds any words that may be selected from their reading lessons; and pupils that are not able to analyze the sounds of words promiscuously chosen, should receive special attention until this standard is attained.

§ 79. *Spelling.*—Spell one hundred words selected from the advertising columns of the newspapers. Five or more dictation exercises, in writing entire advertisements selected from newspapers. Fifty or more words selected from the lessons in geography.

The spelling exercises of this grade may be about

References.—§ 79. Northend's Dictation Exercises.

---

taken, great general principles have been substituted for innumerable useless details; the value of map drawing, already acknowledged, has been still more effectively insisted upon; the intimate connection between geography and history has been pointed out, and, in other ways, a new and stronger interest has been excited."—*George B. Emerson.* See, also, Fifteenth Annual Report of Secretary of Massachusetts Board of Education, by Dr. Sears, p. 65.

half oral and half written. But spelling exercises should be conducted chiefly in writing, as soon as pupils are sufficiently expert with a pen to write legibly, in the usual time for a recitation, ten or fifteen of the more difficult words in the lesson.* As the pupils become more ready in the use of the pen, the number of words may be increased. Oral exercises in spelling should not be entirely dispensed with in any of the grades.

Written exercises in spelling should in all cases be regarded as lessons in penmanship as well as in orthography, and examples of carelessness in writing should be charged as errors.

In the 1st, 2d, and 3d grades, written exercises in spelling should be put in suitable blank books, and preserved for the inspection of the School Directors, and others. Every word misspelled should afterward be rewritten correctly by the pupil, in his manuscript speller. See, also, § 2.

§ 80. *Drawing.*—Special attention should be given in this grade to the principles of drawing, preparatory to map drawing. Pupils should also have lessons in drawing various mathematical lines and

---

* "Spelling by writing, when the pupil can write, appears to have great advantage over spelling orally. In the business of life, we have no occasion to spell orally, and thousands of cases have made it certain, that the same person may be a good speller with the lips, who is an indifferent one with the pen."—*Mann.*

"The orthography of a language should be taught by *writing;* an opinion, we believe, that is now pretty well established, but not sufficiently put into practice."—*London Quarterly Journal of Education.*

figures, architectural figures, etc., and in copying pictures from books and other sources.* See, also, §§ 33 and 71½.

Writing.—See § 3.

§ 81. *Arithmetic.*—Teachers should be careful to secure a thorough acquaintance with the principles of notation and numeration. As soon as pupils are able to add figures together, the teacher should dictate several numbers to them orally, requiring them to place units under units, tens under tens, etc., and add them together. Examples of this class should be made more and more difficult, as the pupils are able to write them, embracing from five to ten numbers each, some of them extending to trillions or quadrillions, and containing more ciphers than significant figures, so that the pupils will frequently be left to fill whole periods and parts of periods with ciphers. These exercises will furnish a valuable review of addition, and a still more valuable review of notation and numeration.

Rapid exercises in adding long columns of numbers. See § 71.

References.—§ 81. Northend's Teachers' Assistant, letter 17; Holbrook's Normal Methods; Davies' Logic of Mathematics.

---

* "Linear Drawing, which supplies the deficiencies of descriptive language, is another acquirement indispensable to the instructor. It may be made a most useful instrument of teaching, even in the humblest school. In the exact, the natural, and the experimental sciences, especially, he who has a command of this art is never at a loss how to render the most intricate details clear, intelligible, and interesting to his auditory."—*Marcel on Language.*

Recitations in arithmetic require constant watchfulness on the part of the teacher, to secure fullness and accuracy of expression. The following are illustrations of common faults:

1. "If one cord of wood cost $5, six cords will cost 5 times 6," instead of "6 times $5."

2. "If one cord of wood cost $5, six will cost 6 times 5," instead of "six cords will cost 6 times $5." [Two errors.]

3. "In $\frac{36}{9}$ of a dollar, there are as many dollars as 9 is contained in 36," instead of "as many dollars as the number of times 9 is contained in 36," or "as many dollars as 9 is contained times in 36."

4. "To subtract one fraction from another, reduce the fractions to a common denominator and subtract the numerators," or "subtract one numerator from the other," instead of "subtract the numerator of the subtrahend from the numerator of the minuend."

See, also, §§ 4, 6, 7, 9, 10, 12, 13, 14, 15, 16.

THIRD GRADE.

[GRAMMAR DEPARTMENT.]

REGULAR COURSE.

Oral Instruction.—Historical sketches; air and water; electricity and magnetism; minerals; morals and manners; familiar exercises in grammar, embracing the parts of speech and construction of sentences. The time devoted to oral instruction each week, tc be equal in amount to fifteen minutes a day.

Geography, through United States, with map drawing.

Third Grade.

Grammar to the verb, with lessons in the use of language—to follow oral exercises in grammar.

Third Reader (or corresponding number of the series) completed, and first third of Fourth Reader, with punctuation, definitions and illustrations, and elementary sounds.

Written and oral spelling, with definitions, from speller and from reading lessons.

Writing.

Mental arithmetic continued, with thorough reviews. Slate arithmetic to addition of denominate numbers, and reviewed. Rapid exercises in adding columns of figures. Extemporaneous exercises in combining series of numbers. See § 5.

Declamations and recitations.

Physical exercises from two to four minutes at a time, not less than three times a day. See § 105.

DIRECTIONS.

Oral Instruction.—See §§ 8 and 18.

§ 82. *History.*—Brief sketches of prominent characters and events in history, both ancient and modern: Babylon, its walls and hanging gardens; Pyramids of Egypt, Trojan War, Homer, Founding of Rome, Alexander, Demosthenes, Virgil, Julius Cæsar, Mohammed, the Crusaders, Columbus, Washington, Franklin, Napoleon, etc.

§ 83. *Air and Water.*—Component element of air; of water. Proportion of oxygen and nitrogen in the air. Relation of oxygen to life; to combustion; most abundant of all known substances. Properties of nitrogen; of hydrogen, weight of hydrogen.

§ 84. *Electricity and Magnetism.*—Illustrate the

References.—§ 82. Mansfield's American Education.

§ 83. Norton & Porter's First Book of Science, part 2; Science of Common Things, index; Reason Why, index.

production of electricity, and properties of attraction and repulsion, by a piece of dry paper rubbed briskly with a piece of india-rubber. Conductors and non-conductors, lightning and lightning conductors, Franklin's kite.

Properties of the magnet. Magnetic needle, mariner's compass, horseshoe magnet, telegraph.

§ 85. *Minerals.*—Oral exercises on the following topics, with illustrations as far as specimens can be obtained:

Common quartz, quartz crystal, common limestone, marble, coral, gypsum, soapstone, anthracite coal, bituminous coal, slate, clay, loam, gravel, etc., together with various stones used for ornament, as agate, topaz, carnelian, amethyst, emerald, and some of the compound rocks, as granite, sandstone; kinds of stone employed in buildings, sidewalks, etc.; bricks, quicklime, mortar.

§ 86. *Geography.*—"In the progress of every successive lesson, the teacher should call in the aid of association, by naming the products and staple commodities of the several States, historical facts, remarkable curiosities, high mountains, manufactories,

---

References.—§ 84. Child's Book of Nature, part 3; Norton & Porter's First Book of Science, part 1; Science of Common Things, index; Reason Why, index; Barnard's Object Teaching, art. 4; Brande's Cyclopædia.

§ 85. Fireside Philosophy, index; Mayo's Lessons on Objects; Brande's Cyclopædia; Webster's and Worcester's Quarto Dictionaries.

§ 86. Northend's Teacher's Assistant, letter 16.

etc., occasionally naming each separately. Say—this is a lumber State, this a wheat State, cotton State, sugar, tobacco, rice, etc. Here is gold; there lead, iron, coal, etc. Then pointing, review interrogatively—what State? its capital, rivers, moun tains? What productions here? What in this This," etc.*

§ 87. *Map Drawing.*—The first steps in map drawing should consist of a series of exercises similar to the following:†

(1.) At a given signal let every member of the class draw on the blackboard or slate a continuous straight line, of any length, and in any direction; a second; a third; a fourth; a fifth. In the same manner, let five dotted lines be drawn. At successive signals, let all the pupils place ten points on the slate or blackboard, without any reference to each other. Now let all the pupils draw a straight line between any two of these points. This exercise should be continued, at successive signals, till all the points are connected.

(2.) The second exercise consists in making the

Reference.—§ 87. Calkins's Object Lessons.

* S. W. Seton.

† The directions for map drawing here given, have been kindly furnished by Messrs. Willard Woodard, Principal of the Jones School, Chicago, and E. C. Delano, Teacher of the Normal Department of the Chicago High School. Though brief, they are sufficiently full and explicit to enable teachers to introduce a systematic course of instruction in this important art,—an improvement greatly needed in nearly all the schools of the country.

pupils familiar with the smaller units of length, which may be done by the use of the common foot measure. Let the class, at a given signal, draw lines one foot in length, and teacher and pupils test the accuracy of the work by applying the standard. After successful trials, represent combinations of the standard in lines of two and three feet. Now let the pupils apply these units to space and objects in the room.

Again, let the pupils draw lines one foot in length, and divide each line into two equal parts; each of these parts into two other equal parts; continuing the division till the line has been divided into inches. Having a clear idea of the above units, assume points at the distance of an inch, a foot, two feet, and a yard, and let them be connected first by continuous lines, and afterward by dotted lines.

(3.) Let the pupils draw straight lines, of given lengths, in different directions, as vertical, horizontal, and oblique. These terms may be illustrated by reference to the walls and floor of the school-room.

(4.) The class should be required to combine straight lines in the formation of triangles—right, acute, and obtuse angled,—quadrilaterals and other rectilinear figures. After the first figure is drawn, other similar figures may be inscribed or circumscribed at given distances.

(5.) Draw curves and parallel curves of different degrees of curvature, and at different distances.

(6.) Around a given point, as a center, at a distance of one inch, let a circumference be drawn.

Around the same center, at the distance of two inches, a second circumference; at the distance of three inches, a third. In this manner let successive circumferences be drawn until the distance from the center to the last is twelve inches. The exercise may be varied by increasing or diminishing the distances.

(7.) Let the above exercise be reversed.

(8.) The division of straight lines into equal parts by the application of a given scale, which should be represented on the board by each pupil.

(9.) The representation of the axes, poles, parallels, meridians, and zones of spheres of different diameters.

(10.) Representation of familiar surfaces, with objects on them, as the school-room, play-grounds, and fields.

(11.) Representation of mountains.

(12.) Representation of rivers.

(13.) Representation of coast lines.

All the foregoing exercises should be repeated till a high degree of accuracy and rapidity is secured. It is important that the first nine exercises should be performed simultaneously by all the members of the class.

Select a county or State having regular outlines. Select a scale with some convenient unit of measure. After determining the position of the cardinal points, draw two dotted lines at right angles to each other, one representing the central meridian, the other the central parallel. Apply the scale to the meridian as many times as the distance represented by it is contained in the distance between the north and south points of the country to be drawn. Through the points of division, draw dotted lines at right angles to the meridian, which will represent parallels or latitude. Apply, in like manner, to the central parallel, such part of the scale as a degree of longitude is of a degree of latitude. Through the points of division draw dotted lines at right angles to the parallel. These will represent meridians. Designate the parallels and meridians by numbers expressing the position of points or places through which they pass, learned from an atlas.

The frame of the map being complete, represent by a dot the prominent points of the boundary, the latitude and longitude of which have been previously learned. Having fixed in the mind the nature and direction of the bounding line, it should be drawn wholly from memory. The boundary completed, the most prominent natural features should be represented.

The pupil now has before him a map of his own construction, in which he can not fail to be interested. See, also, § 80.

§ 88. In illustration of the foregoing principles we will proceed to draw a map of Europe, the most irregular and difficult of all the Grand Divisions.

The pupils having been thoroughly drilled in the application of latitude and longitude, and the relative length of a degree of longitude in different latitudes, the following prominent points in the boundaries of Europe should be written by the teacher on the blackboard and copied by the pupils into a blank book for preservation, to be committed to memory in lessons of five or ten each, according to the ability of the class. Commencing at

	Lat.		Lon.	
North Cape	71°	N.,	26°	E.
The Naze	58	"	7	"
Tornea	66	"	24	"
St. Petersburg	60	"	30	"
Lubeck	54	"	11	"
Mouth of the Elbe . . .	54	"	9	"
Brest	48	"	4½	W.
Bayonne	43	"	1½	"
Ortegal	44	"	8	"
Straits of Gibraltar . . .	36	"	5	"
Genoa	44½	"	9	E.
Cape Spartivento	38	"	16	"
Venice	45	"	12	"
Cape Matapan	36	"	22	"
Constantinople	41	"	29	"
Sevastopol	44	"	33	"
Intersection of Caucasus Mts. and Caspian Sea . .	40	"	50	"
Northeast point of Ural Mts.	67	"	60	"
Mouth of Ural River . .	47	"	52	"
Mouth of Volga River . .	46	"	48	"

The above points are deemed sufficiently accurate for practical purposes, not differing from the true position more than one half of a degree.

Teachers will increase or diminish the number of points at their discretion; but care should be taken not to burden the memory with more numbers than are really necessary to secure accuracy in the form of the map. Some teachers would have more points fixed in the map of Europe than the number here given. Very few maps require more than half as many of these points as the map of Europe.

Suppose the first lesson to be a map of the coast line from Cape North to St. Petersburg. The points essential to this exercise are Cape North, The Naze, Tornea, and St. Petersburg.

The latitude and longitude of these points having been learned, recitation may be required in the following manner:

Cape North is situated 21° N., 26° E. The general direction of the coast line is southwesterly to The Naze at the south point of Norway, with many small indentations; thence northeasterly to Christiana, coast line regular; thence southeasterly to the most southern point of Sweden, very regular. The position of the remaining points and the regularity and direction of the coast line should be learned and recited in a similar manner.

The class is now prepared to draw. First each pupil draws upon the board a vertical line called the scale, representing 5° or 10° of latitude, according to the size of the map. A dotted vertical line should now be drawn representing the central meridian in Europe, the 20th degree. Supposing our scale to represent 5° of latitude, the most southerly point being about 35°, the most northerly 70°, the difference will contain seven spaces of 5° each; hence there will be eight parallels. Now divide the meridian into seven equal parts, each equal in length to the scale assumed, and draw dotted curved lines through the points of division, representing parallels of latitude. Next draw the meridians. On the parallel of the 70th degree, a degree of longitude is nearly one-third of a degree of latitude. The most easterly point being in longitude 60°, and the most westerly nearly 10° W., there will be eight spaces and eight meridians east of the meridian of 20°, and six spaces and six meridians west of it.

Now set off on the parallel of 70°, eight spaces equal to one-third of the scale, east of the meridian of 20°, and two on the west. A degree of longitude on the parallel of 35° is $\frac{4}{5}$ of a degree of latitude, nearly. Now proceed to lay off the same number of spaces as before, each being $\frac{4}{5}$ of the scale, and connect the parallels of 70° and 35° with straight or curved dotted lines.

The frame being completed, let the points learned and described be located with dots and connected with lines, in conformity with the description previously given. After the class has acquired the ability to represent with accuracy and rapidity the first lesson, another section of the boundary, together with that previously drawn, should be assigned for the next lesson. Let successive sections be assigned until the outline is completed. The teacher can not overestimate the value of rapid execution in map drawing, which is attainable only by frequent reviews.

The mode of representing lakes, rivers, mountains, and prominent towns, will be readily suggested to the teacher.

§ 89. *Grammar and Composition.*—One of the most common faults in teaching grammar, is that of requiring pupils to commit too many rules and observations to memory. The most important principles only should be learned and recited directly from the text-book, and always in connection with illustrative examples furnished by the pupils. The less important principles, embracing more than half of the remarks, observations, etc., of the different school-grammars, should be learned chiefly as they are called into use by the grammatical study of selected passages of prose and verse.

As fast as the principles of grammar are learned, let the pupils be required in all cases to embody them in sentences of their own construction. The ability to use language correctly, and the demonstration of this ability by actual performance, should ever be regarded as the only satisfactory test of the pupil's attainments in this branch. "The art of speaking and writing correctly," is something more than "the art of knowing how to speak and write correctly." The knowledge of pupils is generally found to be far in advance of their practice. It is

References.—89. Mansfield's American Education, chap. 11; Page's Theory and Practice, chap. 7.

true that most teachers give some attention to the language employed by their pupils, especially during recitations; but it would be a very great improvement if still more time was spent in cultivating habits of freedom and accuracy in the use of language. If one-fourth of the time usually devoted to the regular recitation in grammar was distributed through the day, and employed in cultivating the art of conversation, and propriety and elegance of expression on all occasions, the loss would prove a great gain.*

The rule adopted by Dr. Johnson deserves a place in the memory of every pupil. "Sir Joshua Reynolds once asked him by what means he had attained his extraordinary accuracy and flow of language. He told him, that he had early laid it down as a fixed rule to do his best on every occasion and in every company; to impart whatever he knew in the most forcible language he could put it in; and that by constant practice, and never suffering any careless

* "Unless the principles of the science are applied in daily practice, and fixed in the mind by habitual exercise, comparatively little is gained from theoretical study of the formulas and parts of speech. The ability to think clearly, and express one's thoughts elegantly and perspicuously, in one's own spoken or written words, is a great acquisition, and a rare one in our grammar schools."—*Report of School Committee, Lowell, Mass.*

"The deficiency alluded to is in the lack of appliances in our school studies and exercises for the proper cultivation of the faculty of expression."—*Isaac J. Allen, Superintendent of Schools, Cincinnati.*

"No teaching of grammatical rules will counteract the injurious effect of the frequent hearing and use of ungrammatical language." —*Report of Boston Committee.*

expressions to escape him, or attempting to deliver his thoughts without arranging them in the clearest manner, it became habitual to him."*

The oral lessons of the course should in all cases be regarded as exercises for the cultivation of the conversational powers of the pupils, and they should always be conducted with special reference to the accomplishment of this object.†

§ 90. *Reading.*—The standard of excellence in reading should be set a little higher in each successive grade. Pupils of the third grade should be able to read with good expression and effect in every variety and style. Take care that all the voices, especially those of the girls, are kept up to the proper

References.—§ 90. Northend's Teacher and Parent, chap. 23; Page's Theory and Practice, chap. 4; Bates's Institute Lectures, lect. 4; Holbrook's Normal Methods; Zachos's Analytic Elocution.

* Boswell's Life of Johnson.

† "Oral lessons cultivate in young people the talent of rational conversation, which, in ordinary education, is entirely left to chance, although it is the most useful, the most social, and the most intellectual of all talents. They impart that free excursive acquaintance with various learning which makes the pleasing and instructive companion; and if they were generally adopted, they would not fail, in the course of time, to raise the tone of conversation in society. The powers of language of the learners being constantly called forth in proposing and answering questions, in stating the results of their observations, and in making verbal or written summaries of the subjects on which they have conversed, they will necessarily acquire great facility of expression in connection with great clearness of thought. And if they excel in conversation, they have every prospect of success in public speaking."—*Marcel on Language.*

degree of loudness and force. Low voices should always be regarded as great defects in reading; and, except in cases of ill health, pupils who fail to make themselves plainly heard in every part of an ordinary school-room should receive marks of error. If pupils are inspired with a suitable degree of ambition to give the proper expression to the pieces they read, there will generally be very little difficulty in regard to fullness of voice.

§ 91. *Spelling.*—Spell one hundred or more words selected from the geography of the United States. Dictation exercises.

Write six or more exercises of entire paragraphs, selected from the "Review of the Market," in one of the daily papers, including all the figures, abbreviations, etc. See, also, §§ 2 and 79.

Writing.—See § 3.

Arithmetic.—See §§ 71 and 81.

See, also, §§ 4, 6, 7, 9, 10, 12, 13, 14, 15, 16.

SECOND GRADE.

[GRAMMAR DEPARTMENT.]

REGULAR COURSE.

Oral Instruction.—Properties of matter; laws of motion, etc.; physiology and hygiene; morals and manners. The time devoted to oral instruction each week, to be equal in amount to fifteen minutes a day.

English grammar.

Reference.—§ 91. Northend's Dictation Exercises.

Composition, abstracts, and written reviews.

Geography. to Asia, and reviewed, with use of outline maps and map-drawing from memory. See §§ 87 and 88.

History of the United States, to the Revolution, and reviewed.

Fourth Reader (or corresponding number of the series) completed, with punctuation, definitions and illustrations, and elementary sounds.

Written and oral spelling, with definitions, from speller, and from reading lessons.

Writing.

Mental arithmetic completed and reviewed. Slate arithmetic through vulgar and decimal fractions, and reviewed. Extemporaneous exercises in combining series of numbers. See § 5.

Declamations and recitations.

Physical exercises, from two to four minutes at a time, not less than twice a day. See § 105.

DIRECTIONS.

Oral Instruction.—See §§ 8 and 18.

§ 92. *Properties of Matter, Laws of Motion, etc.*—In presenting the following topics, explain and apply the principles, and introduce illustrations when practicable: General properties of matter—extension, impenetrability, etc. Solids, liquids, gases. Inertia, different kinds of attraction, specific gravity, center of gravity, centripetal and centrifugal forces, flying, swimming, rowing, water-wheels, the action of powder in firing a gun, mechanical powers, the pendulum, air—its common properties and uses, pressure of the air, balloons and soap-bubbles, sailing a boat,

---

References.—§ 92. Norton & Porter's First Book of Science, part 1; Child's Book of Nature, part 3; Fireside Philosophy, index; Science of Common Things, index; Reason Why, index; Barnard's Object Teaching, arts. 2 and 4; Brande's Cyclopædia.

flying a kite, suction-pump, siphon, barometer, friction.

§ 93. *Physiology and Hygiene, etc.*—Let the expansion and application of the following topics be continued and reviewed, till the pupils are able to sustain a satisfactory examination upon all of them: The blood, mastication, the teeth, saliva, digestion, chyme, chyle, nutrition, blood-vessels, structure and office of the heart, circulation of the blood through the system, impurities, waste of the system, how repaired, proper and improper food, eating too much, too fast, too often, late in the evening, irregularity of meals, dyspepsy, alcoholic drinks.

Structure and office of the lungs, respiration, capacity of the lungs, exercises for their healthy development, obstructed action, dangerous habit of bending over desks, process of purifying the blood, different colors; carbonic acid of the breath, how formed, amount, composition of carbonic acid, weight, relation to life, experiment of lighted candle in air that has been held in the lungs a few seconds, carbonic acid in wells, burning charcoal in close room, carbonic acid in the stomach, soda fountains, raising bread; ventilation.

Brief account of the bones, joints, muscles.

The hand. Men and animals compared.

References.—§ 93. Child's Book of Nature, part 2; Beecher's Physiology and Calisthenics, *passim;* Root's School Amusements; Science of Common Things, index; Fireside Philosophy, index; Reason Why, index; Calkins's Object Lessons, Barnard's Object Teaching, art. 4; Brande's Cyclopædia.

Structure and office of the skin, sensible and insensible perspiration, importance of frequent bathing, danger from exposure to currents of air applied to the school-room.*

The brain, excessive use of; nerves of sensation, of motion.

Physical exercise, its relation to health, kind and amount required.

Clothing, kind and quantity required to preserve health; importance of frequent change; danger from cold or damp feet.

Sleep, nature and uses, amount required, effect of sleeping too much, too little; rising early, late; retiring early, late; ventilation of sleeping-rooms.

Recreation and amusement—relation to health. Importance of change and variety of mental labor.†

§ 94. *Reciting by Topics.*—One of the best modes of reciting history, geography, etc., is by the use of topics. Thus, in geography, a pupil passes to an outline map, suspended on the wall, with a set of topics in his hand, as boundaries, rivers, mountains, climate, surface, soil, productions, commerce, etc., and proceeds to describe the country assigned, stating all he recollects under each topic. When his description is completed, other members of the class are called on for corrections and additions, and the teacher makes such suggestions as the case may re-

* "Avoid a current of air as you would an arrow."—*Chinese Proverb.*

† "The mind is as much refreshed by *variety* as by *idleness.*"—*Todd's Student's Manual.*

quire. This made of reciting by topics leaves the pupils in a great degree to their own resources, secures a more thorough and systematic preparation of the lessons, and furnishes important aid in imparting that discipline of mind which is more valuable than knowledge. It will be found particularly adapted to reviews.

Reading.—See §§ 1, 41, 50, 78.

§ 95. *Spelling.*—Spell one hundred words selected from the geography of South America and Europe; thirty words selected from the terms and definitions used in arithmetic; thirty from the lessons and definitions used in grammar. See, also, §§ 2 and 79.

Write five dictation exercises of paragraphs selected from the "Marine Journal" of a newspaper.

Writing.—See § 3.

Arithmetic.—See § 81.

See, also, §§ 4, 6, 7, 9, 10, 12, 13, 14, 15, 16, 89.

FIRST GRADE.

[GRAMMAR DEPARTMENT.]

REGULAR COURSE.

Oral Exercises.—Popular astronomy; elementary book-keeping; government; heat; geology; morals and manners. The time devoted to oral instruction each week to be equal in amount to fifteen minutes a day.

Grammar completed, with parsing and analysis from reading-book.

Reference.—§ 95. Northend's Dictation Exercises.

Compositions, abstracts, and written reviews.

Geography completed and reviewed, with map-drawing from memory, and use of terrestrial globe. See §§ 87 and 88.

History of the United States, completed and reviewed. Outlines of English history, with review.

Fifth Reader (or corresponding number of the series), with explanations, analysis of derivative and compound words, and elementary sounds.

Written exercises in spelling from reading lessons, and other words selected by the teacher. Analysis of derivative and compound words, and a few selected rules of spelling.*

Writing.

Slate arithmetic completed and reviewed. Extemporaneous exercises in combining series of numbers. See § 5. Difficult examples in mental arithmetic reviewed. See § 81.

Declamations and recitations.

Physical exercises, from two to four minutes at a time, not less than twice a day. See § 105.

DIRECTIONS.

Oral Instruction.—See §§ 8 and 18.

§ 96. *Popular Astronomy.*—Ten or more elementary lessons. The earth—its size and motions Change of seasons—how caused; difference in the length of days and nights at different seasons of the year; length of the longest day at the equator;

References.—§ 96. Norton & Porter's First Book of Science, part 1; Child's Book of Nature, part 3; Fireside Philosophy, index; Brande's Cyclopædia; Brownell's How to Use Globes.

---

* "The rules for spelling derivatives are not very commonly learned in our schools, or if memorized they are not comprehended and practically applied. Certainly a large share of the bad spelling which I have witnessed is chargeable to a neglect of these rules."—*B. G. Northrop, Agent of Massachusetts Board of Education.*

tropics; polar circles; at the poles. Tides. Solar System. The sun—its office, distance, magnitude, spots. The moon—its size, distance, telescopic appearance, different phases; eclipse of the moon; of the sun. Name the planets in their order; relative size; satellites of each, and ring of Saturn. Morning and evening stars. Comets. Fixed stars. Teach the pupils to point out in a clear night five or more conspicuous constellations; five or more stars of the first or second magnitude; all the larger planets that are above the horizon.

§ 97. *Elementary Exercises in Book-keeping.*—A dozen simple exercises in single-entry book-keeping, illustrated by the teacher on the blackboard, and written out by the pupils, will be sufficient to enable them to keep ordinary accounts with a good degree of facility and accuracy; and pupils should never be allowed to pass through the Grammar divisions and leave school, without this knowledge.

§ 98. *Government.*—Seven or more elementary lessons on government, embracing the general structure of National, State, city, and town governments, and their relation to each other; government of United States, compared with that of Great Britain, Russia, Switzerland. Legislative, executive, and

---

References.—§ 97. Introduction to Mayhew's Book-keeping.

§ 98. Mansfield's Political Manual; Howe's Young Citizen's Catechism; Shurtliff's Governmental Instructor; Sheppard's Constitutional Text-book; Young's Science of Government; Brande's Cyclopædia, words *Jury*, *Homicide*, etc.; Webster's and Worcester's Quarto Dictionaries.

judicial branches of government; origin of our National government; Declaration of Independence; Constitution; trial by jury. Terms *homicide*, *manslaughter*, *felony*, *arson*, *burglary*, *treason*, *perjury*, *forgery*, etc. Names of the principal sovereigns of Europe.

§ 99. *Heat.*—In expanding the following topics, explain and apply the principles, and illustrate them as far as practicable. Sources of heat; heating by conduction, radiation, convection. Sensation of heat and cold; burning-glasses; good and poor conductors; different kinds of clothing; double windows; ice-houses; use of a fan; protection of the ground by snow. Contraction and expansion; putting tire on a wheel; fire balloons; thermometer; glass cracked by hot water; why clocks go faster in cold weather than in warm; freezing water; heat absorbed by change from solid to liquid state, and from liquid to gaseous; freezing mixture of salt and ice; cooling a heated room by sprinkling water on the floor. Boiling water; how the force of steam is produced. Flame—how produced. Carbon. Flame of a candle—why no combustion in the center; wick—why not consumed; use of circular wick in astral and solar lamps; use of glass chimney; of small hole in top of lamp; gas used in lighting buildings; use of a blower in kindling a fire; action

---

References.—§ 99. Norton & Porter's First Book of Science, part 2; Science of Common Things, index; Reason Why, index; Barnard's Object Teaching, arts. 2 and 4; Brande's Cyclopædia.

of a common chimney; proper construction; advantages of stoves, as compared with open fireplaces; disadvantages.

§ 100. *Geology.*—Five or more oral lessons on the geological formation of the United States; coal fields; mineral ores; geology of the State in which the pupils reside; fossiliferous rocks.

§ 101. *Grammar and use of Language.*—At least half the time appropriated to Grammar in the first grade, should be spent in parsing and analyzing select pieces from Milton, Pope, and other authors, embracing several different varieties of style. The extracts required for this purpose may be selected from the reading-books.

No exercise should be regarded as complete and satisfactory that does not analyze the thought as well as the language of the writer.

Pupils of this grade should receive special instructions in letter-writing, including the form and manner of beginning and ending, with the date; paragraphs; dividing between syllables at the end of a line; margin; folding; superscription; sealing, etc. See, also, §§ 6 and 89.

§ 102. *Use of Globe.*—Pupils should receive so much instruction in the use of the terrestrial globe,

---

References.—§ 100. Norton & Porter's First Book of Science, part 2; Willson's Fifth Reader; Brande's Cyclopædia; Webster's and Worcester's Quarto Dictionaries; any of the Physical Geographies.

§ 102. McIntyre on the Use of the Globes; Keith on the Use of the Globes; Brownell's How to Use Globes.

that they will be able to solve by it, before the class, not less than five common problems; as, To find the length of a degree of longitude at any given latitude: To find the hours of sunrise and sunset, and the length of day and night at a given place on a given day: To find how long the sun shines without setting, at any given place in the north frigid zone, and how long it is invisible, etc.

Reading.—See §§ 1, 41, 78.

§ 103. *Spelling and Analysis of Derivative Words.*—Spell one hundred names selected from the geography of Asia and Africa; the names of fifty islands and groups of islands, situated in any part of the world. Dictation exercises. Special attention to the analysis of derivative and compound words. See §§ 2 and 79.

Writing.—See § 3.

Arithmetic.—See § 81.

See, also, §§ 4, 6, 7, 9, 10, 12, 13, 14, 15, 16, 94.

MUSIC.

§ 104. It is highly important that all the divisions in the Grammar and Primary Departments should have one or more regular lessons in vocal music every week. Each division should also have daily exercises in singing both devotional and secular pieces. In

---

References.—§ 103. Northend's Dictation Exercises; Sanders's Analysis of English Words; Town's Analysis of Derivative Words; McElligott's Analytical Manual.

the Primary divisions, singing should be interspersed among the other exercises several times a day.

CONDITIONS OF TRANSFER FROM ONE GRADE TO ANOTHER.

No pupils should be advanced from one grade to another, till they are able to sustain a thorough and satisfactory examination, by the Principal, on all the branches of the grade from which they are to be transferred, including the oral lessons, use of slate, etc. They should be able to read any of the pieces they have gone over, with proper expression; explain the meaning of any of the words; give the names and uses of the different marks used; and spell any of the words, both by letters and by sounds. In the Grammar divisions, the examinations should be both oral and written. When practicable, all promotions from one grade to another should be made at the commencement of a school month.

Whenever the scholarship of a pupil falls behind the rank of his class, he should be sent into the class next below, unless by extra effort he is able promptly to regain his position.

PHYSICAL EXERCISES.*

§ 105. The following exercises embody the result of many careful experiments, and are believed to combine the elements of the most useful movements that are adapted to the school-room. The best ef-

---

* Most of the "free gymnastics" here presented, have been kindly furnished by Messrs. S. H. White, Principal of the Brown School, Chicago, G. D. Broomell, Principal of the Dearborn School, and E. C. Delano, Teacher of the Normal Department of the High School; assisted by three of the lady teachers.

fects will generally be produced by executing them in order, from first to last; but teachers can at any time make selections from them, at their discretion.

The value of the exercises depends in a great degree upon the energy and force with which they are executed. In all the arm and shoulder movements, the muscles should be kept as rigid as possible, and the rapidity of the movements should not be so great as to prevent the utmost tension of the muscles. In all the body movements the motion should be full and slow.

The directions assume that the regularity and number of motions in each movement are fixed by counting, either by the teacher alone, or by both teacher and class, as may be desired. The number to be counted in the body movements may be eight; and in the others, when counted at all, twelve. In some cases, it may be thought desirable to duplicate the numbers.

The following positions are recommended, preparatory to the execution of the movements:

Position A, Sit erect, hands folded in front.
" B, Turn to the aisle, preparatory to rising.
" C, Rise and face the teacher.

References.—§ 105. Root's School Amusements; Potter & Emerson's School and Schoolmaster, part 2; Calkins's Object Lessons; Beecher's Physiology and Calisthenics; Barnard's Object Teaching, art. 1; Fitzgerald's Exhibition Speaker and Gymnastic Book; Trall's Family Gymnasium; Walker's Manly Exercises; De Laspee's Free Gymnastics; Alfonce's Instructions in Gymnastics; Dio Lewis's New Gymnastics.

Position D, Stand erect, with arms akimbo.
" E, Pupils resume their seats.

These positions may be used in dismissing school, when classes are called to recitation, and at all times when the scholars are called to rise from their seats.

While on the floor, the scholars should stand erect, with the shoulders thrown back, and, unless otherwise directed, with the hands hanging naturally at the sides.

NOTE.

Cases will sometimes occur in which pupils are affected with infirmities that render particular exercises injurious to them. Teachers should give watchful attention to this point, and never require pupils to join in any of the movements against the wishes of their parents.

The windows should generally be raised from the bottom during the physical exercises, so as to furnish a supply of fresh air. All pupils in health are expected to join in these exercises; but if, from ill health or other cause, any one is prevented from engaging in them, he should never be allowed to sit in a current of air.

MOVEMENTS.

(1.) Inhale slowly and fill the lungs to their utmost capacity; retain the air a few seconds, and then exhale slowly until the air is expelled as completely as possible. Six inspirations and expirations.

(2.) Place the clenched hands on the shoulders, the elbows being elevated sidewise to a horizontal line with them. At count *one*, throw the fists forcibly outward, so that the arms shall be in a horizontal position. At count *two*, bring the fists back to the shoulders, keeping them closed firmly during the whole movement. Count twelve.

(3.) Hands hanging at the sides, closed. Counting *one*, pass the fists in front of the shoulders, and raise them so that the arms shall be vertical; *two*, bring the fists down immediately over the shoulders, at the same time throwing the elbows downward and backward; *three*, throw the fists downward, commencing with a short curve by bending the wrists and raising the elbows. Count twelve.

(4.) Position D. At count *one*, incline the body to the right at an angle of 45°. At *two*, incline to the left in the same manner. Count eight.

(5.) Inflate the lungs suddenly with a full breath; retain the breath a short time, and then emit as quickly as possible. Five times.

(6.) Extend the arms forward a little above the horizontal, the fists being side by side, thumbs downward. At *one*, bring the fists immediately in front of the shoulders, turning the thumbs upward, and throwing the elbows downward and backward forcibly, as if to strike them together behind. At *two*, thrust the fists forward to the first position. Count twelve.

(7.) Position D. At *one*, thrust the right fist upward to a vertical position; at *two*, bring the right hand to position D, and then thrust the left fist upward in the same manner. Count twelve.

(8.) Hands hanging in front, clasped. At *one*, throw the hands to the right and as far behind as possible, at the same time turning the body in the same direction, but keeping the face and feet straight forward. At *two*, turn to the left in the same manner. Count eight.

(9.) Position D. Inhale a full breath slowly; emit the breath audibly and slowly, giving the prolonged sound of *a* in *father*.

(10.) Let the arms hang at the sides, hands open. At *one*, throw the hands outward and upward, keeping the arms extended, and bring the hands together directly over the head with a clap; keeping the hands together and arms extended; at *two*, bring the hands down in front to a level with the shoulders; at *three*, throw the hands backward, keeping the arms extended horizontally; at *four*, drop the arms to the sides as in position of starting. Count twelve.

(11.) Position D. At *one*, rise on the toes as far as possible; at *two*, ease back to starting position, being careful to avoid dropping noisily on the heels. Count twelve.

(12.) Hands hanging at the sides, closed. At *one*, bring the fists up under the arms; at *two*, return them to first position. Count twelve.

(13.) Hands hanging naturally at the sides. At *one*, raise both shoulders as forcibly and as high as possible. At *two*, lower them gently. Count twelve.

This exercise may be varied by raising and dropping first one shoulder six times and then the other six; or by raising and dropping one shoulder once and then the other once, alternating to count *twelve*.

(14.) Position D. Thrust the right fist forward, horizontally, while counting *one.* At *two*, bring the right hand back to position D, and then thrust the left fist forward in the same manner. Count twelve.

(15.) Bring the fists together upon the chest, immediately between the shoulders, at the same time elevating the elbows above the horizontal, and bringing them as far forward as possible. At *one*, throw the elbows downward and backward with force, and at *two*, bring the fists and elbows as at first. Count twelve.

(16.) Position D. At *one*, turn the whole body, including the head, to the right as far as possible, keeping the feet stationary. At *two*, twist the body toward the left in the same manner. Count eight.

(17.) Place the fists upon the shoulders, with tho elbows raised sidewise to a horizontal with them. Throw the right fist outward and upward at an angle of 45°, counting *one.* At *two*, bring it back to its former position, at the same time throwing out the left in the same manner. Keep the muscles as rigid as possible. Count twelve.

(18.) Position D. At *one*, look over the right shoulder, at the same time bending the body backward and twisting sidewise sufficiently to allow a downward glance as at the heels. At *two*, look over the left shoulder in the same manner. Count eight. This movement calls into exercise more of the muscles of the body than any of the others, and should be thoroughly executed.

(19.) With the left hand upon the hip, whirl the

right hand and arm in as near a vertical plane as the situation of the scholar will allow, first forward, then backward. Then with the right hand upon the hip, whirl the left in the same manner. Let each arm be whirled six times in both directions, counting at ach time.

(20.) Place the fists upon the shoulders, with the elbows raised in front to a level with them. At *one*, throw the fists suddenly forward, keeping the arms horizontal and opening the hands, palms upward. At *two*, place the fists as before. Count twelve.

(21.) Hold the right palm in front of the eyes, at the distance of about a foot from them, and the left palm similarly, opposite the lower part of the chest. At *one*, change positions of the hands; *two*, reverse, and so on till twelve is counted.

(22.) Position D. At *one*, incline the body forward as in a low bow, and at *two*, incline backward to the same extent. Count eight.

(23.) Inhale slowly. Exhale suddenly and forcibly, with the sound of the letter A. Three times.

In movements 1, 5, 9, 13, 23, the length of time to be occupied by each inhalation should be indicated by some signal, as the raising and lowering of the teacher's hand; the raising of the hand being the signal for the inhalation, and the breath being retained while the hand is kept up, and sent out as the hand is lowered.

Other movements, selected from works on gymastics, or devised by the teacher, or combined from the foregoing, may be introduced, as the taste and ingenuity of the teacher may direct. The following is given as an example of several movements combined in one exercise:

(24.) Hands hanging at the sides, closed. At *one*, bend the elbows and describe a curve with the hands, by bringing them up in front of the chest and head, and over outward, so that the arms will come to the horizontal, sidewise; *two*, bring the fists against the upper and outer portions of the chest; *three*, throw the right fist forward to the horizontal; *four*, bring it back against the chest again; *five* and *six*, describe the same movements with the left arm; *seven* and *eight*, the same with both arms; after which the fists are to be thrust downward to the sides, as at first, with count *one*. The same movement may be repeated, always giving the same numbers to the same parts of the movement. The second time the fists are brought down to their first position, it should be with count *two*; the third time, *three*, and so on. The advantage of this is, that at the close of the repetitions, say nine, the class will all stop at once and there will be no break in the exercise.

(25.) *Marching.*—All the lower divisions should have exercises in marching as often as once or twice a day. By exercising a little ingenuity, the teacher will be able to arrange the files so that all the pupils will commence marching at the same time, and end at the same time. The children should keep together in their time, and this should be regulated by appropriate singing. If the singing can not be secured, the pupils may repeat verses in concert, and march to the measure of the poetry.

(26.) *Military Movements.*—Occasional exercises in marching, counter-marching, facing, dressing, and halting, with military precision, may be profitably introduced. They will not require the use of arms nor any substitute for them. For full directions respecting these movements, teachers are referred to Root's School Amusements, and The Boy Soldier, by the same author.

§ 106. Teachers should guard their pupils against all constrained and unnatural postures. The position "*hands behind*" induces a stooping posture, and should generally be avoided.* The habit of stooping over desks while engaged in exercises requiring the use of the pen or pencil, is one of the most serious evils now existing in schools, and its deleterious influence upon the health and form of pupils is abundantly manifest.

It is true that many teachers devote special attention to this matter, but in most cases the cure is by no means radical or permanent, and a more efficient and systematic course of treatment is required. There are many schools in which the pupils are required to give special attention to physical movements, at frequent and regular intervals, and yet lose more every day by indulging in this dangerous habit than they gain by the gymnastic exercises.

* See Report of S. W. Seton, Assistant Superintendent of Schools, New York, 1856.

As a first step toward the correction of this evil, teachers should inform themselves and their pupils of its nature and magnitude. The next step of progress should be a firm resolve to overcome it, whatever may be the effort required.

With most pupils, a frequent admonition from the teacher will be sufficient to establish the habit oi sitting erect, and when this habit is once formed, very little attention will be needed to perpetuate it.

But when this measure is found to be ineffectual, a persistent habit of stooping at the desk should be treated as a misdemeanor, affecting the deportment average of the pupil the same as any other example of misconduct.*

* "The training of children in sitting, standing, and walking, and in the use of the organs of respiration and of utterance, are among the first things to be attended to in the physical education at school."—*John D. Philbrick, Superintendent of Schools, Boston.*

COURSE OF INSTRUCTION

FOR A

HIGH SCHOOL,

EMBRACING

A GENERAL COURSE

AND

A CLASSICAL COURSE.

THE circumstances of different cities and towns are so various, that it is impossible to devise a course of study equally adapted to all high schools.

The following outline embodies substantially the course adopted in the Chicago High School. Some of its features have been borrowed from the course of study adopted in Philadelphia, St. Louis, Cincinnati, Boston, and other cities, and some of them are the fruit of observation and experiment during a period of six years.

The greatest danger, even with the time extended to four years, is that of crowding too much labor into each period of the course. It is not always sufficient to arrange the course so that pupils will not be required to carry a large number of studies at a time. Cases will frequently arise in which certain portions of a text-book may, without serious loss, be either omitted altogether, or used only for occasional reference. These should by all means be marked in the class, and treated accordingly. A reasonable amount well learned, is better than more learned imperfectly; and either of these is far better than the highest intellectual acquisitions obtained in exchange for good health.

When the time of the course is reduced to three years, still greater care will be required to avoid tasking pupils beyond their strength, and to prevent them from overtasking themselves. The tendency to this evil will be greatly diminished, if pupils can be retained in the grammar schools till they are thoroughly prepared to enter the high school. No pupil should be received to the high school under twelve years of age, and in many cases thirteen years would be a better limit to establish.

The highest standard of requirement in all the classes should be attainable by pupils of average capacity, without the necessity of studying during hours required for exercise and relaxation. But in attempting to remove the evil of overtasking pupils, we should remember that there is also danger of falling into the opposite extreme. If pupils are tasked beyond their strength, the school is justly chargeable with blame. But if the standard is dropped so low that it fails to stimulate the scholars to habits of thoroughness and self-reliance, then is the school itself a failure, and every community would so regard it.

HIGH SCHOOL.

SYNOPSIS OF THE GENERAL COURSE.

FIRST YEAR.

First Term.—Algebra; German or Latin; Descriptive Geography.

Second Term.—Algebra; German or Latin; English Grammar and Analysis.

Third Term.—Arithmetic; German or Latin; Physical Geography.

SECOND YEAR.

First Term.—Algebra; German or Latin; Universal History.

Second Term.—Geometry; German or Latin; Universal History.

Third Term.—Geometry; German or Latin; Universal History; Botany.

THIRD YEAR.

First Term.—Geometry; German, or Latin, or French; Physiology; Rhetoric.

Second Term.—Trigonometry; German, or Latin, or French; Natural Philosophy; English Literature.

Third Term.—Mensuration, Navigation, and Surveying; German, or Latin, or French; Natural Philosophy; English Literature

FOURTH YEAR.

First Term.—Astronomy; German, or Latin, or French; Intellectual Philosophy; Constitution of United States and Book-keeping.

Second Term.—Chemistry; German, or Latin, or French; Logic · Political Economy.

Third Term.—Geology and Mineralogy; German, or Latin, o French; Moral Science; Political Economy.

Drawing during the second, third, and fourth years. Such attention to reading, spelling, and penmanship, through the course, as may be necessary to secure satisfactory attainments in these branches. Rhetorical exercises, music, and physical exercises through the course.

At the beginning of the third year, those in the General Department are allowed to continue their Latin or German, or choose French instead, for the remainder of the course. Thus no pupil in the General Department studies more than one foreign language at the same time, and all are permitted to take two at some time in the course.

Those pupils who elect to take Latin during the first and second years, can defer their choice between the Classical and the General Course till the commencement of the third year.

SYNOPSIS OF THE CLASSICAL COURSE.

FIRST YEAR.

FIRST TERM. Algebra; First Latin Book; Descriptive Geography.

SECOND TERM.—Algebra; First Latin Book; English Grammar and Analysis,

THIRD TERM.—Arithmetic; Latin Reader; Physical Geography.

SECOND YEAR.

FIRST TERM.—Algebra; Latin Reader; Universal History.

SECOND TERM.—Geometry; Cæsar; Universal History.

THIRD TERM.—Geometry; Cæsar; Universal History; Botany.

THIRD YEAR.

FIRST TERM.—Greek; Cæsar or Cicero; Physiology.

SECOND TERM.—Greek; Cicero; Natural Philosophy.

THIRD TERM.—Greek, Anabasis; Cicero; Natural Philosophy.

FOURTH YEAR.

FIRST TERM.—Greek, Anabasis; Virgil, Eclogues; Cicero; Latin Prose.

SECOND TERM.—Greek ; Virgil, Æneid and Georgics ; Latin Prose.
THIRD TERM.—Greek, Iliad ; Virgil, Æneid ; Review of Latin.

Drawing during the second, third, and fourth years. Rhetorical exercises, music, and physical exercises, through the course. Such attention, through the course, to reading, spelling, and penmanship, as may be necessary to secure satisfactory attainments in these branches. Classical antiquities, military affairs, during the second year. Classical antiquities, civil affairs, during the third year. Classical antiquities, mythology, during the fourth year. Ancient geography, in connection with the literature and history of Greece and Rome.

DIFFERENT FORMS OF ORGANIZATION.

In the organization of high schools, three different forms have been adopted by different cities and towns.

1. That which embraces a general course and a classical course in the same school ; the parents or guardians of the pupils being allowed to elect between the two courses.

2. A division into two distinct schools, an English high school, and a classical school, each independent of the other.

3. A union of the two courses in one classical and English school, in which all the pupils are required to study both the English branches and the classics.

The first of these forms is illustrated by the course already presented, and by the course adopted in the St. Louis High School.

The second form is illustrated by the high schools of Boston.

The third form is illustrated by the high schools of Cincinnati.

COURSE OF STUDY

IN THE

ENGLISH HIGH SCHOOL,

BOSTON.

FIRST YEAR.

1. Review of preparatory studies, using the text-books authorized in the grammar schools of the city; 2. Ancient Geography; 3. General History; 4. Algebra; 5. French Language; 6. Drawing.

SECOND YEAR.

1. Algebra, continued; 2. French Language, continued; 3. Drawing, continued; 4. Geometry; 5. Book-keeping; 6. Rhetoric; 7. Constitution of the United States; 8. Trigonometry, with its application to surveying, navigation, mensuration, astronomical calculations, etc.; 9. Evidences of Christianity,—a Monday morning lesson.

THIRD YEAR.

1. Trigonometry, with its applications, etc., continued; 2. Evidences, continued,—a Monday morning lesson; 3. Drawing, continued; 4. Astronomy; 5. Natural Philosophy; 6. Moral Philosophy; 7. Political Economy; 8. Natural Theology; 9. English Literature; 10. French, continued; or the Spanish language may be commenced by such pupils as in the judgment of the master have acquired a competent knowledge of the French. Physical Geography is *permitted.*

For the pupils who remain at the school the fourth year, the course of study is as follows:

1. Astronomy; 2. Intellectual Philosophy; 3. Logic; 4. Spanish; 5. Geology; 6. Chemistry; 7. Mechanics, Engineering, and the higher mathematics, with some option.

The several classes shall also have exercises in English composition and declamation. The instructors shall pay particular attention to the penmanship of the pupils, and give constantly such instruction in spelling, reading, and English grammar, as they may deem necessary to make the pupils familiar with these fundamental branches of a good education.

COURSE OF STUDY

IN THE

LATIN HIGH SCHOOL,

BOSTON.

FIRST YEAR.

1. Latin Grammar; 2. English Grammar; 3. Reading English; 4. Spelling; 5. Mental Arithmetic; 6. Geographical Questions; 7. Declamations; 8. Penmanship; 9. Latin Lessons; 10. Latin Reader.

SECOND YEAR.

1, 2, 3, 4, 7, 8, continued. 11. Viri Romæ; 12. Written Translations; 13. Arithmetic; 14. Cornelius Nepos; 15. Latin Prose Composition.

THIRD YEAR.

1, 2, 3, 4, 7, 8, 12, 13, 15, continued. 16. Greek Grammar; 17. Greek Lessons; 18. Cæsar's Commentaries; 19. French Grammar; 20. Exercises in speaking and reading French, with a native French Teacher.

FOURTH YEAR.

1, 2, 3, 4, 7, 8, 12, 13, 15, 16, 19, 20, continued. 21. Ovid's Metamorphoses; 22. Greek Prose Composition; 23. Greek Reader; 24. Algebra; 25. English Composition; 26. Le Grandpère.

FIFTH YEAR.

1, 2, 3, 4, 7, 8, 15, 16, 19, 21, 22, 23, 24, 25, continued. 27. Virgil; 28. Elements of History; 29. Translations from English into Latin.

SIXTH YEAR.

1, 7, 15, 16, 19, 20, 21, 22, 23, 25, 27, 28, 29, continued. 30. Geometry; 31. Cicero's Orations; 32. Composition of Latin verses; 33. Composition in French; 34. Ancient History and Geography.

The instructors shall pay particular attention to the penmanship of the pupils, and give constantly such instruction in spelling, reading, and English grammar, as they may deem necessary to make the pupils familiar with those fundamental branches of a good education.

COURSE OF STUDY

IN THE

CINCINNATI HIGH SCHOOLS.

FIRST YEAR.

FIRST SESSION.—Latin Lessons, with Latin Grammar, five lessons per week; English History, five lessons per week; Algebra, five lessons per week.

SECOND SESSION.—Latin Lessons, with Latin grammar, five lessons per week; Anatomy and Hygiene, five lessons per week; Latin Grammar, five lessons per week; Algebra, five lessons per week; Lectures by Principal, on Morals, Manners, etc., once per week, during year; Rhetoric, once per week, during year; Reading and Vocal

Music; Composition and Declamation, by Sections, once in three weeks.

SECOND YEAR.

FIRST SESSION.—Latin Lessons completed, with Latin Grammar, five lessons per week; Geometry, five lessons per week; Natural Philosophy, to Pneumatics, five lessons per week.

SECOND SESSION.—Cæsar, three Books, or Sallust, one Book, four lessons per week; Geometry, to Book IX., five lessons per week; Natural Philosophy, completed, five lessons per week; Reading, Elemental Sounds, one exercise per week; Rhetoric and Vocal Music, one exercise per week; Composition and Declamation, by Sections, once in three weeks.

THIRD YEAR.

FIRST SESSION.—Chemistry, five lessons per week; Virgil's Æneid, three Books, four lessons per week; German or French, four lessons per week; Algebra and Spherics, completed, five lessons per week.

SECOND SESSION.—Cicero, three Orations, four lessons per week; German or French, four lessons per week; Chemistry, five lessons per week; Trigonometry, completed, five lessons per week; Constitution of the United States, completed, one exercise per week; Reading, Rhetoric, and Vocal Music, one exercise per week; Composition and Declamation, by Sections, once in three weeks.

FOURTH YEAR.

FIRST SESSION.—Horace, five Satires and the Ars Poetica, four lessons per week; German or French, four lessons per week; Astronomy completed, five lessons per week; Physical Geography and Geology completed, five lessons per week; Moral Philosophy, by Lectures, one exercise per week; Logic, completed, one exercise per week.

SECOND SESSION.—German or French, four lessons per week; Mental Philosophy, completed, five lessons per week; General History, completed, five lessons per week; Navigation and Surveying, completed, five lessons per week; Evidences of Christianity, by Lectures, one exercise per week; Critical Readings, Vocal Music, one exercise per week; Composition, by Sections, once in three weeks; Original Addresses.

COLLEGE CLASS.

In view of preparation to enter college, this class is permitted to substitute the following studies for the regular ones, in the fourth year:

Greek Grammar, completed; Greek Reader, completed; Cicero's Orations, six in number; Virgil's Æneid, six Books; Cæsar or Sallust, completed.

ADMISSION TO HIGH SCHOOLS.

John S. Hart, LL. D., formerly principal of the Philadelphia High School, is entitled to the credit of having first perfected a thorough and satisfactory system of examining candidates for admission to a high school.* The main features of the method employed by Mr. Hart in the Philadelphia High School, nearly twenty years ago, have since been extensively adopted, with various minor changes, in all parts of the country.

The following is an outline of the form of examination adopted in Chicago.

On the morning of the examination a card is presented to each candidate, with a number written on it by which the candidate is known during the day. On the back of this card are printed several directions and explanations.

* The Reports of Mr. Hart, for the years 1846 and 1850, were documents of uncommon value, containing elaborate and graphic sketches of the organization and management of a large high school, with an extended course of study.

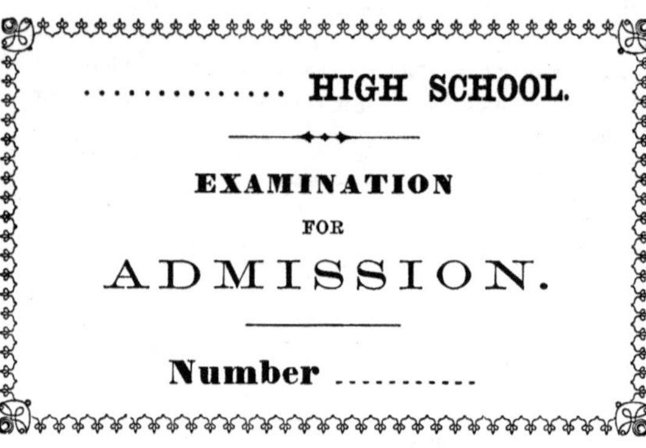

.... HIGH SCHOOL.

EXAMINATION

FOR

ADMISSION.

Number ....

DIRECTIONS TO CANDIDATES.

1. Throughout the examination, you will be known only by the number on the opposite side of this card.

2. Do not write your name upon any of your exercises.

3. Write your number very plainly at the upper left-hand corner of each exercise; your age in years and months at the upper right-hand corner; and the date in the middle, so that they will all be on the same line.

4. You can make any use of slates and pencils while preparing your answers; but the answers on the paper which you pass in must all be written in *ink*.

5. Number each answer to correspond with the number of the question, leaving for this purpose a margin on the left of each page.

6. Avoid all communication with other candidates.

7. Be careful not to lose this card. Candidates admitted will bring their cards with them at the opening of the school.

Small slips of paper are next distributed among the candidates, on which they write their names and the numbers on their cards. These papers are collected and immediately locked in one of the desks till after the Board has decided on the admissions. They are then used to identify the successful applicants.

After attending to these preliminaries, the candidates are distributed in different rooms, and arranged at separate desks, so as to prevent, as far as possible, any opportunity for communication with one another. Each candidate is furnished with a slate and pencil, and with pen, ink, and paper. The questions for the first exercise, previously prepared by the superintendent, or by the teachers of the high school, are now distributed at the same moment in all the rooms, and the candidates are allowed a definite time to write out their answers,—usually from an hour to an hour and a half, according to the number and difficulty of the questions. Every effort is made to put the candidates as much at ease as possible, and to secure them from all unnecessary embarrassment. If they do not understand any of the requirements, or lack any little convenience for writing out their work, they are requested to make known their difficulties with the utmost freedom. When the time appointed for the first exercise expires, the answers written by the candidates are collected together, whether completed or not, and the next set of questions is distributed as before, and so on, through the day.

Besides the teachers of the high school, on whom the examination chiefly devolves, one or more members of the Board of Education and the superintendent are also in attendance during a portion or all of the examination, but no other spectators are admitted.

Most of the labor still remains to be performed, after the candidates are dismissed. Several days are now spent by the teachers in examining the papers that have been written. Every answer is read with care, and its value, estimated on a scale of 100, is marked in the margin. The sum of these estimates standing against the several answers on any one paper, divided by the number of questions assigned, gives the *average* for that exercise. The *averages* of each candidate, in all the different branches, are set against the card-number by which he is known during the examination; but the averages in arithmetic and English grammar are multiplied by two when they are entered, because the examination in these branches affords a safer test of the candidate's ability to sustain a position in the high school than the examination in branches that are more mechanical, or that depend more upon the pupil's memory, and less upon his powers of reasoning and judging. The sum of the averages now standing against any number, divided by the number of branches increased by two, gives the *general average* of the candidate designated by this number. To render the result of the examination still more reliable, the teachers usually select the papers of all the candidates whose general averages are within five or ten per cent. of the lowest rank that will probably be admitted, whether above or below, and revise the estimates with special care. This measure insures the correction of any slight errors that may have occurred in estimating the answers of any candidate who could possibly be affected by such errors. The names of the candidates are never seen by any one, from the time when they are received on the morning of the examination till after this revision of estimates, and the final decision of the Board upon the admissions.

As the question of a candidate's admission or rejection depends entirely upon the *general average* of his examination, it is hardly possible that injustice should be done to any of the applicants. There are frequent cases in which candidates are not able to do justice to *themselves;* and these instances would be far more numerous if the examinations were conducted orally. A large number and variety of experiments have been tried by different boards of examiners, and they have almost invariably resulted in the decision that written examinations afford the most reliable test of qualifications, and are on the whole the most just and satisfactory to all parties.

If any instance occurs in which an applicant is supposed to be rejected for insufficient reasons, the answers on which this rejection is based are always on file at the school, or at the office of the Board of Education, in the applicant's own hand, and can be examined at any time by the candidate or his friends.

In estimating the examinations in reading, each candidate is requested to read two short passages, one in poetry and one in prose. The estimates in penmanship are based upon the written answers that are given in other branches.

SCHOOL RECORDS.

[The importance of securing greater uniformity in school statistics has long been felt, and numerous educational reports have sent out earnest calls for improvements in the methods of making and preserving school records. The report of Cincinnati for 1856, by A. J. Rickoff, Esq., Superintendent of Schools, contained several valuable recommendations on this subject.

The following views were embodied in the author's annual report for 1858–9, in the hope that by presenting in tangible form the leading objects to be sought, and offering a few practical suggestions respecting the best means to be employed, one step of actual progress would be made in lessening the evils that existed. Several important efforts in the same direction have since been made by school officers and educational conventions, and it is now safe to say that considerable progress has been made toward the accomplishment of the desired end.]

The subject of school records demands more careful attention from teachers and school directors than it has hitherto received. If the records of a school are properly kept, in the hands of a judicious teacher they become an important auxiliary to the healthful discipline and progress of the school, and at the close of a term or year the general summaries and averages afford valuable information respecting the character and success of the school, and its just claims to continued favor and support.

In many schools the records are so meager or so

inaccurate that very little practical benefit can be derived from them. In others they are so complicated and minute, that teachers find it impossible to devote the time required by them, without neglecting other important duties.*

Such records only should be required as will be of some practical value or general interest, and the greatest care should be taken to make the directions for keeping them so plain and explicit that even an inexperienced teacher, with ordinary care, will be in no danger of falling into errors.

The three essential elements of the records which are designed more particularly to aid the teacher in raising the standard of scholarship and discipline, are *attendance*, *scholarship*, and *deportment*.

In respect to the records from which the general summaries are prepared at the close of the year, it is to be regretted that so little uniformity exists in different cities and towns. The practice of exchanging school reports now prevails in all parts of the country, and comparisons are constantly made respecting the cost of instruction, regularity of attendance, etc.; but the data from which these results are obtained are so different in different places that the comparisons, in a majority of cases, are entirely unreliable. In one city or town the cost of instruction

* "School statistics are far inferior, in completeness and accuracy, to the commercial, manufacturing, and agricultural statistics of the day. It ought not to be so, for certainly the products of the school-room can vie in value with the products of the farm or the factory." —*A. J. Rickoff, Superintendent of Schools, Cincinnati.*

for each scholar is based on the *average number enrolled* during the year, and in another on the *whole number.* In one, the cost of instruction embraces all the expenditures for school purposes, including permanent investments; in another, it includes the current expenses for tuition, supplies, and repairs, together with five or six per cent. on the whole valuation of the school estates, which is regarded as rent; and in a third it includes only tuition, supplies, and repairs.

In one city or town, a pupil who is absent from school a single week, is marked as *left*, and his absences no longer affect the attendance averages. In another, the name of a pupil is crossed from the roll when he has been absent two weeks; in another, when he has been absent a month; and there are instances in which the absences continue to count to the end of the term, even though the pupil may have left at the close of the first week.

Of the various statistical results which are embodied in the reports of different cities and towns, the following are generally regarded as the most important:

1. Average number belonging.
2. Average daily attendance.
3. Per cent. of daily attendance on average number belonging.
4. Whole number of different scholars.
5. Expense per scholar on average number belonging.

The first of these, the *average number belonging*,

is, in many respects, the most important of the five. It is the basis of all reliable estimates in regard to the accommodations required, the number of teachers, and the expense of sustaining the schools.

The point which chiefly concerns us in this connection, is the condition on which a pupil shall forfeit his seat in school. If we can secure uniformity of practice in this particular, one important object will be accomplished. In the public schools of Chicago, when a pupil is suspended from school by any of the rules of the Board of Education, he is recorded as having left, and in all other cases, when a pupil is absent more than five consecutive school-days, he is recorded as having left—the date of leaving being at the close of the fifth day. This rule is adopted, not because we have any very strong preference for the exact period of one week, but because this limit is found on trial to be as convenient as any other, and because it is the period adopted in many other cities.

The second item of the foregoing list, *average daily attendance*, is easily obtained, and the practice of different cities and towns is nearly uniform in regard to it.

The per cent. of daily attendance on the *average number belonging* is, in most cases, a pretty safe index to the general character and progress of the school. The accuracy of this result depends mainly upon the accuracy of the record from which the *average number belonging* is obtained.

The *whole number of different scholars*, when compared with the *average number belonging*, shows approximately the per cent. of changes that take place in the membership of a school. This per cent. varies greatly in different places.

The *cost of instruction per scholar* is an item of special importance, and it is to be regretted that so little uniformity has heretofore prevailed in respect to the manner of obtaining it. That this estimate should properly be based on the *average number belonging*, and not on the *whole number of different scholars* during the year, nor on the *average daily attendance*, must, I think, be evident to any one who will carefully examine the subject. The *whole number of different scholars* may vary from year to year to any extent, without affecting materially the number of seats required, or the number of teachers, or the actual expense of sustaining the schools, provided the *average number belonging* remains unchanged. In a city having accommodations for 10,000 scholars, the whole number of different pupils may be swelled by constant changes to 20,000, without increasing the actual enrollment at any time beyond the original 10,000. If, now, we estimate the cost of instruction per scholar on the *whole number enrolled*, it will appear to be only one half as great as it would if the membership of the school remained unchanged. Here, then, is an apparent reduction of one half the cost of instruction per scholar, without any reduction whatever in the actual expenditures. The truth is, the city is taxed for the instruction of 10,000 children, and not for the instruction of 20,000, and the estimates should be made to correspond with the facts.

So also of the *average attendance;* it may be high or low, but so long as the *average number belonging* is the same, the labor and expense are but slightly affected. Each pupil enrolled as a member of the school, must have a seat, whether present or absent.

In some cases, two separate averages are made, one giving the cost per scholar on the *average number belonging*, and the other on the *whole number.* To this practice there can be no objection, as it will not be likely to mislead.

The foregoing suggestions respecting school records, are presented in the hope that they may contribute, in some degree, to the introduction of greater uniformity of practice in this important department of school economy.

At a meeting of the National Teachers' Association, held at Buffalo, in 1860, a valuable report on school statistics was presented by C. S. Pennell, Esq., of St. Louis, chairman of a special committee appointed for this object at a previous meeting. The following extracts are copied from Mr. Pennell's report:

"The committee have corresponded with superintendents and teachers, and have examined school reports as extensively as they have been able. They find the sentiment very prevalent that our school statistics, as now collected and presented, have far less value than they ought to possess; and they are compelled to believe this sentiment founded in truth. This does not, however, in the least diminish our estimate of the value of reliable records, nor weaken our confidence that our school records may serve a very valuable purpose. Theoretic views must be subjected to actual trial and the results of the trials can be presented in no better way than in statistical tables.

* * * * * *

"The *record of attendance* must embrace the following particulars, and may be much extended.

"1st. *Whole number of pupils enrolled during the year.*

"This must not be confounded with the whole number in the district or town of legal age to attend school, as shown by the census.

"2d. *Number transferred during the year.*

"These names will have been entered twice, and their number must be deducted from the first item in order to give the number of different pupils that have attended during the year.

"3d. *Average number belonging to the school or town.*

"4th. *Average daily attendance.*

"In order that these statistics may possess value, *the original entries must be correct*. This, it is believed, has too often not been the case. The records required by committees and superintendents, instead of being few and simple, have often been complex and voluminous, and teachers seeing little use made of them, have grown negligent. The popular distrust which has arisen in consequence of carelessness, has been urged as an excuse for continued want of care. Cases are found in which the average attendance is greater than the whole number registered, and also greater than the number of seats in the building. Such want of care admits of no justification. Correctness is the demand of honesty.

"*The meaning of the several headings should be made perfectly obvious.* There is oftener fault in this particular than those who make the forms and reports are aware of.

* * * * * *

"We believe the 'average number belonging' to be the proper number for all estimates of expenses, per cent. of attendance, number of pupils to a teacher, etc. We find no dissent from this opinion where we have been able to consult.

"How shall the 'average number belonging' to the school be determined? To obtain the 'whole number of names enrolled' is easy; so of the 'average attendance;' but with this quite otherwise.

* * * * * *

"We would suggest the following modes of determining who are members, as either of them would be better than the present want of method:

"1st. That, without the present attempt at uniformity, the school report should always contain an intelligible account of the method by which the 'average number belonging' is obtained. The consideration of these different methods will have a tendency, year by year, to produce uniformity. Or,

"2d. That the account of membership, for this purpose, be entirely disconnected from the exclusions from school which are of a penal kind; and that, whatever the cause of the absence may be, decease alone being excepted, the pupil be considered a member for a certain number of days, say four, after he has ceased to attend that on the fifth day the name be dropped."

The following extract is taken from the report of a committee of the Massachusetts State Teachers Association, prepared by John D. Philbrick, Esq., Superintendent of Schools, Boston:

"To ascertain the average whole number *belonging* with uniformity and exactness, is the most difficult matter connected with educational statistics. The percentage of attendance based on this, and ascertained by dividing the average daily attendance by the average whole number belonging, is what has been aptly denominated, by the late president of this association, in an article on the subject, in the March number of the *Massachusetts Teacher*, the true merit of attendance. Now this percentage may be increased in two ways; first, by making the dividend as large as possible, that is, the daily attendance; and so far as teachers and scholars are concerned, all the merit lies here. As a general rule, the attendance of a pupil should not be counted, unless he is present during the session, or long enough to substantially accomplish the work of the session."

In 1860, Ira Divoll, Esq., Superintendent of St. Louis Public Schools, issued a circular on this subject to superintendents and school commissioners, from which the following extracts are taken:

School Records.

"*Registration of Pupils and Attendance.*—This portion of statistical matter should embrace—

"1. The whole number of pupils enrolled, of each sex (exclusive of duplicate registrations caused by transferring).

"2. The average number *belonging*, for the year.

"3. The average number in daily attendance, for the year.

"The character of the attendance of pupils determines the de gree of usefulness of schools. Records of tardiness and punctuality are also important.

"The ages of the pupils enrolled are important in determining the standing and grades of different schools. It is also desirable to know the *minimum* and *maximum* ages at which pupils are admitted to school in different cities.

"Statistics showing the number of children represented by parents in particular occupations, are valuable, in determining, as nearly as possible, to what degree the different classes of society avail themselves of the advantages of public schools.

"The nativity of children is important enough to be noted in school reports. The degree of homogeneity among the scholars has its influence on the standing of the school.

"The number of pupils in different studies also determines the grade and standing of the schools.

"Whenever evening schools are a part of the public-school system, they should be as carefully and reliably reported as the day schools.

"A clear distinction should be made in items of cost, between those for the schools proper, and for other purposes.

"If any thing useful is to come from comparing the school statistics of one city with those of another, they must not only be correct, but they must be uniform. Suppose the average number of pupils *belonging* (as this is the number for which accommodations and instruction must be provided), be taken as the basis for estimating cost, the question at once arises, 'How shall this *average number belonging to school* be determined?' After a child has been registered as a member of the school, when, and for what causes, shall his connection be severed; and how long shall he be considered a member while he is absent? Shall his name be stricken from the roll immediately, or shall it remain for a day, a week, a month, or a quarter? Shall the reasons of his absence be considered in determining this matter? He may be absent on account of truancy, sickness of himself, sickness in the family, doing errands, visiting, working, and a variety of excuses.

"The rules on this subject, in St. Louis, are as follows:

"1. A pupil may be suspended (not expelled) for a variety of causes, and while under suspension his name is stricken from the roll.

"2. If a pupil has deceased, or has positively left the city without the intention of returning, his name is stricken from the roll immediately.

"3. If his continued absence is caused by his own sickness, his name is retained on the roll for one week, and no longer.

"4. For all other causes of absence, and when no cause is known to the teacher, the name is dropped from the record after two days, if the pupil do not return.

"These regulations are strictly observed in our schools; the number *belonging*, the number *present*, and the *per cent.* of attendance, are recorded every half-day in every department."

USE OF SCHOOL RECORDS.

A judicious use of the Class-Book, in which a record is made of the pupil's standing and progress from day to day, is one of the most important instrumentalities that teachers can bring to their aid in securing punctual attendance and an elevated standard of scholarship and deportment. The consciousness that these elements of character and scholarship are permanently recorded, is an abiding and potent influence with every pupil who has not lost all self-respect and all regard for the good opinion of his friends.

No other agency has yet been devised, which is half so effective as this in preventing the necessity for resorting to corporal punishment in school. If a teacher *created* the necessity for corporal punishment, even in a single instance, he would be regarded as unworthy to retain his office. If he can, by a proper use of school records, *lessen* the necessity for punishment, and neglects to avail himself of this means, how much less culpable is he to be regarded?

In the grammar divisions, the results of these records should, if practicable, be sent to the parent of the pupils at the close of every month. The salutary influence of these frequent *reckonings* with pupils, in the presence of their parents, cannot be over-estimated.

In the primary divisions, also, these records should be made to bear directly and constantly upon the character and progress of the pupils. Frequent and pointed allusions should be made to them, for the purpose of stimulating exertion and checking irregularity. When several marks of misdemeanor have accumulated against the name of a pupil, he may be called to the desk, or detained after school, and warned of the consequences. When pupils pass an entire week, or other prescribed period, without a demerit mark, they may receive a mark of special credit. At the close of every day or week, the names of all the children that have not been marked for misconduct, may be read before the school; and at the close of every month, the names of those that have secured the highest rank in deportment may be printed on the blackboard. By these and other similar means, a gentle pressure of influence may be brought to bear at all times upon the children, which will serve as a substitute for more than half of all the corporal punishment that is now inflicted by teachers who have not learned the use of school records.

Similar remarks might also be made respecting the records of attendance and scholarship, and similar lessons drawn from them, respecting the importance of obtaining the best results by the best means.*

In compiling and arranging the forms herewith presented, the two great objects sought were simplicity and completeness. The writer examined and compared a large number of the blanks used in different cities, and endeavored to copy their best features. A trial of over four years in the schools of Chicago, has proved the efficiency of these forms in accomplishing the object for which they were prepared.

The form marked **A** is the upper portion of a single folio of the *Class-Book*, arranged for a month of five weeks. When the month contains only four weeks, the last week of the form will be left blank.

* "As a general rule, the teacher, as well as the merchant or man of business, who keeps his accounts in a loose, irregular manner, and seldom posts his books, is the one most likely to meet with failure, without knowing the cause."—*Rochester Report.*

"Those teachers who so employ a well-adjusted method as to reach the highest results, deem the practice of keeping records not only a most valuable agency in the whole management of a school, but quite indispensable, for which no equivalent can be found as a substitute."—*Ariel Parish, Member of Mass. Board of Education.*

The following *directions* and *explanations* will be a sufficient guide to the use of the *Class-Book.*

A small *a* denotes absence, *t* tardiness, and *d* dismissal ; to be placed at the lower left-hand corner of the square for A. M., and at the lower right hand for P. M. A blank space at the upper left hand corner denotes good scholarship ; at the upper right-hand corner, good deportment. Marks at the upper left hand denote bad lessons ; at the upper right hand, bad conduct. Entries of special credit may be made by turning a pencil on its point, so as to leave a dot in the same corner that is devoted to the marks of error or demerit.

The highest degree of excellence in the *Average* columns is denoted by 100. The column headed *General Average* combines the three averages of *Attendance, Scholarship*, and *Deportment.* The pupil having the highest rank in the *General Average*, is marked 1 in the column headed *Relative Standing ;* the next highest, 2 ; and so on through the class.

The daily record of scholarship and deportment should be made with such fullness and care that the averages at the close of the month, may, in the main, be based upon it. In the lower classes of the primary divisions, these daily marks will necessarily be less full and exact than in the more advanced classes, and the teachers will be obliged to rely more upon general impressions, and less upon the daily record ; but even in the lowest classes, some account should be kept of the daily lessons and deportment of the pupils.

At the close of the school month, the results should be carried out in the columns of the Monthly Report, and the name of the teacher affixed. The *averages* should all be carried out in *whole numbers.* When there is a fraction of one half or more, add one to the whole number. All fractions less than one half should be dropped.

The numbers under *Punctual, Late, Absent*, and *Dismissed* represen *half-days.* These columns should all be footed up at the close of the month.

Each half-day's absence, unless for sickness, may deduct two from 100 in the *Attendance Average*, and each tardiness or dismissal may deduct one. Absences and dismissals occasioned by sickness, are carried out in their respective columns, but do not affect the *Attendance Average.*

The Scholarship and Deportment Averages may be found by deducting the number of marks for bad lessons and bad conduct from 100, provided the pupil has been present through the month; but if the pupil has been absent any part of the month, the number should be proportionally larger. If teachers give their pupils marks of special credit, these may, at the discretion of the teacher, be applied to cancel a limited number of errors or marks of demerit. Thus, one or two special credit marks may cancel one error or mark of demerit; two or four credit marks may cancel two errors or marks of demerit, etc. But rules for removing marks of error or demerit should be applied with great caution. Pupils should never be suffered to feel that it is an easy matter to secure the removal of errors or marks of demerit which have once been placed against their names.

When the month contains five weeks, the *Averages* may be found by deducting four-fifths of the marks from 100. When the month contains only two weeks, the *Averages* may be found by deducting four halves of the number of marks, or twice the number; and for three weeks, four-thirds of the number may be deducted. The same principle applies to the *Attendance Average.*

It may in some cases be proper to deduct more or less than the exact number of marks for bad lessons or bad conduct. Whatever rule is adopted, the results arrived at in the *General Average* should be such that ranks from 95 to 100 may be designated as *highest;* from 90 to 95, *high;* from 80 to 90, *mediate;* from 70 to 80, *low;* and under 70, *lowest.*

In noting the *Relative Standing* of different members in a class, it will often be found that several pupils have the same *General Average.* In such cases they should be marked alike. Thus, if two pupils have each a rank of 98, and that is the highest rank attained by any one in the class, they should both be marked 1 in the column of *Relative Standing*, and so of any lower rank.

The *Monthly Report to Parents* is copied directly from the right-hand column of the Class-Book. See accompanying form marked **B.**

SELF-RELIANCE.

THE two great objects of intellectual education, are mental discipline and the acquisition of knowledge. The highest and most important of these objects is mental discipline, or the power of using the mind to the best advantage. The price of this discipline is effort. No man ever yet made intellectual progress without intellectual labor. It is this alone that can strengthen and invigorate the noble faculties with which we are endowed.

However much we may regret that we do not live a century later, because we can not have the benefit of the improvements that are to be made during the next hundred years, of one thing we may rest assured, that intellectual eminence will be attained during the 20th century just as it is in the 19th—by the *labor of the brain.* We are not to look for any new discovery or invention that shall supersede the necessity of mental toil; we are not to desire it. If we had but to supplicate some kind genius, and he would at once endow us with all the knowledge in the universe, the gift would prove a curse to us, and not a blessing. We must have the discipline of *acquiring* knowledge, and in the manner established by the Author of our being. Without this discipline our intellectual stores would be worse than useless.

The general law of intellectual growth is manifestly this;—whatever may be the mental power which we at any time possess, it requires a repetition of mental efforts, equal in degree to those which we have put forth before, to prevent actual deterioration. Every considerable step of advance from this point must be by a new and still higher intellectual performance.

There are many impediments in the path of the student, which it is desirable to remove; but he who attempts to remove all difficulties, or as many of them as possible, wars against the highest law of intellectual development. There can not be a more fatal mistake in education, than that of a teacher who adopts the sentiment, that his duty requires him to render the daily tasks of his pupils as easy as possible.

There is, perhaps, no error in our schools at the present time more deeply seated or more widely extended than the ruinous practice of aiding pupils in doing work which it is all-important they should do for themselves. Our progress in the art of cultivating habits of earnest, independent thought, has not kept pace with our improvements in other departments of education. Familiar explanations, and illustrations, and simplifications, and dilutions, too often spare the pupil the labor of thinking for himself, and thus dwarf the intellect, and defeat the highest object for which our schools are established.

To secure from a pupil the solution of a difficult problem will often cost time which the teacher can ill afford; it may often cost more effort to secure a solution from the pupil, than it costs the pupil to do the work. The pupil has tried the problem, and satisfied himself that he is not able to solve it; the teacher may be satisfied that the pupil can perform it, but if he can not make the pupil think so too, it will be difficult to bring his best energies to bear upon it; and even after the pupil is persuaded that he is able to accomplish the task, it may still be necessary for the teacher to adopt special measures to set the pupil's mind at work. The pupil may have the ability to solve the problem; he may believe that he has this ability; and he may have a willing mind; and, after all, fail entirely of doing it. And this brings to view what must be regarded as the highest gift of the teacher: namely, the ability to teach his pupils how to think and act, without doing their thinking and acting for them.

When a pupil has failed to overcome an obstacle, his mind may often be quickened to action by requesting him to explain the steps he has taken. "Great thoughts," says Dr. Channing, "are never fully possessed till he who has conceived them has given them fit utterance." So with a pupil attempting to surmount a difficulty; the very effort required to express a thought in language often aids materially in grasping the thought itself.

A scholar had become discouraged over a difficult question. He had gone through the solution again and again, but could not obtain the answer sought. The teacher availed himself of a favorable opportunity, and requested the pupil to go through the work slowly and carefully in his presence. As the pupil proceeded the teacher required him to explain each step of the process; and when he reached the point where his previous error occurred, as the teacher asked him to give his reason, the pupil's eye flashed with delight and he exclaimed, "I see my mistake!" Without further assistance he soon reached a correct result. The teacher had not furnished the slightest hint in respect to the solution of the problem. He had only taken measures which brought the pupil's own strength to bear upon it.

There are, however, peculiar cases which no such method will reach. The pupil may be required to repeat his solution a hundred times, in the presence of the teacher or alone, with reasons or without, and all to no purpose. The result, if he reaches one, is sure to be wrong. It is not time, even now, for the teacher to give over in despair. Let him ask the pupil such questions as will call to mind the principles which he has occasion to apply, and, in a majority of cases, the pupil will need no further aid.

The same end may usually be gained by giving the pupil an example involving the difficulty over which he has stumbled, but less complicated in other respects; or by giving him several examples, leading gradually to the main obstacle to be overcome. I believe the cases are exceedingly rare in which minds properly disciplined would ever be benefited by direct assistance, in an ordinary course of mathematical study. But if it be thought best, in extreme cases, to afford this assistance, let the pupil, by all means, be required to *repeat the process*, after the teacher's work has been entirely erased; and thus derive, at least, the benefit of *reproducing*, though he has not the power to *originate*.

The teacher will find it a highly useful exercise to give his pupils an occasional *model of thinking*. Let him take a problem to the blackboard, and *think aloud* as he proceeds with the solution; so that the pupils may witness the action of the teacher's mind, and observe the questions he asks himself, and the various associations and comparisons that arise, as he advances from step to step in the process.

I am aware that in many schools the teachers can not dwell upon particular points with the same degree of thoroughness that I have recommended; but this does not affect the importance of the principle, which should be applied whenever the circumstances permit.

In most of our schools pupils indulge, to a greater or less extent, in the practice of assisting one another in the solution of difficult questions. I need not say that we should labor most assiduously to eradicate this injurious practice. Pupils should be taught to regard it as dishonorable, either to assist others or to receive assistance, except under the special cognizance and direction of the teacher.

Permit me, in this connection, to allude to one of the *helps* kindly furnished by a large class of publishers and authors, for the special benefit of teachers; but which many pupils have thought to be quite as well suited to their wants as to the wants of instructors. I refer to printed *keys*, containing solutions of all the more difficult problems in arithmetic and other branches of mathematics.

There are undoubtedly cases in which the *time* of the teacher is so limited that it is necessary for him to resort to the use of a key; but with pupils their effect is always injurious, sapping the very foundation of every thing adapted to promote manly, independent thought. Even with teachers who are compelled to resort to the use of keys for the purpose of saving time, it must be confessed that the *tendency* of the practice is to render instruction superficial. The very best that can be said of them is that they are *necessary evils.**

The practice of introducing young children to the study of English grammar as a science, and assigning them daily lessons to be prepared from a text-book, is exceedingly injurious in its influence upon their mental habits. A thorough and intelligent analysis of the structure of language is beyond the capacity of children eight or nine years of age.

Instruction in the use of language should be commenced as soon as children enter school, and all the primary classes should have frequent oral and written exercises in cultivating this important art; but the practice of requiring pupils under ten years of age to prepare set lessons from a grammatical textbook, often accomplishes little more than to form and strengthen the habit of studying without thinking.

* I refer, in these remarks, to keys that contain the solution of difficult questions, and not to those which contain only the *answers* of the problems. No such evils could arise from the use of keys containing answers only.

Few of us have any just conception of the latent energies of our own minds. It was eloquently said by Prof. B. B. Edwards, that "Genius lies buried on our mountains and in our valleys;" and he might with equal truth have added, that genius lies buried in our schools and colleges.

A successful teacher, of many years' experience, was accustomed to say to his pupils that he did not believe their average intellectual progress was ever half so great as they were capable of making. But it would be absurd to suppose that pupils do not generally devote half so much *time* to study as their duty requires. Most of the pupils in our higher seminaries study too many hours in a day already. The loss is in the *manner* of studying. The mind is not perfectly abstracted from every thing except the subject in hand. The mental energies are not all aroused and concentrated on a single point.

A young man was employed, some years ago, as an assistant teacher in a flourishing New England academy. Among the classes which he was called to instruct was one composed mostly of older pupils, in Day's Algebra. He had been over the greater part of this text-book before, but there were two or three problems which he had never been able to solve. There was one in particular on which he had already tried his strength a number of times without success. His class was now rapidly approaching this portion of the book, and he must be prepared for any emergency. He accordingly set himself at work, and devoted several hours to the unsolved problem; but still the desired result was as far from his grasp as ever.

Mortifying as the alternative was, he decided at length to go to one of the teachers of the school, and ask for assistance. The teacher kindly engaged to examine the question, but remarked that it was some time since he had been over this portion of the work, and he really was not quite sure that the method of solving it would readily occur to him. The class had now reached the section in which his difficulty occurred, and there was no time to be lost. After waiting one or two days the problem was returned to him, without a solution. What could be done? To go before his class and acknowledge that he was unable to master it, would be to lose caste at once. The necessity of the case suggested one more expedient. He had a friend, in an adjoining city, who was quite distinguished as a teacher of mathematics. To the house of his friend he now directed his course with as little delay as possible, but on arriving he learned that his friend had left the city and would not return for several days.

His last hope had fled, and his heart sunk within him. With a burden of chagrin and mortification that was almost insupportable, he commenced retracing his steps. "What," thought he to himself, "am I doing? Why am I here?" And his steps gradually quickened, as the excitement of his mind increased. He walked a few moments in silence; but his emotions soon found audible utterance. "I *can* solve the problem," he said, with emphatic gesture, "and I *will* solve it!" He went to his room, seated himself at his table, and did not rise till the task was accomplished.

This single triumph was worth more to him than a year of ordinary tuition, and the pleasure it afforded seemed to him like the concentration of a life of bliss. The solution was written out in full, and at the end of it there still stands a memorandum of the date and the hour of the night when the desired answer was obtained.

If we examine the intellectual efforts of our pupils we shall probably find that nine-tenths of them fall below the maximum of their own previous efforts, and can not therefore be taken into the account in estimating their intellectual progress.

Two pupils of equal abilities have the same lesson to prepare for recitation. One accomplishes the task by putting forth twenty distinct mental efforts. Eighteen of these cost him no greater energy or activity of mind than he has often brought into exercise before. The other two relate to difficulties which can not be overcome without efforts one degree *higher* than any that he has previously made. But the appearance of new difficulties only stimulates his mind to action, and the task is accomplished.

The other pupil puts forth the eighteen efforts that come within the range of his previous attainments, and leaves the two difficulties which would cost a *new* effort, to be explained at the recitation. To a superficial observer, these two pupils may seem to progress in the ratio of 20 to 18; but the true philosopher will tell us that their progress, so far as intellectual growth is concerned, is in the ratio of 2 to 0.

It is our misfortune that we have no means of measuring and recording from day to day the successive steps of mental growth. Heat and cold, the lapse of time, the speed of lightning, are made tangible, and measured with ease and exactness. We can even form a tolerably correct estimate of the amount of knowledge acquired in a single day or hour; but our estimates of progress in intellectual strength are exceedingly uncertain and often fallacious. It is to be feared that we often give our pupils credit for having passed a very profitable day in school, when they have actually deteriorated in mental power. We are in danger of forgetting that they may add to their stores of *knowledge*, without increasing their intellectual *strength.*

Let me here suggest the importance of having lessons recited by *pupils*, and not by *teachers.* Many teachers fall into the habit of supplying all the *ellipses* made by their pupils during recitation. A pupil rises in his place with an air of assurance, and proceeds with a full voice till he meets with some trifling difficulty, when the teacher supplies the desired word or hint, and the pupil proceeds as before, till another difficulty arises, and the teacher again comes to his aid.

In this way a very fair recitation is made out; and neither teacher nor pupil appears to know that if the pupil had been left to stand independent and alone he would have made almost an entire failure.

The practice of asking questions that suggest, directly or indirectly, the desired answer, has been exposed and condemned again and again in educational conventions and educational journals, but it has not yet been banished from the school-room. Many teachers who are careful to avoid *leading questions*, still ask altogether too *many* questions. Instead of giving the pupil a general topic, and expecting him to exhaust it, they kindly throw in a number of *additional* questions, to draw out the particulars which the pupil ought to associate with the main thought, and present in full, without this aid. Younger pupils require more questions than those more advanced; but even younger pupils should be allowed to carry some portion of a recitation without assistance. See *ante*, p. 99, § 94.

Let me not be misunderstood in the views I have expressed respecting the importance of requiring pupils to rely upon their own resources. The first germs of knowledge must come from *without*, and not from *within*, and very much of the knowledge acquired by younger classes, must be imparted directly by teachers and others. There are many branches of learning which we must all derive, in a greater or less degree, from teachers and books. The treasures of knowledge that have been accumulating for nearly 6000 years, are not to be rejected nor lightly esteemed. They are a precious inheritance; but he who contents himself in idleness and ease, and neglects to put his inheritance to usury, will find that his riches are little better than shadows.

But there are other departments of study, in which the value of our acquisitions depends almost entirely upon the action of our own minds; and it is upon these branches that we depend in a great degree for intellectual growth. Here, then, I would apply most rigidly the rule—never do for a pupil what he is capable of doing for himself.

Passive instruction is always attended with danger to the mental habits of pupils. A happy faculty of explaining and illustrating the principles of a lesson is an exceedingly valuable gift, but it is a gift that is often exercised to the detriment of learners. Whatever instruction we attempt to impart orally, should be given in such a manner that it will not fail to find a lodgment in the mind of the pupil. It is not sufficient to illustrate principles by examples and then leave them. They may even be *understood* at the time, and yet not fully *possessed.* The learner must *go through the process himself*, to be sure he is master of it.

Five boys of a class had failed to solve a difficult example in their lesson. The teacher went to the blackboard, and explained very carefully the manner in which the work was to be performed. He then requested those that understood the explanation to manifest it, and the five hands were all promptly raised. "Well," said the teacher, removing his work from the board, "you may all perform it now on your slates." The effort was made, but the result showed that only two of the five were able to perform the task. The others were perhaps right in saying that they *understood* the work, as the teacher explained it, step by step, on the board; but it was quite another thing *to do it.*

In our efforts to cultivate habits of self-reliance on the part of our pupils, one of the best and most feasible measures to which we can resort, is the practice of introducing frequent written reviews.

Several topics are written distinctly on the blackboard, and the pupils are required to expand them as fully and accurately as possible. Each pupil is seated by himself, and furnished with pen and paper; but receives no assistance, direct or indirect, from either teacher or text-book. See *ante*, p. 31, § 9.

There are too many teachers who seem to regard it as their chief business to exercise and develop their *own* minds, instead of attending to the minds of their pupils. There are those who even manage to sustain a very good degree of popularity, in school and in the community, by a display of themselves. "What stores of knowledge he possesses," says one. "How beautiful his illustrations," says another. This display of the teacher's knowledge may serve for *exhibition*, but it will prove of little value to the pupils in after life. The scholar whose attainments at school are but the echo of what the teacher has learned, will be sure to become one of that large class of citizens whose opinions and actions are always governed by those who have the independence to think and act for themselves.

I have dwelt at considerable length upon the subject of this article, because I believe that very few pupils are taught to rely sufficiently upon their own resources, and because I believe that many of the modern appliances in schools militate directly against the accomplishment of this object.

A few brief quotations will close the article.

"One preliminary truth is to be kept steadily in view in all the processes of teaching, and in the preparation of all its instruments, viz., that though much may be done by others to aid, yet the effective labor must be performed by the learner himself."—*Horace Mann.*

"Alas! how many examples are now present to our memory, of young men the most anxiously and expensively be-schoolmastered, be-tutored, be-lectured, any thing but *educated;* who have received arms and ammunition, instead of skill, strength, and courage; varnished rather than polished; perilously over-civilized, and most pitiably uncultivated! And all from inattention to the method dictated by nature herself, to the simple truth, that as the forms in all organized existence, so must all true and living knowledge proceed from within; that it may be trained, supported, fed, excited, but can never be infused or impressed."—*Coleridge.*

"A man can no more learn by the sweat of another man's brains than he can take exercise by getting another man to walk for him. All mental improvement resolves itself ultimately into self-improvement."—*Dr. Booth, of Wandsworth, England.*

"The prevailing notion, that we must be taught every thing, is a great evil. The most extensive education given by the most skillful masters often produces but inferior characters; that alone which we give to ourselves elevates us above mediocrity. The eminence attained by great men is always the result of their own industry."—*Marcel.*

"The first error in education is teaching men to *imitate*, or *repeat*, rather than *to think*. We need to take but a very cursory glance at the great theater of human life, to know how deep a root this radical error has struck into the foundations of education."—*Mansfield's American Education.*

PRIMARY SCHOOLS.

PRIMARY SCHOOLS are the basis of our whole system of public instruction. If evils are suffered to exist here, they will manifest themselves in all the higher stages of the pupil's progress, and cling to him through life.*

"Scratch the green rind of a sapling, or wantonly twist it in the soil;
The scarred and crooked oak will tell of thee for centuries to come."

It is in the Primary Schools that more than half of all public instruction is imparted, and a large portion of the children gathered here do not remain in school long enough to pass into the higher departments at all.

In most cities and towns, the Primary Schools suffer in a greater or less degree from the general impression that the teachers occupy positions less honorable than those of the teachers in the higher divisions, and perhaps still more from the pecuniary distinction that is often made in favor of teachers in the higher grades.

* "As parts of a great system of public instruction, it is scarcely possible to attach too much importance to the Primary Schools. They are the base of the pyramid, and in proportion as the base is enlarged and its foundations strengthened, the superstructure can be reared with ease and rapidity in graceful proportions, and to a towering height."—*Report of Boston School Committee.*

It is no disparagement to the teachers to say, that Primary classes are not generally taught so well as classes more advanced.* This would probably still be true if the Primary classes were taught by the teachers of the upper grades.

Of all the applicants examined by School Directors and Superintendents, there are more who are found qualified to instruct in the Grammar Schools than there are who are qualified to instruct in the Primary Schools.†

To excel as a Primary teacher, requires peculiar natural gifts, a thorough acquaintance with the first principles of knowledge, special fondness for young children, and an abiding consciousness that there is really no higher department of useful labor than that of giving direction to the first efforts of minds that are opening to an endless existence.‡

---

* "The weakest point in the whole system of American education, is its deficiency in thoroughness in all the elementary courses." —*Dr. Sears.*

† "In my search for teachers to fill vacancies, I find ten qualified to teach Geometry in a High School, to one who is qualified to teach reading in a Primary School; and in general, it is more difficult to find teachers adapted to give instruction in the lower grades, than in the higher."—*A. Freeze, Superintendent of Schools, Cleveland.*

‡ "*The best teachers are needed for Primary Schools.* At no point in the whole course of study are the results of incompetent teaching so disastrous, as at the commencement. If utter inexperience or desperate mediocrity must sit at the teacher's desk, let it be anywhere, everywhere, save in the Primary School: for anywhere and everywhere else will its ability to do irreparable mischief be less. At the subsequent stages of education, the mind emerging from the state of implicit trust in the mere dicta of the master, begins to

There is no other grade of schools in which the personal character of the teacher is so directly felt, as in the Primary. In the Grammar School, lessons are learned from text-books, and very much of the

---

assert itself, to sift what it receives, and find corrections when they are needed—but at the beginning, the mind takes the impress of the instruction given, with unquestioning faith, exact as the print of the seal upon the wax. The position is confidently assumed, that the wise discipline and sound philosophic mental training of the children in our Primary Schools, is more important and more difficult than that of any other department; and hence that the very best teachers should be assigned to that post of duty. It requires the clearest insight into the laws of mental life and action and the springs of feeling, the broadest views of the philosophy of education considered both as a science and an art, and the rarest combination of personal qualities, intellectual, moral, and social, that can well be conceived. When such teachers are found, they should be secured at almost any price. The common notion, that it matters little who teaches the little ones, or who is the assistant, provided an able man is obtained for the advanced scholars, or for principal, is exceedingly pernicious. With the exception, perhaps, of the principal of a union or graded school, the teachers of the Primary Departments should be the best qualified and the best paid."—*Newton Bateman, State Superintendent of Public Instruction, Illinois.*

"Especially should those to whom the education of the Primary classes is committed, be not only competent and apt to teach, but equable, dignified, and gentle in their deportment, kind and affectionate in their disposition, accustomed to self-control, and familiar with the wants and peculiarities of the children intrusted to their care. As a general rule, much greater maturity of mind is necessary and desirable for the proper development and discipline of this class of pupils, than for those of a more advanced grade; while, in the selection and arrangement of teachers, the youngest and least experienced are most frequently assigned to the duties of the former. While greater age, of itself, affords no criterion of ability to succeed in this department of instruction, the judgment, the dispo-

pupil's progress is made without the direct assistance of the teacher. But in the Primary Schools, the teacher is herself the text-book, the living oracle; and nearly all the impressions received by the pupil are a direct reflection from her own mind and heart.

But a teacher may possess every desirable mental and moral endowment, and yet, if a position in a Primary School is regarded as secondary in importance, and a situation in a higher department is continually before the mind as an object of ambition and desire, it is vain to expect the same degree of success that would be realized if no such distinction existed.

Since the duties of Primary teachers are really more arduous and responsible than those of teachers in the higher grades, and since most teachers would prefer situations in the higher grades, even if the compensation was the same as that of the Primary teachers, it would be difficult to find a reason, except in the power of custom, for paying the lowest salary to teachers of the Primary classes. In St. Louis, Chicago, and several other cities, the salaries are alike in the Grammar and Primary grades. By applying the same scale of salaries to both departments, the two positions are made equally honorable, and School Directors are enabled to secure for

---

sition, the temper, and the demeanor of the teacher should be narrowly scrutinized before committing to her guidance the intellectual and moral instruction of the elementary classes in our public schools."—*S. S. Randall, Superintendent of Schools, New York.*

the pupils of each grade the teachers best qualified to instruct them.*

It is to be regretted that so few Primary teachers receive any *special training* before entering upon the peculiar duties of their office. They are generally well educated, but their education has been conducted without any particular reference to the positions they are called to occupy. It is seldom that an examination of teachers occurs in which a majority of the applicants are not found to be radically deficient in some of the elementary principles of Primary instruction. Examples are constantly presented in which a candidate who is requested to give the sounds of the letters as they occur in some common word, replies, with the utmost composure,

* "Those active sympathies, winning ways, intuitive perceptions, womanly grace and delicacy, which captivate the hearts of all children, united with a well-balanced, well-cultivated mind, and a sincere desire to make children happy, are indispensable to the success of the Primary teacher. To secure these advantages, teachers must be selected with special reference to the labor to be done; and instead of testing the fitness of teachers for higher grades in the Primary Schools, it is respectfully submitted that it would be wisest to begin and work in the other direction. And let the scale of wages be also inverted, to correspond with the inverted order of rank. Let the best wages be paid to the most successful Primary teacher. Tradition and reverence for usage hang heavily upon all school management and all modes of instruction, but nowhere are these more conspicuous or more oppressive, than in the common opinion that *anybody* is competent to teach the little child."—*M. F. Cowdery, Superintendent of Schools, Sandusky, Ohio.*

"It requires a nicer tact, more instinctive talent, to manage successfully a Primary School, than one of a higher grade."—*Rhode Island State Commissioner's Report.*

that she has never attended to the sounds of the letters. Many applicants seem wholly unconscious that there is any necessary connection between their familiarity with the *rudiments* of learning and their fitness to teach a Primary School.

But while the Primary Schools are still suffering greatly from the evils which I have here pointed out, it is gratifying to know that the number of well-qualified Primary teachers is constantly increasing. The attention of educators has been specially turned to this subject, and a large number of model Primary teachers are now found in every section of the country; and among those that entered upon their labors as teachers with inadequate preparation, there are many who have made the most earnest efforts to improve their qualifications for the positions which they occupy. In no department of educational labor has improvement been more manifest during the last ten years, than in the instruction and discipline of Primary Schools

DISCIPLINE.

THE system of discipline adopted in schools should ever be guarded with special care. The constant aim of the teacher should be not merely to secure the best discipline, but to secure it by the best means.

That good order and a ready compliance with the directions and wishes of the teacher are essential to the success of every school, is a point on which all are agreed; but different teachers adopt widely different measures to attain this end. One labors chiefly to secure the confidence and kind regard of his pupils, and to satisfy them that all his requirements are dictated by a sincere and ardent desire to advance their best interests. Another appeals mainly to the necessity and justice of connecting suffering with wrong-doing, and follows every offence with some form of punishment. He may even succeed in satisfying both his pupils and their parents that the steps he is taking are necessary to the order and improvement of his school.

One commences his efforts before the tendencies to misconduct have ripened into action, and avoids the necessity for punishment except in extraordinary cases; while the other delays till his rules are violated, and is then compelled either to punish the offender or abandon his rules, and with them all hope of subordination and improvement.

If, now, we reason from cases like these, that a necessity for punishment implies incapacity on the part of the teacher to govern, we shall do great injustice to many of the most worthy and successful teachers in our schools. Cases will sometimes arise in which the best teacher would find it necessary to resort to the infliction of punishment for the misconduct of his pupils. Instances not unfrequently occur in which no other course will bring a wayward scholar to reflect long enough to afford an opportunity for higher and better influences to gain a lodgment in his mind.

If, then, on the one hand, we rest satisfied that a teacher has done his whole duty when we find that his punishments, though frequent and severe, are not disproportionate to the offences committed, we are in danger of giving sanction to punishments which, under the management of a more skillful teacher, would have been wholly unnecessary. And, on the other hand, if every punishment inflicted by a teacher is to be a means of rendering his name odious; if he is not to be sustained by the sympathy and approval of school directors and parents, the right arm of his authority is paralyzed. This very lack of sustaining influence will be the means of increasing greatly the necessity for punishment, which might be avoided if the right to inflict it was never called in question.

The ability to manage a school with the least possible amount of punishment, is an attainment of the highest order; and the teachers who possess this power should everywhere receive the highest honors of the profession and the most liberal rewards.

The main question at issue respecting corporal punishment, is not whether it can be entirely dispensed with, but how far can the necessity for resorting to it be reduced, without detriment to the order and discipline of schools.

In the efforts of the teacher to remove, as far as possible, the necessity for school punishments, he will have occasion to exercise all the judgment and skill he possesses, in employing other means to control the tendency of wayward pupils to irregularity and insubordination.* The first, and most important of these, must be found in the personal influence of the teacher himself. He must have the ability to inspire his pupils with a love of virtue and every adorning excellence, and his own life must be a model worthy of their imitation.

* "The following appear to be the principal means of which the educator can avail himself for maintaining an influence over his pupil:

1. The pupil's sense of duty.
2. The pupil's sense of his future interests.
3. The pupil's desire for knowledge.
4. The pupil's desire for occupation and intellectual action.
5. The pupil's desire for praise.
6. The pupil's desire to surpass others.
7. The pupil's love of, and respect for, the teacher.
8. The example of the teacher.
9. The hope of a reward.
10. The fear of punishment."—*Reid's Principles of Education.*

No effort should be spared to lead the pupils to govern themselves. This is a cardinal point in school discipline, and every thing short of this should be regarded as defective and unsatisfactory. Even arbitrary government by the teacher, when necessary, should tend to self-government on the part of the pupil, as an ultimate object.

There are two kinds of obedience, which are radically distinct from each other: obedience that is yielded in compliance with the dictates of reason and from a sense of duty; and obedience that is yielded to arbitrary authority, without any regard to reason and duty. The first requires no sacrifice of honor or self-respect on the part of the governed. It is simply recognizing the true and natural relation of the parent to his child, and of the teacher to his pupil. When the child's mind acts in accordance with reason, this obedience is yielded cheerfully and from choice. When the pupil will not acknowledge his duty to submit to the rightful authority of the teacher, when the will of the pupil gains control over his reason and judgment, then the teacher must take such measures as may be necessary to bring this wayward will to bow. The authority of the teacher in school must be complete and unquestioned.

But the teacher should never forget that love of freedom, love of independence, love of power, are all implanted in the natures of children for wise and important ends; and no unskillful teacher should be allowed to lay his hand ruthlessly upon them. No degree of eminence is ever attained without them. No high order of effort is ever made without them. They are committed to the teacher to be controlled and regulated, not to be crushed out.

The habit of yielding to arbitrary power against reason, is the condition of a slave; and mere servile obedience is degrading in its influence, destroys self-respect, breaks down all laudable ambition, and paralyzes every noble and worthy effort.

Of all the special instrumentalities that have been devised to aid teachers in securing the discipline of their schools, the most important is the use of the School Register, in which a permanent record is made of the pupil's deportment from day to day, and a general average carried out at the end of every month, to be sent, when practicable, to the parent or guardian. See *ante*, p. 139.

The subject of School Discipline is exceedingly fruitful, and I can not here attempt to discuss it in all its bearings. After introducing two or three quotations, I will pass to the consideration of a kindred topic.

"The value of any given result in school government depends very much upon the motives which produced it. We have seen pupils benumbed with fear and still as the grave, and heard their teacher—whose only *rule* was a reign of terror—lauded by the committee as a model disciplinarian. The stillest school is not always the most studious. Pupils may be controlled for a time by motives which will ultimately debase the character and enfeeble the will, or they may be stimulated to the highest effort by incentives which will be healthful and permanent in their influence upon the mind and heart."—*B. G. Northrop.*

Quotations.

"Another principle that is kept constantly in view in the government of the school, is to produce results by steadiness and perseverance, rather than by violent measures. Few students are found so obstinate or wayward as not to yield, eventually, even to a moderate pressure, steadily applied. This method of procedure is rendered the more easy and efficacious, by the consciousness of both the parties, that there is always in reserve ample power for more decisive measures, if they should become necessary. Students not previously accustomed to a mild method of discipline, sometimes mistake it at first for want of firmness. But such mistakes are soon rectified. The whole machinery of the school, like an extended piece of net-work, is thrown over and around him, and made to bear upon him, not with any great amount of force at any one time or place, but with a restraining influence just sufficient, and always and everywhere present. Some of the most hopeless cases of idleness and insubordination that I have ever known, have been found to yield to this species of treatment."—*Report of John S. Hart, Principal of Philadelphia High School.*

"Where all other means, both of prevention and of persuasion, reasoning and argument, have been faithfully and perseveringly tried, and have failed,—when the incorrigible offender is proof against all the gentler influences and agencies which the teacher has at his command, and continued forbearance involves a permanent injury, not only to the obstinate transgressor, but to his associates and companions, and to the welfare of the entire school,—the teacher should be clothed with the power of effectual chastisement. But this power should be exercised as sparingly as possible, and exercised, when it becomes inevitable, in such a manner as to produce the most salutary effect—*without passion, without anger or undue severity, and never in the presence of the school or the class.* Its infliction should, as far as possible, partake of the character of a *judicial punishment*,—resorted to with the utmost reluctance,—upon the fullest evidence of guilt, and of contumacy, *and only as a last resort.*"—*S. S. Randall, Superintendent of Schools, New York.*

LESSONS OF OBEDIENCE.

SOCIETY is so constituted, that the influence of government must everywhere be felt. A cheerful and hearty submission to rightful authority, is perfectly consistent with the freest and fullest development of a manly, independent spirit. It is impossible for any nation to maintain an existence, if the people have not learned this first great lesson of life; least of all can a free republic like ours continue, if the people have learned to govern, but not to obey. It becomes, then, an important inquiry, when and where shall this lesson of obedience be acquired. If delayed to adult years, there is no reason to expect it will ever be learned. It must be in the period of childhood and youth, and it must be either in the family or in the school. But it is painfully manifest, that a large portion of the children of every community, never learn to yield to authority at home, unless it be against their wills. In the public schools, all must be brought to the same standard. A spirit of implicit obedience must be secured, before any thing else can be attempted; not stolid, unreasoning, servile obedience, which crushes all manliness and self-respect out of the soul, but that intelligent, kindly obedience, which recognizes the true relation between parent and child, teacher and pupil, and bows cheerfully and from choice to the decision of another, whose character and position render it incumbent upon him to direct.

Here it is, in the public schools, that all the pupils learn a lesson which many of them would never learn elsewhere; a lesson which is essential to the perpetuity of our free government. This, if I mistake not, is the most important bond of connection between the free-school system and the State, and in this alone is found a sufficient argument for the support of schools at the expense of the State.*

* "Of all the dangers which threaten the future of our country, none, not even the fetid tide of official corruption, is so fearful as the gradual decrease in our habits of obedience. This is a result of the 'inalienable right of liberty' which we enjoy so fully; and is shown in the impaired force of parental influence, a greater disregard of the rights and comforts of others, and an increasing tendency to evade or defy the authority of law. Young America is now exuberant in its independence; but the greatest blessing it can have, is to be saved from itself, and to be taught that liberty rising above law, destroys its victim; untempered by humanity, is mere selfishness; and unregulated by law, becomes anarchy. This discipline is the work of education, and can only be accomplished by its broadest and most thorough operation."—*Report of Andrew H. Green, President of New York Board of Education*, 1857.

HEATING AND VENTILATION.

The improvements that have been made during the last thirty years in the principles and modes of teaching, are without a parallel in the history of the world.

In school architecture very great progress has also been made, and most of the principal cities and villages now possess neat and commodious school-buildings. It must, however, be confessed, that in the art of heating and ventilating school-houses, we have not made the same degree of progress.

In attempting a few practical suggestions on the heating and ventilation of school-buildings, I will first introduce some of the more important principles relating to the subject.

TEMPERATURE.

We are so constituted that a certain degree of heat is essential to health and comfort. The proper temperature of a school-room, according to the testimony of a large number of the best physicians and educators, is about 68° Fahrenheit. When the thermometer in a room rises above 70°, measures should immediately be taken to reduce the temperature; and when it sinks below 65°, measures should be taken to raise the temperature. If at any time the thermometer sinks below 60°, pupils can not be confined in their seats without an exposure of health.

RESPIRATION.

The healthy action of both mind and body requires a constant supply of fresh air for the lungs. A pure atmosphere is composed of about 80 per cent. of nitrogen, and 20 per cent. of oxygen. The life-giving principle is the oxygen. Air that has once passed through the lungs, is deprived of a large portion of its oxygen and charged with a poisonous gas. If it is retained in the lungs a few seconds, it will not even support ordinary combustion. Any one desirous of satisfying himself on this point, can do so by the following simple experiment. Provide a vessel containing a few quarts of water, a short tube of sufficient size for the breath to pass freely through it, a common drinking-glass, and a piece of candle about half an inch in length, attached to a few inches of wire, by which it may be suspended. Now plunge the glass into the water, and when the air is all expelled, invert and raise it gradually till most of the glass rises above the water; the open part being still below the surface, and the glass being still filled with the water. Next inhale a full breath of air and hold it in the lungs for fifteen or twenty seconds; then breathe it through the tube under the edge of the glass. It will of course displace the water, and the glass will be filled with air from the lungs. Before taking the glass out of the water, plunge in a small plate or board, and close the opening of the glass. It may now be removed from the water and set on a table, and is ready for use. Having lighted the candle, remove the cover from the glass and drop the candle into the impure air, and the flame will be instantly extinguished.

Besides the impurities sent out from the lungs, the insensible perspiration from all the pupils in a room contributes very considerably to increase the pernicious quality of the atmosphere.

To those who value the health of their children, it needs no argument to prove that this devitalized, poisonous air should be constantly removed from the school-room, and pure, life-giving air be introduced in its stead.

In estimating the amount of fresh air to be supplied, we ought not merely to consider what the system can be made to tolerate, but what amount will sustain the highest state of health for the longest time. Dr. Reid recommends at least ten cubic feet per minute as a suitable average supply for each individual; and states that his estimate is the result of an "extreme variety of experiments, made on hundreds of different constitutions, supplied one by one with given amounts of air, and also in numerous assemblies and meetings, where there were means of estimating the quantity of air with which they were provided."*

---

* Reid on Ventilation.

No physiologist estimates the amount required by each individual at less than five cubic feet per minute; and yet not one school in a hundred receives even this supply. The consequence is, that most of the pupils in our schools are compelled to inhale a small amount of poison at every breath. But most constitutions can bear a gradual undermining by slow poison, without any sudden or alarming symptoms of disease, and so the process is allowed to go on.

It is a reproach to the age in which we live, that with so many opportunities for advancement, the heating and ventilation of most of the school-buildings in every section of the country are still so unsatisfactory.

Let us not, however, neglect to avail ourselves of the knowledge we possess, nor regard all efforts to introduce improvements as failures, because they are only partially successful.

HOT-AIR FURNACES.

Hot-air furnaces are natural ventilators. The heated air that is sent into the room by them, necessarily forces the same amount of impure air out of the room. But the heated air itself, with which the room is constantly supplied, is rendered more or less impure by contact with the overheated surface of the furnace.

STEAM-HEATING.

Heating by steam is in many respects more satis factory than by hot-air furnaces, but even this mode of heating has not yet been fully perfected.

In most of the school-buildings that are now heated by steam, the radiators are placed in the rooms to be warmed. When due care is exercised to furnish a liberal supply of radiating surface, a satisfactory amount of heat is usually secured, with a reasonable consumption of fuel; and in the coldest days of winter, when there is a great difference between the temperature of the outside and of the inside air, there is little difficulty in securing a moderate degree of action in the ventiducts. In milder weather the ventilation is necessarily very imperfect.

To insure the safety of the school, the boiler should, if practicable, be located outside of the main building.

HOT-WATER HEATING.

When air is heated by passing over pipes that contain hot water, or over other surfaces heated by water, it retains its purity and possesses all the substantial advantages of air heated by steam. This mode of heating has already been adopted in a large number of school-houses and other buildings, but it has not yet met with so general favor as steam-heating. The choice between steam and hot water is simply a question of convenience and expense. Neither of these modes of heating, as ordinarily applied, affords good ventilation.

IMPROVED METHODS OF HEATING BY STEAM AND HOT WATER.

The following improved method of heating by steam and hot water, is worthy of special consideration: The heating pipes are brought together in a chamber in the basement of the building. This chamber is supplied by conductors with cold air from the outside of the building, and the heated air passes by conductors from the hot-air chamber into the different rooms, in the same manner as from an ordinary hot-air furnace. The consumption of fuel is somewhat greater than in the buildings heated by pipes which are placed in the rooms to be warmed; but this increased expenditure is mainly owing to the fact that rooms heated by pipes around the walls are of necessity poorly ventilated. The saving is made by heating the air once, and then breathing it over and over; whereas, by the improved arrangement, the air is heated, used once, and then removed by introducing a fresh supply.

This may safely be pronounced one of the best methods of heating school-buildings yet devised, since it secures the requisite degree of heat, furnishes a constant supply of fresh, warm air, and insures a good action of the ventiducts.

Another mode of heating by steam or hot water, combines the two modes already described. A portion of the pipes are placed around the rooms to be warmed, and a portion in the hot-air chamber under

the building. The object of this arrangement is to bring as much of the radiating surface as possible into the rooms, and at the same time secure a satisfactory action of the ventiducts.

PERKINS HEATER.

The Perkins Heater has a pot for the fire and a hot-air chamber, similar to an ordinary hot-air furnace; but instead of sending the heated air of this chamber into the school-rooms, a large number of metallic tubes are made to pass through the chamber, communicating below with cold-air conductors from without, and above with hot-air conductors to the several rooms; the air being heated as it passes through these tubes, which extend from the bottom to the top of the hot-air chamber. To increase the action of the hot air upon these tubes, open pans of water are placed around the fire-pots, which are constantly sending off vapor or steam into the hot-air chamber. This arrangement furnishes a constant supply of pure air, raised to the proper degree of heat, and secures an efficient action of the ventiducts.

Other furnaces, similar in principle to the Perkins Heater, have also been employed successfully in the heating and ventilation of buildings.

Whatever form of apparatus may be employed, it the air is heated in chambers below, it is important that the rooms should be warmed by the introduction of a large volume of moderately heated air. When air is introduced into a room at a very high temperature, it rises at once to the top and will not readily mingle with the cold air below. In rooms heated by hot-air furnaces, it is not uncommon to find a difference of fifteen or twenty degrees between the temperature of the upper part of the room and that of the lower.

IMPROVED STOVES.

There are two serious objections to the use of common stoves in schools. The first is the inequality of temperature in different parts of the room. Children sitting near the stove are often obliged to endure a temperature of 75° or 80°, while those more remote are exposed to a temperature of only 55° or 60°. The other principal objection to common stoves, is their lack of ventilating power.

The air surrounding a stove rises as it becomes heated, and the cold air near the floor of the room is drawn toward the stove to supply the place of the air that rises. In this way, the feet of the children are obliged to remain in the coldest air of the room, and the evil is increased by the action of the stove, which is constantly giving this stratum of cold air a greater or less degree of motion.*

* "When a stove stands uninclosed in a room, and without any direct connection with the outer atmosphere, there is a constant current of air toward it from every side of the apartment, both to supply the draft of combustion within the fire-chamber, and to seek contact with the outer surface of the hot plates, and then pass upward in a heated, and consequently more rarefied condition. This current, which is not at all impeded by the ordinary movable screens, owing to their being open below and at the sides, enters

To obviate these objections, stoves have been constructed with double cylinders, the space between the cylinders being open at the top and bottom. This secures a constant and rapid flow of air between the cylinders, which is heated in passing, rises to the top of the room, and then diffuses itself like the air that is introduced from a hot-air furnace.

It is obvious that this action will have the effect to distribute in different parts of the room the heat that would otherwise be radiated from the stove to the space immediately around it, and thus remove one of the most serious objections to the use of stoves.

The lower opening of the space between the cylinders may draw its supply of air directly from the room, or by a little extra expense it may be made to communicate with the air outside of the building.

If the air is carried to this lower opening by conductors from the outside, the stove becomes a *ventilating stove.* Pure, warm air is constantly introduced by it, and the vitiated air of the room is forced out through the ventiducts.

---

the apartment at the bottom of the doors and windows, and the chinks and openings in the floor and washboard, passes most strongly close along the floor, where the air is coldest and densest, and thus comes in direct contact with the feet and ankles of the occupants. This effect is extremely unpleasant, at the same time that it is most injurious to health. Children, especially in the country, often enter school with damp feet, and exposure to this cold current of air, in a state of inaction for hours together, is the sure but unsuspected cause of many a severe cold and hard cough."—*Pennsylvania School Architecture, by Thomas H. Burrowes, LL.D*

If the lower opening, under the stove, is fed by air from the room, the effect is to consume rapidly the cold air near the floor and equalize the temperature in all parts of the room. A constant circulation is secured, and the warm air from the upper portion of the room is necessarily drawn down near the floor, to take the place of the air that is carried up through the stove.

Since the improved stoves I have described can be procured at a moderate increase of expense above the cost of common stoves, and since they combine most of the substantial advantages of steam and hot-water apparatus, and of hot-air furnaces, their limited use can only be accounted for by the fact that their advantages are not generally known.

VENTILATION.

The construction and arrangement of ventiducts is a question of vital importance, in connection with the heating of school-rooms.

Since the essential element of all ventilation consists in the ingress and egress of air, the subject would seem at first view exceedingly simple; but in practice it has been found one of the most difficult of all the questions that have tasked the ingenuity of educators and philanthropists.

The first ventilator of which the author has any recollection, was made about twenty-five years ago, and used in connection with one of Orr's air-tight stoves. It opened directly into a smoke-flue, and was placed at the bottom of a room, the lower part being even with the floor. This secured a strong and certain action, and removed the air from the bottom of the room where it is coldest.

In many of our modern houses the ventilating registers are placed at the top of the rooms instead of the bottom. If a school-room is properly heated, that is, heated by the injection of a constant supply of fresh warm air, a ventilator placed at the top carries off the warmest and purest air of the room. The heated air conducted into the room rises directly to the top, and if it there finds a register opening into the ventiducts, it will of course pass directly off without being used at all. But if, on the other hand, the ventilating registers are placed either in the floor or in the bottom of the wall, the heated air sent into the room will first rise to the top, and then as the impure air near the floor is removed by the ventilators, the warm air above will pass down to take its place, and after being used and vitiated will pass off in the same way. The principal ventilators should not only be placed at the bottom of the room, but at the greatest distance from the inlet of the warm air.

A very excellent heating furnace, patented by Mr. Sawyer, is based on the principle of securing active ventilation from the lowest portion of the room. His ventilating registers are placed in the floor, and the impure air is conducted by tubes under the floor to the smoke-flues. This not only takes the coldest and most impure air from the room, but the ascending current in the smoke-flues necessarily secures a strong and constant action of the ventilators. It is worthy of observation that this arrangement is substantially a reproduction of the ventilators used twenty-five years ago in connection with Orr's air-tight stoves.

In constructing school-buildings, ventilating registers should generally be placed both at the top and the bottom of the rooms. In houses heated by common stoves, or by steam or hot-water pipes placed in the rooms, both the upper and the lower registers should ordinarily be kept open.

The foregoing remarks relate to the ventilation of school-rooms during the cold season. In the summer, when no artificial heat is required, the impure air from the lungs naturally ascends, and the upper registers should be constantly open.

It is not too much to say, that half the ventilators now found in our school-rooms are nearly useless. In rooms heated by steam with the pipes in the rooms, or by common stoves, it is very difficult to secure any but the most sluggish action, even when the ventiducts are properly constructed; and in most of the houses heated by the injection of warm air, the ventiducts are found to be either too small, or so badly obstructed as to be wholly inefficient. There are also hundreds of examples in which the ventiducts are made to terminate in close attics.

In a room intended for the accommodation of fifty or sixty pupils, the ventiduct should be not less than fifteen inches by eighteen, with a register having an equal amount of clear opening. In the construction of ventiducts, care should be taken to give them a smooth surface, and to avoid all sudden turns or angles. The Emerson ventilating caps, placed at the outlets, are also important auxiliaries to the successful operation of ventilating flues.

If a smoke-pipe, or steam or hot-water pipe, can be made to pass through a ventiduct, its value will be greatly increased. When this is impracticable, the ventiduct should at least be carried up by the side of a smoke-flue. In one of the school-buildings of Chicago, a steam-pipe is carried through the length of each ventiduct. In the Philadelphia High School, the ventiducts all terminate in two ventilating chambers in the loft. In each of these is placed a large coal-stove, and from the top is a large cylindrical exit-tube. A large amount of heat may be generated by these stoves, at any season of the year, and an impetus given to the ascending current to any extent desired.*

When all other resources for ventilation fail, the teacher should resort to the windows. These can be opened freely before and after school, and at the

* "The important points in the construction of a ventilator are, that it should, when possible, be a warm tube, and that it should open near the floor of the apartment to be ventilated. When warm, it constantly acts, from the mechanical tendency of a column of heated air to rise; whereas, if cold, it acts only when air is, by some means, forced into the room to be ventilated. In every other case, a cold ventilator is not to be relied on. A second point is, that its opening should be near the floor of the apartment, for it then carries off the stratum of air in contact with the floor, which is always the coldest, and usually the foulest in the room."--*North American Review.*

recesses; and they can be let down from the top, a few inches, during school hours, when the air of the room becomes unfit for use.

The following extract from a report prepared by a special committee of the New York Board of Education, embodies a condensed summary of nearly all the valuable results that have yet been reached on the subject of heating and ventilation:

"That the building be warmed throughout (except the janitor's rooms, halls, and stairways) with fresh air, heated by contact with hot-water or steam pipes, or radiators, placed beneath the building; that the quantity of such radiating surface be at least one square foot to every fifty feet of the cubical content of the portion of the building to be heated; that if this do not amount to four square feet of radiating surface for each scholar to be accommodated in the building, then that amount be put in; that the boilers shall be capable of boiling the water, or of generating abundant steam in the coldest weather, and the smoke-pipe shall not in any case show a temperature of above 350°; that the draught of air into the furnace of the boiler, of water into the boiler, and of cold air into the stacks of pipes or radiators, be governed by automatic regulators; that the boilers shall not require replenishing with fuel oftener than once in every four hours; that the radiating surface be divided into separate stacks, one or more for each room, and that the ventilating flues be separate, with openings into the room both at the top and the bottom of the room, and equal in aggregate sectional area to the sectional area of the cold-air boxes, which shall not be less than one square foot for every hundred feet of radiating surface; that the contractor shall give security satisfactory to the Board of Education that he will keep the apparatus in repair for five years, and that it shall in all weathers heat every portion of the house to 70°, and furnish ventilation at the rate of ten cubic feet of air per minute to each scholar to be accommodated by the building, the air to be so introduced into the rooms as to produce no unpleasant draught."

BOOKS OF REFERENCE

FOR THE

ORAL COURSE OF INSTRUCTION.

In conducting oral exercises on the various subjects relating to common life, teachers are often at a loss to know what sources of information are most available. The following catalogue will serve as a general guide to works of this class. The list is by no means complete; but it embraces the most useful of those which have fallen under the author's observation.

Teachers will generally derive more aid from such works as "The Science of Common Things," "First Book of Science," "Fireside Philosophy," etc., than from the more elaborate text-books prepared for the use of High Schools and Academies. By cultivating a familiarity with elementary and practical works on the different subjects to be presented, teachers will more readily adopt a style of instruction and illustration that is adapted to the wants of their classes, than by studying works which are more extended and more strictly scientific. One of the greatest dangers in giving oral lessons, is that of attempting too much. The principles of science must be drawn upon sufficiently to give the pupils a clear and satisfactory explanation of most of the common phenomena around them, without attempting to exhaust the different sciences to which they relate.

ACKERMAN.—First Book of Natural History, by A. Ackerman, 12mo, pp. 286, New York.

ABBOTT.—Learning about Common Things, by Jacob Abbott, 16mo, pp. 193, New York.

BARNARD.—Object Teaching and Oral Lessons on Social Science and Common Things, with various Illustrations of the Principles and Practice of Primary Education, as adopted in the Model and Training Schools of Great Britain; republished from Barnard's American Journal of Education; 8vo, pp. 434, New York and Chicago. $1.50.

This volume contains a reprint of several of the most valuable English works on Oral Teaching.

BEECHER.—Physiology and Calisthenics, by Catharine E. Beecher, 16mo, pp. 151, New York. 50 cts.

BROWNELL.—How to Use Globes, by F. C. Brownell, 12mo, pp. 33, New York and Chicago. 10 cts.

BATEMAN.—Third Biennial Report of the Superintendent of Public Instruction of the State of Illinois, for 1859–60, by Hon. Newton Bateman, Springfield, Illinois.

Mr. Bateman's Report embraces an article of sixteen octavo pages on object lessons; the value and use of the slate and blackboard, and of cards and charts; the best methods of cultivating habits of observation and reflection; and the relative importance of Primary Schools in a graded course of instruction.

Calkins.—Primary Object Lessons for a Graduated Course of Development, by N. A. Calkins, 12mo, pp. 362, New York. $1.00.

Carll.—Child's Book of Natural History, illustrating the Animal, Vegetable, and Mineral Kingdoms, with application to the Arts, by M. M. Carll, 16mo, pp. 148, New York. 38 cts.

Cowdery.—Elementary Moral Lessons, for Schools and Families, by M. F. Cowdery, Superintendent of Public Schools, Sandusky, Ohio, 12mo, pp. 261, Philadelphia. 63 cts.

Cowdery.—Primary Moral Lessons, Part I., by M. F. Cowdery, Superintendent of Public Schools, Sandusky, Ohio, 16mo, pp. 116, Sandusky. 33 cts.

Camp.—Annual Report of the Superintendent of Common Schools of the State of Connecticut for 1861–62, by Hon. David N. Camp.

Mr. Camp's Report contains an article of twenty-five octavo pages on Methods of Teaching, embracing Object Lessons and a Course of Study for Primary, Intermediate, and Grammar Schools.

Emerson and Flint.—Manual of Agriculture, for the School, the Farm, and the Fireside, by Geo. B. Emerson and Chas. L. Flint, 12mo, pp. 306, Boston.

Fitzgerald.—Exhibition Speaker; to which is added a Complete System of Calisthenics and Gymnastics, with Instructions for Teachers and Pupils. Illustrated with fifty engravings, 12mo, pp. 268, New York. 75 cts.

The Gymnastics and Calisthenics occupy forty-six pages.

Gregory.—Catalogue of the Michigan State Teachers' Institutes, Spring Series of 1862, held under the direction of the Superintendent of Public Instruction. Pamphlet, pp. 80. Lansing, Michigan.

Fifty pages of this Catalogue are devoted to Object Lessons, Physical Education, Moral Education, Primary Teaching, and an extended Course of Study for a Graded School, by J. M. Gregory, Superintendent of Public Instruction.

Most of these articles are also embraced in Mr. Gregory's Annual Report for 1861.

Hill.—First Lessons in Geometry, by Thomas Hill, President of Antioch College, 24mo, pp. 144, Boston.

Hazen.—Popular Technology, or Professions and Trades, by Edward Hazen, A. M., 2 vols., 16mo, pp. 536, Harper's Family Library.

Hooker.—Child's Book of Nature, in three parts. Part I., Plants; Part II., Animals; Part III., Air, Water, Heat, Light, etc. By Worthington Hooker, M. D., 16mo, square, pp. 469, New York.

Hooker.—Natural History for the use of Schools and Families, by Worthington Hooker, M. D., 12mo, pp. 382, New York.

Hailman.—Outlines of a System of Object Teaching, by William N. Hailman, 8vo, pp. 38, Louisville, Ky.

Mayo.—Manual of Elementary Instruction, by Elizabeth Mayo, 2 vols., 16mo, pp. 609, London, Home and Colonial School Society. $2.50.

MAYO.—Lessons on Objects, by Elizabeth Mayo, 16mo, pp. 229, London. $1.50.

An American edition of this work will soon be issued by J. B. Lippincott & Co., Philadelphia.

MAYO.—Lessons on Shells, by Elizabeth Mayo, 16mo, London. $2.00.

MARCEL.—Language as a Means of Mental Culture and International Communication, by C. Marcel, French Consul, 2 vols., 12mo, pp. 841, London.

This is an elaborate and philosophical system of mental, moral, and physical culture, practically applied. The title is not well chosen.

NORTON AND PORTER.—First Book of Science, designed for Public and Private Schools, by W. A. Norton and J. A. Porter. Part I., Natural Philosophy and Astronomy; Part II., Chemistry and Allied Sciences. 12mo, pp. 419, New York. $1.00.

NORTHEND.—Exercises for Dictation and Pronunciation, by Charles Northend, A. M., 18mo, pp. 252, New York. 40 cts.

PHILBRICK.—Boston Primary School Tablets, by John D. Philbrick, Superintendent of Public Schools of Boston. Twenty Tablets, mounted on ten cards, illustrating the Alphabet, Penmanship, Drawing, Punctuation, Numerals, Sounds of the Letters, etc. Boston. $5.00.

PHILBRICK.—Primary School Manual, by John D Philbrick, Superintendent of Public Schools, Bos ton, 12mo, about 400 pages. $1.00. In press.

A treatise on the Principles and Methods of Elementary Education.

PETERSON.—Familiar Science, by R. E. Peterson, 12mo, pp. 558, Philadelphia.

ROOT.—School Amusements; or, How to Make School Interesting. Embracing Simple Rules for Military and Gymnastic Exercises, and Hints upon the General Management of the School-room. By N. W. Taylor Root, 12mo, pp. 225, New York. $1.00.

ROOT.—Infantry Tactics for Schools; Explained and Illustrated for the use of Teachers and Scholars. By the Author of School Amusements, 18mo, pp. 180, New York. 50 cts.

SANDERS.—Elocutionary Chart, by C. W. Sanders, A. M., New York.

TRALL.—The Illustrated Family Gymnasium; containing the most Improved Methods of applying Gymnastic, Calisthenic, Kinesipathic, and Vocal Exercises to the Development of the Bodily Organs, the Invigoration of their Functions, the Preservation of Health, and the Cure of Diseases and Deformities. By R. T. Trall, M. D., 8vo, pp. 215, New York. $1.25.

WILLEMENT.—Catechism of Familiar Things; their History, etc., with a brief Explanation of some of the Principal Natural Phenomena. By Emily Elizabeth Willement, 12mo, pp. 206, Philadelphia.

WELCH.—Object Lessons, prepared for Teachers of Primary Schools and Primary Classes, by A. S Welch, Principal of Michigan State Normal School 18mo, pp. 173, New York. 50 cts.

WELLS.—Familiar Science; or, the Scientific Explanation of the Principles of Natural and Physical

Science, and their Practical and Familiar Applications to the Employments and Necessities of Common Life. By David A. Wells, A. M., 8vo, pp. 566, Philadelphia.

WELLS.—The Science of Common Things; a Familiar Explanation of the First Principles of Physical Science; for Schools, Families, and Young Students. By David A. Wells, A. M., 12mo, pp. 323, New York. 75 cts.

WATTS on the Mind, with Questions, 18mo, New York. 34 cts.

WALKER.—Manly Exercises, containing Rowing, Sailing, Riding, Driving, Racing, Leaping, Balancing, Hunting, Shooting, Exercises with Indian Clubs, etc. From the 9th London edition, 12mo, pp. 323, Philadelphia.

WATSON.—National Phonetic Tablets, by J. Madison Watson. Eight Tablets. New York. $3.00.

WILLARD.—Morals for the Young, by Emma Willard, 16mo, New York. 50 cts.

YOUMANS.—Hand-Book of Household Science; a Popular Account of Heat, Light, Air, Aliment, and Cleansing, in their Scientific Principles and Domestic Applications. By Edward L. Youmans, 12mo, pp. 470, New York. $1.25.

The Reason Why; General Science. A careful collection of many hundreds of Reasons for Things which, though generally believed, are imperfectly understood. 12mo, pp. 346, New York. $1.00

Fireside Philosophy; or, Familiar Talks about Common Things. 12mo, pp. 360, New York. $1.00

GENERAL LIBRARY FOR TEACHERS.

"We, and the community, would look with distrust, if not with contempt, upon the man who should commence the practice of law without having in his possession a single treatise on law. Are we not, then, justified in withholding respect from one who attempts to teach without the opportunity of daily reference to the excellent works which have been prepared to aid teachers? The teacher should have a professional library, and should replenish it yearly, as regularly as he does his wardrobe, and as liberally as circumstances will allow."—*Dr. A. D. Lord, of Columbus, Ohio.*

The character of schools must always depend mainly upon the character of the teachers, and the progress and improvement of the schools generally bear a direct relation to the efforts made by the teachers for their own improvement.

The teacher who is satisfied with present attainments, and whose ambition in school rises no higher than a mere repetition of past efforts, will be sure to furnish an example in which both teacher and school are constantly deteriorating.

It is the manifest duty of the teacher to strive every day to make some positive advance upon the labors of the previous day. To this end he must not only be fruitful in expedients, and assiduous in studying the character and dispositions of his different pupils, but he must also avail himself of the wisdom and experience of others who are engaged in the same work.

The study of educational works embodying the results of the best efforts of successful educators in this and other countries, is an indispensable auxiliary to the labors of the teacher who is desirous of advancing to a high standard in his profession.

Abbott.—The Teacher; or, Moral Influences employed in the Government and Instruction of the Young. By Jacob Abbott, 12mo, New York. $1.00.

Arnold.—Life and Correspondence of Thomas Arnold, D. D., late head master of Rugby School, by A. P. Stanley. Reprinted from London edition. 8vo, pp. 490, New York.

Alcott.—Confessions of a Schoolmaster, by William A. Alcott, 12mo, pp. 316, New York. 75 cts.

Burton.—The District School as it was, by Warren Burton, 18mo, pp. 156, Boston.

Barnard.—National Education in Europe; being an Account of the Organization, Administration, Instruction, and Statistics of Public Schools of different Grades in the different States. By Henry Barnard, LL. D., 8vo, pp. 890. $3.00.

Barnard.—Educational Biography; or, Memoirs of Teachers, Educators, and Promoters and Benefactors of Education, Literature, and Science. By Henry Barnard, LL. D., vol. 1, 8vo, pp. 524, New York and Hartford. $3.50.

Barnard.—American Journal of Education, from 1855 to the present time, edited by Henry Barnard, LL. D., 11 vols., 8vo, each about 800 pages, Hartford and New York. First five volumes, $12.50. Annual subscription, $4.00.

Barnard—School Architecture; or, Contributions

to the Improvement of School-houses in the United States. By Henry Barnard, LL. D., 8vo, pp. 366, New York. $2.00.

BARNARD.—Normal Schools, and other Institutions, Agencies, and Means designed for the Professional Education of Teachers, by Henry Barnard, LL. D., 8vo, pp. 659, Hartford and New York. $2.00.

BARNARD.—Educational Aphorisms and Suggestions, Ancient and Modern, republished from Barnard's American Journal of Education, 8vo, pp. 753, New York and Chicago. $1.50.

BURROWES.—Pennsylvania School Architecture; a Manual of Directions and Plans for Grading, Locating, Constructing, Heating, Ventilating, and Furnishing Common-school Houses; by Thomas H. Burrowes, LL. D., royal 8vo, pp. 276, Harrisburg, Pa.

BATES.—Lectures on Mental and Moral Culture, by Samuel P. Bates, A. M., 12mo, pp. 319, New York. $1.00.

BATES.—Method of Teachers' Institutes, and the Theory of Education, by Samuel P. Bates, A. M., 12mo, New York.

CRAIG.—The Philosophy of Training; or, The Principles and Art of a Normal Education. By A. R. Craig, 12mo, pp. 377, London.

DWIGHT.—The Higher Christian Education, by Benjamin W. Dwight, 12mo, pp. 347, New York. $1.0C

DAVIES.—Logic and Utility of Mathematics, with he best Methods of Instruction explained and illustrated, by Charles Davies, LL. D., 8vo, pp. 375. $1.00.

DUNN.—Principles of Teaching; or, The Normal Manual: containing Practical Suggestions on the Government and Instruction of Children. By Henry Dunn, 12mo, pp. 274, London. $1.25.

DE TOCQUEVILLE.—American Institutions and their Influence, by Alexis de Tocqueville, with Notes by John C. Spencer, 12mo, pp. 460, New York. $1.00.

FOWLE.—The Teachers' Institute; or, Familiar Hints to Young Teachers. By William B. Fowle, 12mo, pp. 258, Boston.

HALL.—The Instructor's Manual; or, Lectures on School-keeping. By S. R. Hall, A. M., 16mo, pp. 233, Boston.

HALL.—Teaching, a Science; the Teacher an Artist. By Baynard R. Hall, A. M., 12mo, pp. 305, New York. $1.00.

HOLBROOK.—The Normal; or, Methods of Teaching the Common Branches, Orthoëpy, Orthography, Grammar, Geography, Arithmetic, and Elocution. By Alfred Holbrook, 12mo, pp. 456, New York. $1.00.

JOHONNOT.—Country School-Houses; containing Elevations, Plans, and Specifications, with Estimates, Directions to Builders, Suggestions as to School Grounds, Furniture, Apparatus, etc., and a Treatise on School-house Architecture. By James Johonnot, New York. $2.00.

MAYHEW.—Means and Ends of Universal Education, by Ira Mayhew, A. M., 12mo, pp. 447, New York. $1.00.

MANSFIELD.—American Education, its Principles

and Elements, by Edward D. Mansfield, 12mo, pp 330, New York. $1.00.

MANN.—Lectures on Education, by Horace Mann, 12mo, pp. 338, Boston. $1.00.

MANN.—The Common-School Journal, from 1838 to 1848. Ten volumes. Edited by Horace Mann, 8vo, Boston.

MILLER.—My Schools and Schoolmasters; or, The Story of my Education. By Hugh Miller, 12mo, pp. 551, Boston.

NORTHEND.—The Teacher and Parent; a Treatise upon Common-school Education: containing Practical Suggestions to Teachers and Parents. By Charles Northend, A. M., 12mo, pp. 327, New York. $1.00.

NORTHEND.—The Teacher's Assistant; or, Hints and Methods in School Discipline and Instruction. By Charles Northend, A. M., 12mo, pp. 327, New York. $1.00.

ORCUTT.—Hints to Common-School Teachers, Parents, and Pupils; or, Gleanings from School-Life Experience. By Hiram Orcutt, A. M., 16mo, pp. 144, Rutland, Vt. 38 cts.

OGDEN.—The Science of Education and Art of Teaching, by John Ogden, A. M., 12mo, Cincinnati.

PAGE.—Theory and Practice of Teaching; or, The Motives and Methods of Good School-keeping. By David P. Page, A. M., 12mo, pp. 349, New York. $1.00.

PHILBRICK.—Report on Truancy and Compulsory Education, by John D. Philbrick, Superintendent of

Public Schools, Boston, 8vo, pp. 74. Published with the Report of the School Committee of Boston, for 1861.

Palmer.—The Teacher's Manual; being an Exposition of an Efficient and Economical System of Education, suited to the Wants of a Free People. By Thomas H. Palmer, A. M., 12mo, pp. 263, Boston.

Pillans.—The Rationale of Discipline, as exemplified in the High School of Edinburgh, by Professor Pillans, 8vo, pp. 259, Edinburgh and London.

Potter and Emerson.—The School and Schoolmaster; a Manual for the use of Teachers, Employers, Trustees, Inspectors, etc., of Common Schools. In two parts. By Alonzo Potter, D. D., and George B. Emerson, LL. D., 12mo, pp. 552, New York.

Richards.—Manual of School Method, for the Use of Teachers in Elementary Schools, by W. F. Richards, 16mo, pp. 188, London.

Reid.—The Principles of Education; an Elementary Treatise, designed as a Manual or Guide for the Use of Parents, Guardians, and Teachers, 12mo, pp. 292, London. $1.50.

Russell.—The American Journal of Education, from 1826 to 1830. Five volumes. Conducted by William Russel, 8vo, Boston.

This was the first periodical devoted exclusively to the interests of education.

Randall.—Mental and Moral Culture and Popular Education, by S. S. Randall, Superintendent or Schools, New York, 16mo, pp. 236, New York.

SAWYER.—A Plea for Amusements, by Frederick W. Sawyer, 16mo, pp. 320, New York.

SMITH.—Education. Part I., History of Education, Ancient and Modern; Part II., a Plan of Culture and Instruction. By H. J. Smith, A. M., 12mo pp. 340, New York.

STOWE.—The Training System, Moral Training School, and Normal Seminary for preparing School-Trainers and Governesses, by David Stowe, 8vo, pp. 560, London. $2.50.

SPENCER.—Education—Intellectual, Moral, and Physical; by Herbert Spencer, 8vo, pp. 283, New York.

Four articles, reprinted from the Westminster, North British, and British Quarterly Reviews.

TATE.—The Philosophy of Education; or, The Principles and Practice of Teaching. In five parts. Part I., On Method as Applied to Education; Part II., The Intellectual and Moral Faculties considered in relation to Teaching; Part III., On Systems and Methods of Instruction; Part IV., On Systems and Methods as applied to the various Branches of Elementary Education; Part V., On School Organization and Discipline. By T. Tate, F. R. A. S., London.

TAYLOR.—Method of Classical Study; illustrated by Questions on a few Selections from Latin and Greek Authors. By Samuel H. Taylor, LL. D., 12mo, pp. 154, Boston.

THOMPSON.—Locke Amsden; or, The Schoolmaster. By D. P. Thompson, 12mo, pp. 231, Boston. 75 cts.

Todd.—The Student's Manual, by John Todd, D. D., 12mo.

Woodbridge.—American Annals of Education, from 1830 to 1837. Seven volumes. Conducted by William C. Woodbridge, assisted in the 7th volume by William A. Alcott, 8vo, Boston.

This is a continuation of the American Journal of Education.

The Sessional School Collection: consisting of Religious and Moral Instruction; a Selection of Fables; Descriptions of Animals, Places, Manners, etc., 12mo, pp. 298, Edinburgh.

The History and Progress of Education in Europe and America, collected from the most reliable sources. By Philobiblius. With an Introduction, by Henry Barnard, LL. D., 12mo, New York. $1.00.

Lectures before the American Institute of Instruction, an annual volume, from 1830 to the present time, 12mo, Boston. 50 cts. a volume.

THE END.

THE NATIONAL SERIES OF READERS.

COMPLETE IN TWO INDEPENDENT PARTS.

I.
THE NATIONAL READERS.

By PARKER & WATSON.

No. 1.—National Primer, ... *64 pp., 16mo,*
No. 2.—National First Reader, . . . *128 pp., 16mo,*
No. 3.—National Second Reader, . . *224 pp., 16mo,*
No. 4.—National Third Reader, . . *288 pp., 12mo,*
No. 5.—National Fourth Reader, . . *432 pp., 12mo,*
No. 6.—National Fifth Reader, . . *600 pp., 12mo,*

National Elementary Speller, . . . *160 pp., 16mo,*
National Pronouncing Speller, . . . *188 pp., 12mo,*

II.
THE INDEPENDENT READERS.

By J. MADISON WATSON.

The Independent First (or Primary) Reader, *80 pp., 16mo,*
The Independent Second Reader, . *160 pp., 16mo,*
The Independent Third Reader, . . *240 pp., 16mo,*
The Independent Fourth Reader, . . *264 pp., 12mo,*
The Independent Fifth Reader, . . *336 pp., 12mo,*
The Independent Sixth Reader, . . *474 pp., 12mo,*

The Independent Child's Speller (Script), *80 pp., 16mo,*
The Independent Youth's Speller (Script), *168 pp., 12mo,*
The Independent Spelling Book, . . *160 pp., 16mo,*

*** The Readers constitute two complete and entirely distinct series, either of which is adequate to every want of the best schools. The Spellers may accompany either Series.

PARKER & WATSON'S NATIONAL READERS.

The salient features of these works which have combined to render them so popular may be briefly recapitulated as follows:

1. THE WORD-BUILDING SYSTEM.—This famous progressive method for young children originated and was copyrighted with these books. It constitutes a process with which the beginner with *words* of one letter is gradually introduced to additional lists formed by prefixing or affixing single letters, and is thus led almost insensibly to the mastery of the more difficult constructions. This is one of the most striking modern improvements in methods of teaching.

2. TREATMENT OF PRONUNCIATION.—The wants of the youngest scholars in this department are not overlooked. It may be said that from the first lesson the student by this method need never be at a loss for a prompt and accurate rendering of every word encountered.

3. ARTICULATION AND ORTHOEPY are considered of primary importance.

4. PUNCTUATION is inculcated by a series of interesting *reading lessons*, the simple perusal of which suffices to fix its principles indelibly upon the mind.

5. ELOCUTION. Each of the higher Readers (3d, 4th and 5th) contains elaborate, scholarly, and thoroughly practical treatises on elocution. This feature alone has secured for the series many of its warmest friends.

6. THE SELECTIONS are the crowning glory of the series. Without exception it may be said that no volumes of the same size and character contain a collection so diversified, judicious, and artistic as this. It embraces the choicest gems of English literature, so arranged as to afford the reader ample exercise in every department of style. So acceptable has the taste of the authors in this department proved, not only to the educational public but to the reading community at large, that thousands of copies of the Fourth and Fifth Readers have found their way into public and private libraries throughout the country, where they are in constant use as manuals of literature, for reference as well as perusal.

7. ARRANGEMENT. The exercises are so arranged as to present constantly alternating practice in the different styles of composition, while observing a definite plan of progression or gradation throughout the whole. In the higher books the articles are placed in formal sections and classified topically, thus concentrating the interest and inculcating a principle of association likely to prove valuable in subsequent general reading.

8. NOTES AND BIOGRAPHICAL SKETCHES. These are full and adequate to every want. The biographical sketches present in pleasing style the history of every author laid under contribution.

9. ILLUSTRATIONS. These are plentiful, almost profuse, and of the highest character of art. They are found in every volume of the series as far as and including the Third Reader.

10. THE GRADATION is perfect. Each volume overlaps its companion preceding or following in the series, so that the scholar, in passing from one to another, is only conscious, by the presence of the new book, of the transition.

11. THE PRICE is reasonable. The National Readers contain more matter than any other series in the same number of volumes published. Considering their completeness and thoroughness they are much the cheapest in the market.

12. BINDING. By the use of a material and process known only to themselves, in common with all the publications of this house, the National Readers are warranted to outlast any with which they may be compared—the ratio of relative durability being in their favor as two to one.

WATSON'S INDEPENDENT READERS.

This Series is designed to meet a general demand for smaller and cheaper books than the National Series proper, and to serve as well for intermediate volumes of the National Readers in large graded schools requiring more books than one ordinary series will supply.

Beauty. The most casual observer is at once impressed with the unparalleled mechanical beauty of the Independent Readers. The Publishers believe that the æsthetic tastes of children may receive no small degree of cultivation from their very earliest school books, to say nothing of the importance of making study attractive by all such artificial aids that are legitimate. In accordance with this view, not less than $25,000 was expended in their preparation before publishing, with a result which entitles them to be considered "The Perfection of Common School Books."

Selections. They contain, of course, none but entirely new selections. These are arranged according to a strictly progressive and novel method of developing the elementary sounds in order in the lower numbers, and in all, with a view to topics and general literary style. The mind is thus led in fixed channels to proficiency in every branch of good reading, and the evil results of 'scattering' as practised by most school-book authors, avoided.

The Illustrations, as may be inferred from what has been said, are elegant beyond comparison. They are profuse in every number of the series from the lowest to the highest. This is the only series published of which this is true.

The Type is semi-phonetic, the invention of Prof. Watson. By it every letter having more than one sound is clearly distinguished in all its variations without in any way mutilating or disguising the normal form of the letter.

Elocution is taught by prefatory treatises of constantly advancing grade and completeness in each volume, which are illustrated by wood-cuts in the lower books, and by black-board diagrams in the higher. Prof. Watson is the first to introduce Practical Illustrations and Black-board Diagrams for teaching this branch.

Foot Notes on every page afford all the incidental instruction which the teacher is usually required to impart. Indices of words refer the pupil to the place of their first use and definition. The Biographies of Authors and others are in every sense excellent.

Economy. Although the number of pages in each volume is fixed at the minimum, for the purpose recited above, the utmost amount of matter available without overcrowding is obtained in the space. The pages are much wider and larger than those of any competitor and contain *twenty per cent* more matter than any other series of the same type and number of pages.

All the Great Features. Besides the above all the popular features of the National Readers are retained except the Word-Building system. The latter gives place to an entirely new method of progressive development, based upon some of the best features of the Word System, Phonetics and Object Lessons.

NATIONAL READERS.

ORIGINAL AND "INDEPENDENT" SERIES.

SPECIMEN TESTIMONIALS.

From D. H. HARRIS, *Supt. Public Schools, Hannibal, Mo.*

The National Series of Readers are now in use in our public schools, and I regard them *the best* that I have ever examined or used.

From HON. J. K. JILLSON, *Supt. of Education, State of South Carolina.*

I have carefully examined your new and beautiful Series of Readers known as "The Independent Readers," and do not hesitate to recommend it as the finest and most excellent ever presented to the public.

From D. N. ROOK, *Sec. of School Board, Williamsport, Pa.*

I would say that Parker & Watson's Series of Readers and Spellers give the best satisfaction in our schools of any Series of Readers and Spellers that have ever been used. There is nothing published for which we would exchange them

From PROF. H. SEELE, *New Braunfels Academy, Texas.*

I recommend the National Readers for four good reasons: (1.) The printing, engraving, and binding is excellent. (2.) They contain choice selections from English Literature. (3.) They inculcate good morals without any sectarian bias. (4.) They are truly *National*, because they teach pure patriotism and not sectional prejudice.

From S. FINDLEY, *Supt. Akron Schools, Ohio.*

We use no others, and have no desire to. They give entire satisfaction. We like the freshness and excellence of the selections. We like the biographical notes and the definitions at the foot of the page. We also like the white paper and clear and beautiful type. In short, we do not know where to look for books which would be so satisfactory both to teachers and pupils.

From PRES. ROBERT ALLYN, *McKendree College, Ill.*

Since my connection with this college, we have used in our preparatory department the Series of Readers known as the "National Readers," compiled by Parker & Watson, and published by Messrs. A. S. Barnes & Co. They are *excellent*; afford choice selections; contain the right system of elocutionary instruction, and are well printed and bound so as to be serviceable as well as interesting. I can commend them as among the excellent means used by teachers to make their pupils proficient in that noblest of school arts, GOOD READING.

From W. T. HARRIS, *Supt. Public Schools, St. Louis, Mo.*

I have to admire these excellent selections in prose and verse, and the careful arrangement which places first what is easy of comprehension, and proceeds gradually to what is difficult. I find the lessons so arranged as to bring together different treatments of the same topic, thereby throwing much light on the pupil's path, and I doubt not adding greatly to his progress. The proper variety of subjects chosen, the concise treatise on elocution, the beautiful typography and substantial binding—all these I find still more admirable than in the former series of National Readers, which I considered *models* in these respects.

From H. T. PHILLIPS, Esq., *of the Board of Education, Atlanta, Ga.*

The Board of Education of this city have selected for use in the public schools of Atlanta the entire series of your Independent Readers, together with Steele's Chemistry and Philosophy. As a member of the Board, and of the Committee on Text-books, the subject of Readers was referred to me for examination. I gave a pretty thorough examination to ten (10) different series of Readers, and in endeavoring to arrive at a decision upon the sole question of merit, and entirely independent of any extraneous influence, I very cordially recommended the Independent Series. This verdict was approved by the Committee and adopted by the Board.

From Report of REV. W. T. BRANTLY, D.D., *late Professor of Belles Lettres, University of Georgia, on "Text-Books in Reading," before the Teachers' Convention of Georgia, May 4, 1870.*

The *National Series*, by Parker & Watson, is deserving of its high reputation. The Primary Books are suited to the weakest capacity; whilst those more advanced supply instructive illustration on all that is needed to be known in connection with the art.

WATSON'S CHILD'S SPELLER.

THE INDEPENDENT CHILD'S SPELLER.

This unique book, published in 1872, is the first to be consistently printed in imitation of writing; that is, it teaches orthography as we use it. It is for the smallest class of learners, who soon become familiarized with words by their forms, and learn to read writing while they spell.

EXTRACT FROM THE PREFACE.

Success in teaching English orthography is still exceptional, and it must so continue until the principles involved are recognized in practice. Form is foremost: the eye and the hand must be trained to the formation of words; and since spelling is a part of writing, the written form only should be used. The laws of mental association, also—especially those of resemblance, contrast, and contiguity in time and place—should receive such recognition in the construction of the text-book as shall insure, whether consciously or not, their appropriate use and legitimate results. Hence, the spelling-book, properly arranged, is a necessity from the first; and, though primers, readers, and dictionaries may serve as aids, it can have no competent substitute.

Consistently with these views, the words used in the Independent Child's Speller have such original classifications and arrangements in columns—in reference to location, number of letters, vowel sounds, alphabetic equivalents, and consonant terminations—as exhibit most effectively their formation and pronunciation. The vocabulary is strictly confined to the simple and significant monosyllables in common use. He who has mastered these may easily learn how to spell and pronounce words of more than one syllable.

The introduction is an illustrated alphabet in script, containing twenty-six pictures of objects, and their names, commencing both with capitals and small letters. Part First embraces the words of one, two, and three letters; Part Second, the words of four letters; and Part Third, other monosyllables. They are divided into short lists and arranged in columns, the vowels usually in line, so as to exhibit individual characteristics and similarity of formation. The division of words into paragraphs is shown by figures in the columns. Each list is immediately followed by sentences for reading and writing, in which the same words are again presented with irregularities of form and sound. Association is thus employed, memory tested, and definition most satisfactorily taught.

Among the novel and valuable features of the lessons and exercises, probably the most prominent are their adaptedness for young children and their being printed in exact imitation of writing. The author believes that hands large enough to spin a top, drive a hoop, or catch a ball, are not too small to use a crayon, or a slate and pencil; that the child's natural desire to draw and write should not be thwarted, but gratified, encouraged, and wisely directed; and that since the written form is the one actually used in connection with spelling in after-life, the eye and the hand of the child should be trained to that form from the first. He hopes that this little work, designed to precede all other spelling-books and conflict with none, may satisfy the need so universally recognized of a fit introduction to orthography, penmanship, and English composition.

The National Readers and Spellers.

THEIR RECORD.

These books have been adopted by the School Boards, or official authority, of the following important States, cities, and towns—in most cases for exclusive use.

The State of Missouri. **The State of Kentucky.**
The State of Alabama.
The State of Florida. **The State of North Carolina.**
The State of Delaware. **The State of Louisiana.**

New York.
New York City.
Brooklyn.
Buffalo.
Albany.
Rochester.
Troy.
Syracuse.
Elmira.
&c., &c.

Pennsylvania.
Reading.
Lancaster.
Erie.
Scranton.
Carlisle.
Carbondale.
Westchester.
Schuylkill Haven.
Williamsport.
Norristown.
Bellefonte.
Wilkesbarre.
&c., &c.

New Jersey.
Newark.
Jersey City.
Paterson.
Trenton.
Camden.
Elizabeth.
New Brunswick.
Phillipsburg.
Orange.
&c., &c.

Delaware.
Wilmington.

D. C.
Washington.

Illinois.
Chicago.
Peoria.
Alton.
Springfield.
Aurora.
Galesburg.
Rockford.
Rock Island.
&c., &c.

Wisconsin.
Milwaukee.
Fond du Lac.
Oshkosh.
Janesville.
Racine.
Watertown.
Sheboygan.
La Crosse.
Waukesha.
Kenosha.
&c., &c.

Michigan.
Grand Rapids.
Kalamazoo.
Adrian.
Jackson.
Monroe.
Lansing.
&c., &c.

Ohio.
Toledo.
Sandusky.
Conneaut.
Chardon.
Hudson.
Canton.
Salem.
&c., &c.

Indiana.
New Albany.
Fort Wayne.
Lafayette.
Madison.
Logansport.
Indianapolis.

Iowa.
Davenport.
Burlington.
Muscatine.
Mount Pleasant.
&c.

Nebraska.
Brownsville.
Lincoln.
&c.

Oregon.
Portland.
Salem.
&c.

Virginia.
Richmond.
Norfolk.
Petersburg.
Lynchburg.
&c.

South Carolina.
Columbia.
Charleston.

Georgia.
Savannah.

Louisiana.
New Orleans.

Tennessee.
Memphis

The *Educational Bulletin* records periodically all new points gained

SCHOOL-ROOM CARDS.

Baade's Reading Case,

A frame containing movable cards, with arrangement for showing one sentence at a time, capable of 28,000 transpositions.

Eureka Alphabet Tablet

Presents the alphabet upon the Word Method System, by which the child will learn the alphabet in nine days, and make no small progress in reading and spelling in the same time.

National School Tablets, 10 Nos.

Embrace reading and conversational exercises, object and moral lessons, form, color, &c. A complete set of these large and elegantly illustrated Cards will embellish the school-room more than any other article of furniture.

READING.

Fowle's Bible Reader

The narrative portions of the Bible, chronologically and topically arranged, judiciously combined with selections from the Psalms, Proverbs, and other portions which inculcate important moral lessons or the great truths of Christianity. The embarrassment and difficulty of reading the Bible itself, by course, as a class exercise, are obviated, and its use made feasible, by this means.

North Carolina First Reader

North Carolina Second Reader

North Carolina Third Reader

Prepared expressly for the schools of this State, by C. H. Wiley, Superintendent of Common Schools, and F. M. Hubbard, Professor of Literature in the State University.

Parker's Rhetorical Reader

Designed to familiarize Readers with the pauses and other marks in general use, and lead them to the practice of modulation and inflection of the voice.

Introductory Lessons in Reading and Elocution

Of similar character to the foregoing, for less advanced classes.

High School Literature

Admirable selections from a long list of the world's best writers, for exercise in reading, oratory, and composition. Speeches, dialogues, and model letters represent the latter department.

ORTHOGRAPHY.

SMITH'S SERIES

Supplies a speller for every class in graded schools, and comprises the most complete and excellent treatise on English Orthography and its companion branches extant.

1. Smith's Little Speller .

First Round in the Ladder of Learning.

2. Smith's Juvenile Definer

Lessons composed of familiar words grouped with reference to similar signification or use, and correctly spelled, accented, and defined.

3. Smith's Grammar-School Speller

Familiar words, grouped with reference to the sameness of sound of syllables differently spelled. Also definitions, complete rules for spelling and formation of derivatives, and exercises in false orthography.

4. Smith's Speller and Definer's Manual

A complete *School Dictionary* containing 14,000 words, with various other useful matter in the way of Rules and Exercises.

5. Smith's Etymology—Small, and Complete Ed's.

The first and only Etymology to recognize the *Anglo-Saxon* our *mother tongue;* containing also full lists of derivatives from the Latin, Greek, Gaelic, Swedish, Norman, &c., &c ; being, in fact, a complete etymology of the language for schools.

Sherwood's Writing Speller
Sherwood's Speller and Definer
Sherwood's Speller and Pronouncer

The Writing Speller consists of properly ruled and numbered blanks to receive the words dictated by the teacher, with space for remarks and corrections. The other volumes may be used for the dictation or ordinary class exercises.

Price's English Speller

A complete spelling-book for all grades, containing more matter than "Webster," manufactured in superior style, and sold at a lower price—consequently the cheapest speller extant.

Northend's Dictation Exercises

Embracing valuable information on a thousand topics, communicated in such a manner as at once to relieve the exercise of spelling of its usual tedium, and combine it with instruction of a general character calculated to profit and amuse.

Wright's Analytical Orthography

This standard work is popular, because it teaches the elementary sounds in a plain and philosophical manner, and presents orthography and orthoepy in an easy, uniform system of analysis or parsing.

Fowle's False Orthography

Exercises for correction.

Page's Normal Chart

The elementary sounds of the language for the school-room walls.

ORTHOGRAPHY—Continued.

Barber's Complete Writing Speller

"The Student's Own Hand-Book of Orthography, Definitions, and Sentences, consisting of Written Exercises in the Proper Spelling, Meaning, and Use of Words." (Published 1873.) This differs from Sherwood's and other Writing Spellers in its more comprehensive character. Its blanks are adapted to writing whole sentences instead of detached words, with the proper divisions for numbering, corrections, etc. Such aids as this, like Watson's Child's Speller and Sherwood's Writing Speller, find their *raison d'être* in the postulate that the art of correct spelling is dependent upon written, and not upon spoken language, for its utility, if not for its very existence. Hence the indirectness of purely oral instruction.

Pooler's Test Speller

The best collection of "hard words" yet made. The more uncommon ones are fully defined, and the whole are *arranged alphabetically* for convenient reference. The book is designed for Teachers' Institutes and "Spelling Schools," and is prepared by an experienced and well-known conductor of Institutes.

ETYMOLOGY.

Smith's Complete Etymology,
Smith's Condensed Etymology,

Containing the Anglo-Saxon, French, Dutch, German, Welsh, Danish, Gothic, Swedish, Gaelic, Italian, Latin, and Greek Roots, and the English words derived therefrom accurately spelled, accented, and defined.

From HON. JNO. G. MCMYNN, *late State Superintendent of Wisconsin.*

I wish every teacher in the country had a copy of this work.

From PRIN. WM. F. PHELPS, *Minn. State Normal.*

The book is superb—just what is needed in the department of etymology and spelling.

From PROF. C. H. VERRILL, *Pa. State Normal School.*

The Etymology (Smith's) which we procured of you we like much. It is the best work for the class-room we have seen.

From HON. EDWARD BALLARD, *Supt. of Common Schools, State of Maine.*

The author has furnished a manual of singular utility for its purpose.

DICTIONARY.

The Topical Lexicon,

This work is a School Dictionary, an Etymology, a compilation of synonyms, and a manual of general information. It differs from the ordinary lexicon in being arranged by topics instead of the letters of the alphabet, thus realizing the apparent paradox of a "Readable Dictionary." An unusually valuable school book.

ENGLISH GRAMMAR.

CLARK'S DIAGRAM SYSTEM.

Clark's Easy Lessons in Language,

Published 1874. Contains illustrated object-lessons of the most attractive character, and is couched in language freed as much as possible from the dry technicalities of the science.

Clark's Brief English Grammar,

Published 1872. Part I. is adapted to youngest learners, and the whole forms a complete "brief course" in one volume, adequate to the wants of the common school.

Clark's Normal Grammar,

Published 1870, and designed to take the place of Prof. Clark's veteran "Practical" Grammar, though the latter is still furnished upon order. The Normal is an entirely new treatise. It is a full exposition of the system as described below, with all the most recent improvements. Some of its peculiarities are—A happy blending of SYNTHESES with ANALYSES; thorough Criticisms of common errors in the use of our Language; and important improvements in the Syntax of Sentences and of Phrases.

Clark's Key to the Diagrams,

Clark's Analysis of the English Language,

Clark's Grammatical Chart,

The theory and practice of teaching grammar in American schools is meeting with a thorough revolution from the use of this system. While the old methods offer proficiency to the pupil only after much weary plodding and dull memorizing, this affords from the inception the advantage of *practical Object Teaching*, addressing the eye by means of illustrative figures; furnishes association to the memory, its most powerful aid, and diverts the pupil by taxing his ingenuity. Teachers who are using Clark's Grammar uniformly testify that they and their pupils find it the most interesting study of the school course.

Like all great and radical improvements, the system naturally met at first with much unreasonable opposition. It has not only outlived the greater part of this opposition, but finds many of its warmest admirers among those who could not at first tolerate so radical an innovation. All it wants is an impartial trial to convince the most skeptical of its merit. No one who has fairly and intelligently tested it in the school-room has ever been known to go back to the old method. A great success is already established, and it is easy to prophecy that the day is not far distant when it will be the *only system of teaching English Grammar*. As the SYSTEM is copyrighted, no other text-books can appropriate this obvious and great improvement.

Welch's Analysis of the English Sentence,

Remarkable for its new and simple classification, its method of treating connectives, its explanations of the idioms and constructive laws of the language, etc.

Clark's Diagram English Grammar.

TESTIMONIALS.

From J. A. T. DURNIN, *Principal Dubuque R. C. Academy, Iowa.*

In my opinion, it is well calculated by its system of analysis to develop those rational faculties which in the old systems were rather left to develop themselves, while the memory was overtaxed, and the pupils discouraged.

From B. A. COX, *School Commissioner, Warren County, Illinois.*

I have examined 150 teachers in the last year, and those having studied or taught Clark's System have universally stood fifty per cent. better examinations than those having studied other authors.

From M. H. B. BURKET, *Principal Masonic Institute, Georgetown, Tennessee.*

I traveled two years amusing myself in instructing (exclusively) Grammar classes with Clark's system. The first class I instructed fifty days, but found that this was more time than was required to impart a theoretical knowledge of the science. During the two years thereafter I instructed classes only *thirty* days each. Invariably I proposed that unless I prepared my classes for a more thorough, minute, and accurate knowledge of English Grammar than that obtained from the ordinary books and in the ordinary way in from one to two years, I would make no charge. I never failed in a solitary case to far exceed the hopes of my classes, and made money and character rapidly as an instructor.

From A. B. DOUGLASS, *School Commissioner, Delaware County, New York.*

I have never known a class pursue the study of it under a *live* teacher, that has not succeeded; I have never known it to have an opponent in an educated teacher who had *thoroughly* investigated it; I have never known an *ignorant* teacher to examine it; I have never known a teacher who has used it, to try any other.

From J. A. DODGE, *Teacher and Lecturer on English Grammar, Kentucky.*

We are tempted to assert that it foretells the dawn of a brighter age to our mother-tongue. Both pupil and teacher can fare sumptuously upon its contents, however highly they may have prized the manuals into which they may have been initiated, and by which their expressions have been moulded.

From W. T. CHAPMAN, *Superintendent Public Schools, Wellington, Ohio.*

I regard Clark's System of Grammar the best published. For teaching the analysis of the English Language, it surpasses any I ever used.

From F. S. LYON, *Principal South Norwalk Union School, Connecticut.*

During ten years' experience in teaching, I have used six different authors on the subject of English Grammar. I am fully convinced that Clark's Grammar is better calculated to make thorough grammarians than any other that I have seen.

From CATALOGUE OF ROHRER'S COMMERCIAL COLLEGE, *St. Louis, Missouri.*

We do not hesitate to assert, without fear of successful contradiction, that a better knowledge of the English language can be obtained by this system in six weeks than by the old methods in as many months.

From A. PICKETT, *President of the State Teachers' Association, Wisconsin.*

A thorough experiment in the use of many approved authors upon the subject of English Grammar has convinced me of the superiority of Clark. When the pupil has completed the course, he is left upon a foundation of *principle*, and not upon the *dictum* of the author.

From GEO. F. MCFARLAND, *Prin. McAllisterville Academy, Juniata Co., Penn.*

At the first examination of public-school teachers by the county superintendent, when one of our student teachers commenced analyzing a sentence according to Clark, the superintendent listened in mute astonishment until he had finished, then asked what that meant, and finally, with a very knowing look, said such work wouldn't do here, and asked the applicant to parse the sentence right, and gave the lowest certificates to all who barely mentioned Clark. Afterwards, I presented him with a copy, and the next fall he permitted it to be partially used, while the third or last fall, he openly commended the system, and appointed three of my best teachers to explain it at the two Institutes and one County Convention held since September.

☞ For further testimony of equal force, see **the Publishers' Special Circular, or current numbers of the Educational Bulletin.**

GEOGRAPHY.

NATIONAL GEOGRAPHICAL SYSTEM.

THE SERIES.

I. Monteith's First Lessons in Geography,
II. Monteith's New Manual of Geography,
II. McNally's System of Geography,

INTERMEDIATE OR ALTERNATE VOLUMES.

1*. Monteith's Introduction to Geography,
2*. Monteith's Physical and Political Geography,

ACCESSORIES.

Monteith's Wall Maps 2 sets (see page 15),
Monteith's Manual of Map-Drawing (Allen's System)
Monteith's Map-Drawing and Object-Lessons,
Monteith's Map-Drawing Scale,

1. PRACTICAL OBJECT TEACHING. The infant scholar is first introduced to *a picture* whence he may derive notions of the shape of the earth, the phenomena of day and night, the distribution of land and water, and the great natural divisions, which mere words would fail entirely to convey to the untutored mind. Other pictures follow on the same plan, and the child's mind is called upon to grasp no idea without the aid of a pictorial illustration. Carried on to the higher books, this system culminates in Physical Geography, where such matters as climates, ocean currents, the winds, peculiarities of the earth's crust, clouds and rain, are pictorially explained and rendered apparent to the most obtuse. The illustrations used for this purpose belong to the highest grade of art.

2. CLEAR, BEAUTIFUL, AND CORRECT MAPS. In the lower numbers the maps avoid unnecessary detail, while respectively progressive, and affording the pupil new matter for acquisition each time he approaches in the constantly enlarging circle the point of coincidence with previous lessons in the more elementary books. In the Physical and Political Geography the maps embrace many new and striking features. One of the most effective of these is the new plan for displaying on each map the relative sizes of countries not represented, thus obviating much confusion which has arisen from the necessity of presenting maps in the same atlas drawn on different scales. The maps of "McNally" have long been celebrated for their superior beauty and completeness. This is the only school-book in which the attempt to make a *complete* atlas *also clear and distinct*, has been successful. The map *coloring* throughout the series is also noticeable. Delicate and subdued tints take the place of the startling glare of inharmonious colors which too frequently in such treatises dazzle the eyes, distract the attention, and serve to overwhelm the names of towns and the natural features of the landscape.

GEOGRAPHY—Continued.

3. THE VARIETY OF MAP-EXERCISE. Starting each time from a different basis, the pupil in many instances approaches the same fact no less than *six times*, thus indelibly impressing it upon his memory. At the same time, this system is not allowed to become wearisome—the extent of exercise on each subject being graduated by its relative importance or difficulty of acquisition.

4. THE CHARACTER AND ARRANGEMENT OF THE DESCRIPTIVE TEXT. The cream of the science has been carefully culled, unimportant matter rejected, elaboration avoided, and a brief and concise manner of presentation cultivated. The orderly consideration of topics has contributed greatly to simplicity. Due attention is paid to the facts in history and astronomy which are inseparably connected with, and important to the proper understanding of geography—and *such only* are admitted on any terms. In a word, the National System teaches geography as a science, pure, simple, and exhaustive.

5. ALWAYS UP TO THE TIMES. The authors of these books, editorially speaking, never sleep. No change occurs in the boundaries of countries, or of counties, no new discovery is made, or railroad built, that is not at once noted and recorded, and the next edition of each volume carries to every school-room the new order of things.

6. SUPERIOR GRADATION. This is the only series which furnishes an available volume for every possible class in graded schools. It is not contemplated that a pupil must necessarily go through every volume in succession to attain proficiency. On the contrary, *two* will suffice, but *three* are advised; and, if the course will admit, the whole series should be pursued. At all events, the books are at hand for selection, and every teacher, of every grade, can find among them one *exactly suited* to his class. The best combination for those who wish to abridge the course consists of Nos. 1, 2, and 3, or where children are somewhat advanced in other studies when they commence geography, Nos. 1*, 2, and 3. Where but *two* books are admissible, Nos. 1* and 2*, or Nos. 2 and 3, are recommended.

7. FORM OF THE VOLUMES AND MECHANICAL EXECUTION. The maps and text are no longer unnaturally divorced in accordance with the time-honored practice of making text-books on this subject as inconvenient and expensive as possible. On the contrary, all map questions are to be found on the page opposite the map itself, and each book is complete in one volume. The mechanical execution is unrivalled. Paper and printing are everything that could be desired, and the binding is—A. S. Barnes & Company's.

8. MAP-DRAWING. In 1869 the system of Map-Drawing devised by Professor JEROME ALLEN was secured *exclusively* for this series. It derives its claim to originality and usefulness from the introduction of a *fixed unit of measurement* applicable to every Map. The principles being so few, simple and comprehensive, the subject of Map-Drawing is relieved of all practical difficulty. (In Nos. 2, 2*, and 3, and published separately.)

9. ANALOGOUS OUTLINES. At the same time with Map-Drawing was also introduced (in No. 2) a new and ingenious variety of Object Lessons, consisting of a comparison of the outlines of countries with familiar objects pictorially represented.

GEOGRAPHY—Continued.

MONTEITH'S INDEPENDENT COURSE.

Elementary Geography

Comprehensive Geography (with 103 Maps)

☞ These volumes are not revisions of old works—not an addition to any series—but are entirely new productions—each by itself complete, independent, comprehensive, yet simple, brief, cheap, and popular; or, taken together, the most admirable "series" ever offered for a common-school course. They present the following features, skillfully interwoven—the student learning all about one country at a time.

LOCAL GEOGRAPHY, or the Use of Maps. Important features of the Maps are the coloring of States as objects, and the ingenious system for laying down a much larger number of names for reference than are found on any other Maps of same size—and without crowding.

PHYSICAL GEOGRAPHY, or the Natural Features of the Earth, illustrated by the original and striking ***Relief Maps,*** being bird's-eye views or photographic pictures of the Earth's surface.

DESCRIPTIVE GEOGRAPHY, including the Physical; with some account of Governments, and Races, Animals, etc.

HISTORICAL GEOGRAPHY, or a brief summary of the salient points of history, explaining the present distribution of nations, origin of geographical names, etc.

MATHEMATICAL GEOGRAPHY, including ASTRONOMICAL, which describes the Earth's position and character among planets; also the Zones, Parallels, etc.

COMPARATIVE GEOGRAPHY, or a system of analogy, connecting new lessons with the previous ones. Comparative sizes and latitudes are shown on the margin of each Map, and all countries are measured in the "*frame of Kansas.*"

TOPICAL GEOGRAPHY, consisting of questions for review, and testing the student's general and specific knowledge of the subject, with suggestions for *Geographical Compositions.*

ANCIENT GEOGRAPHY. A section devoted to this subject, with Maps, will be appreciated by teachers. It is seldom taught in our common schools, because it has heretofore required the purchase of a separate book.

GRAPHIC GEOGRAPHY, or MAP-DRAWING by Allen's "Unit of Measurement" system (now almost universally recognized as without a rival) is introduced throughout the lessons, and not as an appendix.

CONSTRUCTIVE GEOGRAPHY, or GLOBE-MAKING. With each book a set of Map Segments is furnished, with which each student may make his own Globe by following the directions given.

RAILROAD GEOGRAPHY, with a grand Map illustrating routes of travel in the United States. Also, a "Tour in Europe."

MAP DRAWING.

Monteith's Map-Drawing Made Easy.

A neat little book of outlines and instructions, giving the "corners of States" in suitable blanks, so that Maps can be drawn by unskillful hands from any atlas; with instructions for written exercises or compositions on geographical subjects, and Comparative Geography.

Monteith's Manual of Map-Drawing (Allen's System).

The only consistent plan, by which all Maps are drawn on one scale. By its use much time may be saved, and much interest and accurate knowledge gained.

Monteith's Map-Drawing and Object Lessons.

The last-named treatise, bound with Mr. Monteith's ingenious system for committing outlines to memory by means of pictures of living creatures and familiar objects. Thus, South America resembles a dog's head; Cuba, a lizard; Italy, a boot; France, a coffee-pot; Turkey, a turkey, etc., etc.

Monteith's Map-Drawing Scale.

A ruler of wood, graduated to the "Allen fixed unit of measurement."

WALL MAPS.

Monteith's Pictorial Chart of Geography.

The original drawing for this beautiful and instructive chart was greatly admired in the publisher's "exhibit" at the Centennial Exhibition of 1876. It is *a picture* of the Earth's surface with every natural feature displayed, teaching also physical geography, and especially the mutations of water. The uses to which man puts the earth and its treasures and forces, as Agriculture, Mining, Manufacturing, Commerce, and Transportation are also graphically portrayed so that the young learner gets a realistic idea of "the world we live in," which weeks of book-study might fail to convey.

Monteith's School Maps, 8 Numbers.

The "School Series" includes the Hemispheres (2 Maps), United States, North America, South America, Europe, Asia, Africa.—Price, $2.50 each.

Each map is 28 × 34 inches, beautifully colored, has the names all laid down, and is substantially mounted on canvas with rollers.

Monteith's Grand Maps, 8 Numbers.

The "Grand Series" includes the Hemispheres (1 Map), United States, South America, Europe, Asia, Africa, The World on Mercator's Projection, and Physical Map of the World.—Price, $5.00 each. Size 42 × 52 inches, names laid down, colored, mounted, &c.

Monteith's Sunday School Maps,

Including a Map of Paul's Travels ($5.00), one of Ancient Canaan ($3.00), and Modern Palestine ($3.00), or Palestine and Canaan together ($5.00).

MONTEITH'S GEOGRAPHIES

Have been adopted, by official authority, for the schools of the following States and Cities—in most cases for *exclusive* and uniform use.

California,	Tennessee,	Iowa,	Arkansas,	North Carolina,
Missouri,	Texas,	Louisiana,	Florida,	Kansas,
Alabama,	Vermont,	Oregon,	Minnesota,	Mississippi.

Cities.—New York City, Brooklyn, Chicago, New Orleans, Buffalo, Richmond, Jersey City, Hartford, Worcester, San Francisco, Louisville, Newark, Milwaukee, Charleston, Rochester, Mobile, Syracuse, Memphis, Salt Lake City, Nashville, Utica, Wilmington, Trenton, Norfolk, Norwich, Lockport, Dubuque, Galveston, Portland, Savannah, Indianapolis, Springfield, Wheeling, Toledo, Bridgeport, St. Paul, Vicksburg, &c.

Monteith & McNally's National Geographies.

CRITICAL OPINIONS.

From R. A. ADAMS, *Member of Board of Education, New York.*

I have found, by examination of the Book of Supply of our Board, that considerably the largest number of any series now used in our public schools is the National, by Monteith and McNally.

From BRO. PATRICK, *Chief Provincial of the Vast Educational Society of the* CHRISTIAN BROTHERS *in the United States.*

Having been convinced for some time past that the series of Geographies in use in our schools were not giving satisfaction, and came far short of meeting our most reasonable expectations, I have felt it my imperative duty to examine into this matter, and see if a remedy could not be found.

Copies of the different Geographies published in this country have been placed at our command for examination. On account of other pressing duties we have not been able to give as much time to the investigation of all these different series as we could have desired; yet we have found enough to convince us that there are many others better than those we are now using; but we cheerfully give our most decided preference, above all others, to the National Series, by Monteith & McNally.

Their easy gradation, their thoroughly practical and independent character, their comprehensive completeness as a full and accurate system, the wise discrimination shown in the selection of the subject matter, the beautiful and copious illustrations, the neat cut type, the general execution of the works, and *other excellencies*, will commend them to the friends of education everywhere.

From the "HOME MONTHLY," *Nashville, Tenn.*

MONTEITH'S AND MCNALLY'S GEOGRAPHIES.—Geography is so closely connected with Astronomy, History, Ethnology, and Geology, that it is difficult to define its limits in the construction of a text-book. If the author confines himself strictly to a description of the earth's surface, his book will be dry, meager, and unintelligible to a child. If, on the other hand, he attempts to give information on the cognate sciences, he enters a boundless field, and may wander too far. It seems to us that the authors of the series before us have hit on the happy medium between too much and too little. *The First Lessons*, by applying the system of object-teaching, renders the subject so attractive that a child, just able to read, may become deeply interested in it. The second book of the course enlarges the view, but still keeps to the maps and simple descriptions. Then, in the third book, we have Geography combined with History and Astronomy. A general view of the solar system is presented, so that the pupil may understand the earth's position on the map of the heavens. The first part of the fourth book treats of Physical Geography, and contains a vast amount of knowledge compressed into a small space. It is made bright and attractive by beautiful pictures and suggestive illustrations, on the principle of object-teaching. The maps in the second part of this volume are remarkably clear, and the map exercises are copious and judicious. In the fifth and last volume of the series, the whole subject is reviewed and systematized. This is strictly a Geography. Its maps are beautifully engraved and clearly printed. The map exercises are full and comprehensive. In all these books the maps, questions and descriptions are given in the same volume. In most geographies there are too many details and minute descriptions—more than any child out of purgatory ought to be required to learn. The power of memory is overstrained; there is confusion—no clearly defined idea is formed in the child's mind. But in these books, in brief, pointed descriptions, and constant use of bright, accurate maps, the whole subject is photographed on the mind.

MATHEMATICS.

DAVIES' NATIONAL COURSE.

ARITHMETIC.

1. Davies' Primary Arithmetic,
2. Davies' Intellectual Arithmetic,
3. Davies' Elements of Written Arithmetic,.
4. Davies' Practical Arithmetic,
   Key to Practical Arithmetic,
5. Davies' University Arithmetic,
   Key to University Arithmetic,

ALGEBRA.

1. Davies' New Elementary Algebra,
   Key to Elementary Algebra,
2. Davies' University Algebra,
   Key to University Algebra,
3. Davies' New Bourdon's Algebra,
   Key to Bourdon's Algebra,

GEOMETRY.

1. Davies' Elementary Geometry and Trigonometry,
2. Davies' Legendre's Geometry,
3. Davies' Analytical Geometry and Calculus,
4. Davies' Descriptive Geometry,
5. Davies' New Calculus,

MENSURATION.

1. Davies' Practical Mathematics and Mensuration,
2. Davies' Elements of Surveying,
3. Davies' Shades, Shadows, and Perspective,

MATHEMATICAL SCIENCE.

Davies' Grammar of Arithmetic,
Davies' Outlines of Mathematical Science,
Davies' Nature and Utility of Mathematics,
Davies' Metric System,
Davies & Peck's Dictionary of Mathematics,

DAVIES' NATIONAL COURSE of MATHEMATICS.

ITS RECORD.

In claiming for this series the first place among American text-books, of whatever class, the Publishers appeal to the magnificent record which its volumes have earned during the *thirty-five years* of Dr. Charles Davies' mathematical labors. The unremitting exertions of a life-time have placed *the modern series* on the same proud eminence among competitors that each of its predecessors has successively enjoyed in a course of constantly improved editions, now rounded to their perfect fruition—for it seems almost that this science is susceptible of no further demonstration.

During the period alluded to, many authors and editors in this department have started into public notice, and by borrowing ideas and processes original with Dr. Davies, have enjoyed a brief popularity, but are now almost unknown. Many of the series of to-day, built upon a similar basis, and described as "modern books," are destined to a similar fate; while the most far-seeing eye will find it difficult to fix the time, on the basis of any data afforded by their past history, when these books will cease to increase and prosper, and fix a still firmer hold on the affection of every educated American.

One cause of this unparalleled popularity is found in the fact that the enterprise of the author did not cease with the original completion of his books. Always a practical teacher, he has incorporated in his text-books from time to time the advantages of every improvement in methods of teaching, and every advance in science. During all the years in which he has been laboring, he constantly submitted his own theories and those of others to the practical test of the class-room —approving, rejecting, or modifying them as the experience thus obtained might suggest. In this way he has been able to produce an almost perfect series of class-books, in which every department of mathematics has received minute and exhaustive attention.

Nor has he yet retired from the field. Still in the prime of life, and enjoying a ripe experience which no other living mathematician or teacher can emulate, his pen is ever ready to carry on the good work, as the progress of science may demand. Witness his recent exposition of the "Metric System," which received the official endorsement of Congress, by its Committee on Uniform Weights and Measures.

DAVIES' SYSTEM IS THE ACKNOWLEDGED NATIONAL STANDARD FOR THE UNITED STATES, for the following reasons:—

1st. It is the basis of instruction in the great national schools at West Point and Annapolis.

2d. It has received the *quasi* endorsement of the National Congress.

3d. It is exclusively used in the public schools of the National Capital.

4th. The officials of the Government use it as authority in all cases involving mathematical questions.

5th. Our great soldiers and sailors commanding the national armies and navies were educated in this system. So have been a majority of eminent scientists in this country. All these refer to "Davies" as authority.

6th. A larger number of American citizens have received their education from this than from any other series.

7th. The series has a larger circulation throughout the whole country than any other, being *extensively used in every State in the Union.*

Davies' National Course of Mathematics.

TESTIMONIALS.

From L. VAN BOKKELEN, *State Superintendent Public Instruction, Maryland.*

The series of Arithmetics edited by Prof. Davies, and published by your firm have been used for many years in the schools of several counties, and the city of Baltimore, and have been approved by teachers and commissioners.

Under the law of 1865, establishing a uniform system of Free Public Schools, these Arithmetics were unanimously adopted by the State Board of Education after a careful examination, and are now used in all the Public Schools of Maryland.

These facts evidence the high opinion entertained by the School Authorities of the value of the series theoretically and practically.

From HORACE WEBSTER, *President of the College of New York.*

The undersigned has examined, with care and thought, several volumes of Davies' Mathematics, and is of the opinion that, as a whole, it is the most complete and best course for Academic and Collegiate instruction, with which he is acquainted.

From DAVID N. CAMP, *State Superintendent of Common Schools, Connecticut.*

I have examined Davies' Series of Arithmetics with some care. The language is clear and precise; each principle is thoroughly analyzed, and the whole so arranged as to facilitate the work of instruction. Having observed the satisfaction and success with which the different books have been used by eminent teachers, it gives me pleasure to commend them to others.

From J. O. WILSON, *Chairman Committee on Text-Books, Washington, D. C.*

I consider Davies' Arithmetics decidedly superior to any other series, and in this opinion I am sustained, I believe, by the entire Board of Education and Corps of Teachers in this city, where they have been used for several years past.

From JOHN L. CAMPBELL, *Professor of Mathematics, Wabash College, Indiana.*

A proper combination of abstract reasoning and practical illustration is the chief excellence in Prof. Davies' Mathematical works. I prefer his Arithmetics, Algebras, Geometry and Trigonometry to all others now in use, and cordially recommend them to all who desire the advancement of sound learning.

From MAJOR J. H. WHITTLESEY, *Government Inspector of Military Schools.*

Be assured, I regard the works of Prof. Davies, with which I am acquainted, as by far the best text-books in print on the subjects which they treat. I shall certainly encourage their adoption wherever a word from me may be of any avail.

From T. McC. BALLANTINE, *Prof. Mathematics Cumberland College, Kentucky.*

I have long taught Prof. Davies' Course of Mathematics, and I continue to like their working.

From JOHN McLEAN BELL, B. A., *Prin. of Lower Canada College.*

I have used Davies' Arithmetical and Mathematical Series as text-books in the schools under my charge for the last six years. These I have found of great efficacy in exciting, invigorating, and concentrating the intellectual faculties of the young.

Each treatise serves as an introduction to the next higher, by the similarity of its reasonings and methods; and the student is carried forward, by easy and gradual steps, over the whole field of mathematical inquiry, and that, too, in a *shorter* time than is usually occupied in mastering a single department. I sincerely and heartily recommend them to the attention of my fellow-teachers in Canada.

From D. W. STEELE, *Prin. Philekoian Academy, Cold Springs, Texas.*

I have used Davies' Arithmetics till I know them nearly by heart. A better series of school-books never were published. I have recommended them until they are now used in all this region of country.

A large mass of similar "Opinions" may be obtained by addressing the publishers for special circular for Davies' Mathematics. New recommendations are published in current numbers of the *Educational Bulletin.*

MATHEMATICS—Continued.

PECK'S ARITHMETICS.

By the Prof. of Mathematics at Columbia College, New York.

1. Peck's First Lessons in Numbers,

Embracing all that is usually included in what are called Primary and Intellectual Arithmetics; proceeding gradually from object lessons to abstract numbers; developing Addition and Subtraction simultaneously: with other attractive novelties.

2. Peck's Manual of Practical Arithmetic,

An excellent "Brief" course, conveying a sufficient knowledge of Arithmetic for ordinary business purposes.

It is thoroughly "practical," because the author believes the Theory cannot be studied with advantage until the pupil has acquired a certain facility in combining numbers, which can only be had by practice.

3. Peck's Complete Arithmetic,

The whole subject—theory and practice—presented within very moderate limits. This author's most remarkable faculty of mathematical treatment is comprehended in three words: System, Conciseness, Lucidity. The directness and simplicity of this work cannot be better expressed than in the words of a correspondent who adopted the book at once, because, as he said, it is "free from that *juggling with numbers*" practiced by many authors.

From the "Galaxy," New York.

In the "Complete Arithmetic" each part of the subject is logically developed. First are given the necessary definitions; second, the explanations of such signs (if any) as are used; third, the principles on which the operation depends; fourth, an exemplification of the manner in which the operation is performed, which is so conducted that the reason of the rule which is immediately thereafter deduced is made perfectly plain; after which follow numerous graded examples and corresponding practical problems. All the parts taken together are arranged in logical order. The subject is treated as a whole, and not as if made up of segregated parts. It may seem a simple remark to make that (for example) addition is in principle one and the same everywhere, whether employed upon simple or compound numbers, fractions, etc., the only difference being in the *unit* involved; but the number of persons who understand this practically, compared to the number who have studied arithmetic, is not very great. The student of the "Complete Arithmetic" cannot fail to understand it. All the principles of the science are presented within moderate limits. Superfluity of matter—to supplement defective definitions, to make clear faulty demonstrations and rules expressed either inaccurately or obscurely, to make provision for a multiplicity of cases for which no provision is requisite—has been carefully avoided. The definitions are plain and concise; the principles are stated clearly and accurately; the demonstrations are full and complete; the rules are perspicuous and comprehensive; the illustrative examples are abundant and well fitted to familiarize the student with the application of principles to the problems of science and of every-day life.

☞ The Definitions constitute the power of the book. We have never seen them excelled for clearness and exactness.—*Iowa School Journal.*

MATHEMATICS—Continued.

PECK'S HIGHER COURSE.

Peck's Manual of Algebra,

Bringing the methods of Bourdon within the range of the Academic Course.

Peck's Manual of Geometry,

By a method purely practical, and unembarrassed by the details which rather confuse than simplify science.

Peck's Practical Calculus,

Peck's Analytical Geometry,

Peck's Elementary Mechanics,

Peck's Mechanics, with Calculus,

The briefest treatises on these subjects now published. Adopted by the great Universities; Yale, Harvard, Columbia, Princeton, Cornell, &c.

ARITHMETICAL EXAMPLES.

Reuck's Examples in Denominate Numbers,

Reuck's Examples in Arithmetic,

These volumes differ from the ordinary arithmetic in their peculiarly *practical* character. They are composed mainly of examples, and afford the most severe and thorough discipline for the mind. While a book which should contain a complete treatise of theory and practice would be too cumbersome for every-day use, the insufficiency of *practical* examples has been a source of complaint.

HIGHER MATHEMATICS.

Macnie's Algebraical Equations,

Serving as a complement to the more advanced treatises on Algebra, giving special attention to the analysis and solution of equations with numerical coefficients.

Church's Elements of Calculus,

Church's Analytical Geometry,

Church's Descriptive Geometry, 2 vols.,

These volumes constitute the "West Point Course" in their several departments.

Courtenay's Elements of Calculus,

A standard work of the very highest grade.

Hackley's Trigonometry,

With applications to navigation and surveying, nautical and practical geometry and geodesy.

PENMANSHIP.

Beers' System of Progressive Penmanship. Per dozen

This "round hand" system of Penmanship in twelve numbers, commends itself by its simplicity and thoroughness. The first four numbers are primary books. Nos. 5 to 7, advanced books for boys. Nos. 8 to 10, advanced books for girls. Nos. 11 and 12, ornamental penmanship. These books are printed from steel plates (engraved by McLees), and are unexcelled in mechanical execution. Large quantities are annually sold.

Beers' Slated Copy Slips, per set

All beginners should practice, for a few weeks, slate exercises, familiarizing them with the form of the letters, the motions of the hand and arm, &c., &c. These copy slips, 32 in number, supply all the copies found in a complete series of writing-books, at a trifling cost.

Payson, Dunton & Scribner's Copy-B'ks. P. doz.,

The National System of Penmanship, in three distinct series—(1) Common School Series, comprising the first six numbers; (2) Business Series, Nos. 8, 11, and 12; (3) Ladies' Series, Nos. 7, 9, and 10.

Fulton & Eastman's Chirographic Charts,

To embellish the school room walls, and furnish class exercise in the elements of Penmanship.

Payson's Copy-Book Cover, per hundred

Protects every page except the one in use, and furnishes "lines" with proper slope for the penman, under. Patented.

National Steel Pens, Card with all kinds

Pronounced by competent judges the perfection of American-made pens, and superior to any foreign article.

SCHOOL SERIES.	
School Pen, per gross,	$ 60
Academic Pen, do	63
Fine Pointed Pen, per gross	70
POPULAR SERIES.	
Capitol Pen, per gross,	1 00
do do pr. box of 2 doz.	25
Bullion Pen (imit. gold) pr. gr.	75
Ladies' Pen do	63
Index Pen, per gross	75
BUSINESS SERIES.	
Albata Pen, per gross,	40
Bank Pen, do	70
Empire Pen, do	70
Commercial Pen, per gross	60
Express Pen, do	75
Falcon Pen, do	70
Elastic Pen, do	75

Stimpson's Scientific Steel Pen, per gross $1 50

One forward and two backward arches, ensuring great strength, well-balanced elasticity, evenness of point, and smoothness of execution. One gross in twelve contains a Scientific Gold Pen.

Stimpson's Ink-Retaining Holder, per doz. 1 50

A simple apparatus, which does not get out of order, withholds at a single dip as much ink as the pen would otherwise realize from a dozen trips to the inkstand, which it supplies with moderate and easy flow.

Stimpson's Gold Pen, $3 00; with Ink Retainer 4 50

Stimpson's Penman's Card, $0 25

One dozen Steel Pens (assorted points) and Patent Ink-retaining Pen holder.

HISTORY.

Monteith's Youth's History.

A History of the United States for beginners. It is arranged upon the catechetical plan, with illustrative maps and engravings, review questions, dates in parentheses (that their study may be optional with the younger class of learners), and interesting Biographical Sketches of all persons who have been prominently identified with the history of our country.

Willard's United States, School and University Editions.

The plan of this standard work is chronologically exhibited in front of the title-page; the Maps and Sketches are found useful assistants to the memory, and dates, usually so difficult to remember, are so systematically arranged as in a great degree to obviate the difficulty. Candor, impartiality, and accuracy, are the distinguishing features of the narrative portion.

Willard's Universal History.

The most valuable features of the "United States" are reproduced in this. The peculiarities of the work are its great conciseness and the prominence given to the chronological order of events. The margin marks each successive era with great distinctness, so that the pupil retains not only the event but its time, and thus fixes the order of history firmly and usefully in his mind, Mrs. Willard's books are constantly revised, and at all times written up to embrace important historical events of recent date.

Lancaster's English History,

By the Master of the Stoughton Grammar School, Boston. The most practical of the "brief books." Though short, it is not a bare and uninteresting outline, but contains enough of explanation and detail to make intelligible the *cause and effect* of events. Their relations to the history and development of the American people is made specially prominent.

Willis' Historical Reader,

Being Collier's Great Events of History adapted to American schools. This rare epitome of general history, remarkable for its charming style and judicious selection of events on which the destinies of nations have turned, has been skillfully manipulated by Prof. Willis, with as few changes as would bring the United States into its proper position in the historical perspective. As reader or text-book it has few equals and no superiors.

Berard's History of England,

By an authoress well known for the success of her History of the United States. The social life of the English people is felicitously interwoven, as in fact, with the civil and military transactions of the realm.

Ricord's History of Rome

Possesses the charm of an attractive romance. The Fables with which this history abounds are introduced in such a way as not to deceive the inexperienced, while adding materially to the value of the work as a reliable index to the character and institutions, as well as the history of the Roman people.

Hanna's Bible History.

The only compendium of Bible narrative which affords a connected and chronological view of the important events there recorded, divested of all superfluous detail.

Summary of History; American, French and English.

A well-proportioned outline of leading events, condensing the substance of the more extensive text-book in common use into a series of statements so brief, that every word may be committed to memory, and yet so comprehensive that it presents an accurate though general view of the whole continuous life of nations.

Marsh's Ecclesiastical History.

Affording the History of the Church in all ages, with accounts of the pagan world during Biblical periods, and the character, rise, and progress of all Religions, as well as the various sects of the worshipers of Christ. The work is entirely non-sectarian, though strictly catholic. A separate volume contains carefully prepared QUESTIONS for class use.

HISTORY—Continued.

BARNES' ONE-TERM HISTORY

A Brief History of the United States,

This is probably the MOST ORIGINAL SCHOOL-BOOK published for many years, in any department. A few of its claims are the following:

1. **Brevity.**—The text is complete for Grammar School or intermediate classes, in 290 12mo pages, large type. It may readily be completed, if desired, in one term of study.

2. **Comprehensiveness.**—Though so brief, this book contains the pith of all the wearying contents of the larger manuals, and a great deal more than the memory usually retains from the latter.

3. **Interest** has been a prime consideration. Small books have heretofore been bare, full of dry statistics, unattractive. This one is charmingly written, replete with anecdote, and brilliant with illustration.

4. **Proportion of Events.**—It is remarkable for the discrimination with which the different portions of our history are presented according to their importance. Thus the older works being already large books when the civil war took place, give it less space than that accorded to the Revolution.

5. **Arrangement.**—In six epochs, entitled respectively, Discovery and Settlement, the Colonies, the Revolution, Growth of States, the Civil War, and Current Events.

6. **Catch Words.**—Each paragraph is preceded by its leading thought in prominent type, standing in the student's mind for the whole paragraph.

7. **Key Notes.**—Analogous with this is the idea of grouping battles, etc. about some central event, which relieves the sameness so common in such descriptions, and renders each distinct by some striking peculiarity of its own.

8. **Foot Notes.**—These are crowded with interesting matter that is not strictly a part of history proper. They may be learned or not, at pleasure. They are certain in any event to be read.

9. **Biographies** of all the leading characters are given in full in foot-notes.

10. **Maps.**—Elegant and distinct Maps from engravings on copper-plate, and beautifully colored, precede each epoch, and contain all the places named.

11. **Questions** are at the back of the book, to compel a more independent use of the text. Both text and questions are so worded that the pupil must give intelligent answers IN HIS OWN WORDS. "Yes" and "No" will not do.

12. **Historical Recreations.**—These are additional questions to test the student's knowledge, in review, as: "What trees are celebrated in our history?" "When did a fog save our army?" "What Presidents died in office?" "When was the Mississippi our western boundary?" "Who said, 'I would rather be right than President?'" etc.

13. **The Illustrations,** about seventy in number, are the work of our best artists and engravers, produced at great expense. They are vivid and interesting, and mostly upon subjects never before illustrated in a school-book.

14. **Dates.**—Only the leading dates are given in the text, and these are so associated as to assist the memory, but at the head of each page is the date of the event first mentioned, and at the close of each epoch a summary of events and dates.

15. **The Philosophy of History** is studiously exhibited—the causes and effects of events being distinctly traced and their interconnection shown.

16. **Impartiality.**—All sectional, partisan, or denominational views are avoided. Facts are stated after a careful comparison of all authorities without the least prejudice or favor.

17. **Index.**—A verbal index at the close of the book perfects it as a work of reference.

It will be observed that the above are all particulars in which School Histories have been signally defective, or altogether wanting. Many other claims to favor it shares in common with its predecessors.

BARNES' ONE-TERM HISTORY—Continued.

From PROF. WM. F. ALLEN, *State Univ. of Wisconsin.*

I think the author of the new "Brief History of the United States" has been very successful in combining brevity with sufficient fullness and interest. *Particularly*, he has avoided the excessive number of names and dates that most histories contain. Two features that I like *very much* are the *anecdotes* at the foot of the page and the "*Historical Recreations*" in the Appendix. The latter, I think, is quite a *new* feature, and the other is *very* well executed.

From S. G. WRIGHT, *Assist.-Supt. Pub. Inst., Kansas.*

It is with extreme pleasure we submit our recommendation of the "Brief History of the United States." It meets the needs of young and older children, combining concision with perspicuity, and if "brevity is the soul of wit," this "Brief History" contains not only that well-chosen ingredient, but wisdom sufficient to enlighten those students who are wearily longing for a "new departure" from certain old and uninteresting presentations of fossilized writers. We congratulate a progressive public upon a progressive book.

From HON. NEWTON BATEMAN, *Supt. Pub. Inst., Illinois.*

Barnes' One-Term History of the United States is an exceedingly attractive and spirited little book. Its claim to several new and valuable features seems well founded. Under the form of six well-defined Epochs, the History of the United States is traced tersely, yet pithily, from the earliest times to the present day. A good map precedes each epoch, whereby the history and geography of the period may be studied together, *as they always should be.* The syllabus of each paragraph is made to stand in such bold relief, by the use of large, heavy type, as to be of much *mnemonic* value to the student. The book is written in a sprightly and piquant style, the interest never flagging from beginning to end—a rare and difficult achievement in works of this kind.

From the "Chicago Schoolmaster" (Editorial).

A thorough examination of Barnes' Brief History of the United States brings the examiner to the conclusion that it is a superior book in almost every respect. The book is neat in form, and of good material. The type is clear, large, and distinct. The facts and dates are correct. The arrangement of topics is just the thing needed in a history text-book. By this arrangement the pupil can see at once what he is expected to do. The topics are well selected, embracing the leading ideas or principal events of American history. . . . The book as a whole is much superior to any I have examined. So much do I think this, that I have ordered it for my class, and shall use it in my school. (Signed) B. W. BAKER.

A Brief History of France,

By the author of the "Brief United States," with all the attractive features of that popular work (which see), and new ones of its own.

It is believed that the history of France has never before been presented in such brief compass, and this is effected without sacrificing one particle of interest. The book reads like a romance, and, while drawing the student by an irresistible fascination to his task, impresses the great outlines indelibly upon the memory.

Gilman's First Steps in General History,

A "suggestive outline" of rare compactness. Each country is treated by itself, and the United States receive special attention. Frequent Maps, contemporary events in Tables, References to Standard Works for fuller details, and a minute Index constitute the "Illustrative Apparatus." From no other work that we know of can so succinct a view of the world's history be obtained. Considering the necessary limitation of space, the style is surprisingly vivid, and at times even ornate. In all respects a charming, though not the less practical, text-book.

Gilman's "Seven Historic Ages,"

This book is written in the style used by a father talking with his children on the progress of history. As one Age after another is taken up, the author brings before the young reader the prominent men and characteristic events by which it is to be remembered. The object is to stimulate the pupil in school or the child at home to study history, to think of it as a lively picture of the doings of men, and not as a dead list of uninteresting dates.

Baker's Brief History of Texas,

On the plan of "Barnes' Brief Histories," with Constitution of the State, for schools.

DRAWING.

Chapman's American Drawing Book,

The standard American text-book and authority in all branches of art. A compilation of art principles. A manual for the amateur, and basis of study for the professional artist. Adapted for schools and private instruction.

CONTENTS.—"Any one who can Learn to Write can Learn to Draw."—Primary Instruction in Drawing.—Rudiments of Drawing the Human Head.—Rudiments in Drawing the Human Figure.—Rudiments of Drawing.—The Elements of Geometry.—Perspective.—Of Studying and Sketching from Nature.—Of Painting.—Etching and Engraving.—Of Modeling.—Of Composition —Advice to the American Art-Student.

The work is of course magnificently illustrated with all the original designs.

Chapman's Elementary Drawing Book,

A Progressive Course of Practical Exercises, or a text-book for the training of the eye and hand. It contains the elements from the larger work, and a copy should be in the hands of every pupil; while a copy of the "American Drawing Book," named above, should be at hand for reference by the class.

The Little Artist's Portfolio,

25 Drawing Cards (progressive patterns), 25 Blanks, and a fine Artist's Pencil, all in one neat envelope.

Clark's Elements of Drawing,

A complete course in this graceful art, from the first rudiments of outline to the finished sketches of landscape and scenery.

Fowle's Linear and Perspective Drawing,

For the cultivation of the eye and hand, with copious illustrations and directions for the guidance of the unskilled teacher.

Monk's Drawing Books—Six Numbers, per set,

Each book contains *eleven* large patterns, with opposing blanks. No. 1. Elementary Studies. No. 2. Studies of Foliage. No. 3. Landscapes. No. 4. Animals, I. No. 5. Animals, II. No. 6. Marine Views, etc.

Allen's Map-Drawing, Scale,

This method introduces a new era in Map-Drawing, for the following reasons:—1. It is a system. This is its greatest merit.—2. It is easily understood and taught.—3. The eye is trained to exact measurement by the use of a scale.—4. By no special effort of the memory, distance and comparative size are fixed in the mind.—5. It discards useless construction of lines.—6. It can be taught by any teacher, even though there may have been no previous practice in Map-Drawing.—7. Any pupil old enough to study Geography can learn by this System, in a short time, to draw accurate maps.—8. The System is not the result of theory, but comes directly from the school-room. It has been thoroughly and successfully tested there, with all grades of pupils.—9. It is economical, as it requires no mapping plates. It gives the pupil the ability of rapidly drawing accurate maps.

Ripley's Map-Drawing,

Based on the Circle. One of the most efficient aids to the acquirement of a knowledge of Geography is the practice of map-drawing. It is useful for the same reason that the best exercise in orthography is the *writing* of difficult words. Sight comes to the aid of hearing, and a double impression is produced upon the memory. Knowledge becomes less mechanical and more intuitive. The student who has sketched the outlines of a country, and dotted the important places, is little likely to forget either. The impression produced may be compared to that of a traveller who has been over the ground, while more comprehensive and accurate in detail.

BOOK-KEEPING.

Folsom's Logical Book-keeping,
Folsom's Blanks to Book-keeping,

This treatise embraces the interesting and important discoveries of Prof. Folsom (of the Albany "Bryant & Stratton College"), the partial enunciation of which in lectures and otherwise has attracted so much attention in circles interested in commercial education.

After studying business phenomena for many years, he has arrived at the positive laws and principles that underlie the whole subject of Accounts; finds that the science is based in *Value* as a generic term; that value divides into *two classes* with varied species; that all the exchanges of values are reducible to nine equations; and that all the results of all these exchanges are limited to *thirteen* in number.

As accounts have been universally taught hitherto, without setting out from a radical analysis or definition of values, the science has been kept in great obscurity, and been made as difficult to impart as to acquire. On the new theory, however, these obstacles are chiefly removed. In reading over the first part of it, in which the governing laws and principles are discussed, a person with ordinary intelligence will obtain a fair conception of the *double entry* process of accounts. But when he comes to study thoroughly these laws and principles as there enunciated, and works out the examples and memoranda which elucidate the *thirteen results* of business, the student will neither fail in readily acquiring the science as it is, nor in becoming able intelligently to apply it in the interpretation of business.

Smith & Martin's Book-keeping,
Smith & Martin's Blanks,

This work is by a practical teacher and a practical book-keeper. It is of a thoroughly popular class, and will be welcomed by every one who loves to see theory and practice combined in an easy, concise, and methodical form.

The Single Entry portion is well adapted to supply a want felt in nearly all other treatises, which seem to be prepared mainly for the use of wholesale merchants, leaving retailers, mechanics, farmers, etc., who transact the greater portion of the business of the country, without a guide. The work is also commended, on this account, for general use in Young Ladies' Seminaries, where a thorough grounding in the simpler form of accounts will be invaluable to the future housekeepers of the nation.

The treatise on Double Entry Book-keeping combines all the advantages of the most recent methods, with the utmost simplicity of application, thus affording the pupil all the advantages of actual experience in the counting-house, and giving a clear comprehension of the entire subject through a judicious course of mercantile transactions.

The shape of the book is such that the transactions can be presented as in actual practice; and the simplified form of Blanks—three in number—adds greatly to the ease experienced in acquiring the science.

NATURAL SCIENCE.

FAMILIAR SCIENCE.

Norton & Porter's First Book of Science,

By eminent Professors of Yale College. Contains the principles of Natural Philosophy, Astronomy, Chemistry, Physiology, and Geology. Arranged on the Catechetical plan for primary classes and beginners.

Chambers' Treasury of Knowledge,

Progressive lessons upon—*first*, common things which lie most immediately around us, and first attract the attention of the young mind; *second*, common objects from the Mineral, Animal, and Vegetable kingdoms, manufactured articles, and miscellaneous substances; *third*, a systematic view of Nature under the various sciences. May be used as a Reader or Text-book.

NATURAL PHILOSOPHY.

Norton's First Book in Natural Philosophy,

By Prof. NORTON, of Yale College. Designed for beginners. Profusely illustrated, and arranged on the Catechetical plan.

Peck's Ganot's Course of Nat. Philosophy,

The standard text-book of France, Americanized and popularized by Prof. PECK, of Columbia College. The most magnificent system of illustration ever adopted in an American school-book is here found. For intermediate classes.

Peck's Elements of Mechanics,

A suitable introduction to Bartlett's higher treatises on Mechanical Philosophy, and adequate in itself for a complete academical course.

Bartlett's SYNTHETIC, AND ANALYTIC, Mechanics,

Bartlett's Acoustics and Optics,

A system of Collegiate Philosophy, by Prof. BARTLETT, of West Point Military Academy.

Steele's 14 Weeks Course in Philos. (see p. 34)

Steele's Philosophical Apparatus,

Adequate to performing the experiments in the ordinary text-books. The articles will be sold separately, if desired. See special circular for details.

GEOLOGY.

Page's Elements of Geology,

A volume of Chambers' Educational Course. Practical, simple, and eminently calculated to make the study interesting.

Emmons' Manual of Geology,

The first Geologist of the country has here produced a work worthy of his reputation.

Steele's 14 Weeks Course (see p. 34)

Steele's Geological Cabinet,

Containing 125 carefully selected specimens. In four parts. Sold separately, if desired. See circular for details.

Peck's Ganot's Popular Physics.

TESTIMONIALS.

From PROF. ALONZO COLLIN, *Cornell College, Iowa.*

I am pleased with it. I have decided to introduce it as a text-book.

From H. F. JOHNSON, *President Madison College, Sharon, Ms.*

I am pleased with Peck's Ganot, and think it a magnificent book.

From PROF. EDWARD BROOKS, *Pennsylvania State Normal School.*

So eminent are its merits, that it will be introduced as the text-book upon ele mentary physics in this institution.

From H. H. LOCKWOOD, *Professor Natural Philosophy U. S. Naval Academy.*

I am so pleased with it that I will probably add it to a course of lectures given to the midshipmen of this school on physics.

From GEO. S. MACKIE, *Professor Natural History University of Nashville, Tenn.*

I have decided on the introduction of Peck's Ganot's Philosophy, as I am satis fied that it is the best book for the purposes of my pupils that I have seen, com bining simplicity of explanation with elegance of illustration.

From W. S. MCRAE, *Superintendent Vevay Public Schools, Indiana.*

Having carefully examined a number of text-books on natural philosophy, I do not hesitate to express my decided opinion in favor of Peck's Ganot. The matter, style, and illustration eminently adapt the work to the popular wants.

From REV. SAMUEL MCKINNEY, D.D., *Pres't Austin College, Huntsville, Texas.*

It gives me pleasure to commend it to teachers. I have taught some classes with it as our text, and must say, for simplicity of style and clearness of illustration, I have found nothing as yet published of equal value to the teacher and pupil.

From C. V. SPEAR, *Principal Maplewood Institute, Pittsfield, Mass.*

I am much pleased with its ample illustrations by plates, and its clearness and simplicity of statement. It covers the ground usually gone over by our higher classes, and contains many fresh illustrations from life or daily occurrences, and new applications of scientific principles to such.

From J. A BANFIELD, *Superintendent Marshall Public Schools, Michigan.*

I have used Peck's Ganot since 1863, and with increasing pleasure and satisfac tion each term. I consider it superior to any other work on physics in its adapta tion to our high schools and academies. Its illustrations are superb— better than three times their number of pages of fine print.

From A. SCHUYLER, *Prof. of Mathematics in Baldwin University, Berea, Ohio.*

After a careful examination of Peck's Ganot's Natural Philosophy, and an actual test of its merits as a text-book, I can heartily recommend it as admirably adapted to meet the wants of the grade of students for which it is intended. Its diagrams and illustrations are *unrivaled.* We use it in the Baldwin University.

From D. C. VAN NORMAN, *Principal Van Norman Institute, New York.*

The Natural Philosophy of M. Ganot. edited by Prof. Peck, is, in my opinion, the best work of its kind, for the use intended, ever published in this country. Whether regarded in relation to the natural order of the topics, the precision and clearness of its definitions, or the fullness and beauty of its illustrations, it is cer tainly, I think, an advance.

☞ For many similar testimonials, see current numbers of the Illustrated Ed ucational Bulletin.

NATURAL SCIENCE—Continued.

CHEMISTRY.

Porter's First Book of Chemistry,

Porter's Principles of Chemistry,

The above are widely known as the productions of one of the most eminent scientific men of America. The extreme simplicity in the method of presenting the science, while exhaustively treated, has excited universal commendation.

Darby's Text-Book of Chemistry,

Purely a Chemistry, divesting the subject of matters comparatively foreign to it (such as heat, light, electricity, etc.), but usually allowed to engross too much attention in ordinary school-books.

Gregory's Chemistry, (Organic and Inorganic, each)

The science exhaustively treated. For colleges and medical students.

Steele's Fourteen Weeks Course,

A successful effort to reduce the study to the limits of a *single term*. (See page 34.)

Steele's Chemical Apparatus,

Adequate to the performance of all the important experiments.

BOTANY.

Thinker's First Lessons in Botany,

For children. The technical terms are largely dispensed with in favor of an easy and familiar style adapted to the smallest learner.

Wood's Object-Lessons in Botany,

Wood's American Botanist and Florist,

Wood's New Class-Book of Botany,

The standard text-books of the United States in this department. In style they are simple, popular, and lively; in arrangement, easy and natural; in description, graphic and strictly exact. The Tables for Analysis are reduced to a perfect system. More are annually sold than of all others combined.

Wood's Plant Record,

A simple form of Blanks for recording observations in the field.

Wood's Botanical Apparatus,

A portable Trunk, containing Drying Press, Knife, Trowel, Microscope, and Tweezers, and a copy of Wood's Plant Record—composing a complete outfit for the collector.

Willis's Flora of New Jersey,

"*Catalogus Plantarum in Nova Cæsarea repertarum.*" This remarkable flora is of great interest to all botanists, and the Jersey Pines have been termed "the Mecca to which every young botanist hopes some day to make a pilgrimage." This work is indispensable to those botanizing on the ground, and is the most useful book of reference ever published for collectors in all parts of the country. It contains also a Botanical Directory, with addresses of living American botanists.

Young's Familiar Lessons,

Combining simplicity of diction with some degree of technical and scientific knowledge for intermediate classes. Specially adapted for Texas and the South-west.

Darby's Southern Botany,

Embracing general Structural and Physiological Botany, with vegetable products, and descriptions of Southern plants, and a complete Flora of the Southern States.

NATURAL SCIENCE—Continued.

WOOD'S BOTANIES.

TESTIMONIALS.

From PROF. RICHARD OWEN, *University of Indiana.*

I am well pleased with the evidence of philosophical method exhibited in the general arrangement, as well as with the clearness of the explanations, the ready intelligibility of the analytical tables, and the illustrative aid furnished by the numerous and excellent wood-cuts. I design using the work as a text-book with my next class.

From PRIN. B. R. ANDERSON, *Columbus Union School, Wisconsin.*

I have examined several works with a view to recommending some good text-book on Botany, but I lay them all aside for "Wood's Botanist and Florist." The arrangement of the book is in my opinion excellent, its style fascinating and attractive, its treatment of the various departments of the science is thorough, and last, but far from unimportant, I like the topical form of the questions to each chapter. It seems to embrace the entire science. In fact, I consider it a complete, attractive, and exhaustive work.

From M. A. MARSHALL, *New Haven High School, Conn.*

It has all the excellencies of the well-known Class-Book of Botany by the same author in a smaller book. By a judicious system of condensation, the size of the Flora is reduced one-half, while no species are omitted, and many new ones are added. The descriptions of species are very brief, yet sufficient to identify the plant, and, when taken in connection with the generic description, form a complete description of the plant. The book as a whole will suit the wants of classes better than anything I have yet seen. The adoption of the Botanist and Florist would not require the exclusion of the Class-Book of Botany, as they are so arranged that both might be used by the same class.

From PROF. G. H. PERKINS, *University of Vermont and State Agricultural College.*

I can truly say that the more I examine Wood's Class-Book, the better pleased I am with it. In its illustrations, especially of particulars not easily observed by the student, and the clearness and compactness of its statements, as well as in the territory its flora embraces, it appears to me to surpass any other work I know of. The whole science, so far as it can be taught in a college course, is well presented, and rendered unusually easy of comprehension. The mode of analysis is excellent, avoiding as it does to a great extent those microscopic characters which puzzle the beginner, and using those that are obvious as far as possible. I regard the work as a most admirable one, and shall adopt it as a text-book another year.

AGRICULTURE.

Pendleton's Scientific Agriculture,

A text-book for colleges and schools; treats of the following topics: Anatomy and Physiology of Plants: Agricultural Meteorology; Soils as related to Physics; Chemistry of the Atmosphere; of Plants; of Soils; Fertilizers and Natural Manures; Animal Nutrition, etc. By E. M. PENDLETON, M. D., Prof. of Agriculture in the University of Georgia.

From President A. D. WHITE, *Cornell University.*

Dear Sir: I have examined your "Text-book of Agricultural Science," and it seems to me excellent in view of the purpose it is intended to serve. Many of your chapters interested me especially, and all parts of the work seem to combine scientific instruction with practical information in proportions dictated by sound common sense.

From President ROBINSON, *of Brown University.*

It is scientific in method as well as in matter, comprehensive in plan, natural and logical in order, compact and lucid in its statements, and must be useful both as a text-book in Agricultural colleges, and as a hand-book for intelligent planters and farmers.

NATURAL SCIENCE—Continued.

PHYSIOLOGY.

Jarvis' Elements of Physiology,

Jarvis' Physiology and Laws of Health,

The only books extant which approach this subject with a proper view of the true object of teaching Physiology in schools, viz., that scholars may know how to take care of their own health. In bold contrast with the abstract *Anatomies*, which children learn as they would Greek or Latin (and forget as soon), to *discipline the mind*, are these text-books, using the *science* as a secondary consideration, and only so far as is necessary for the comprehension of the *laws of health.*

Hamilton's Vegetable and Animal Physiology,

The two branches of the science combined in one volume lead the student to a proper comprehension of the Analogies of Nature.

Steele's Fourteen Weeks Course,

In the popular style, avoiding technical and purely scientific formulas. It contains beautiful and vivid illustrations, some of them colored, and a blackboard analysis of the skeleton. The sections on diseases and accidents, and their prompt home treatment, give the book great practical value (see p. 34).

ASTRONOMY.

Willard's School Astronomy,

By means of clear and attractive illustrations, addressing the eye in many cases by analogies, careful definitions of all necessary technical terms, a careful avoidance of verbiage and unimportant matter, particular attention to analysis, and a general adoption of the simplest methods. Mrs. Willard has made the best and most attractive *elementary* Astronomy extant.

McIntyre's Astronomy and the Globes,

A complete treatise for intermediate classes. Highly approved.

Bartlett's Spherical Astronomy,

The West Point course, for advanced classes, with applications to the current wants of Navigation, Geography, and Chronology.

Steele's Fourteen Weeks Course,

Reduced to a single term, and better adapted to school use than any work heretofore published. Not written for the information of scientific men, but for the inspiration of youth, the pages are not burdened with a multitude of figures which no memory could possibly retain. The whole subject is presented in a clear and concise form. (See p. 34.)

NATURAL HISTORY.

Carll's Child's Book of Natural History,

Illustrating the Animal, Vegetable, and Mineral Kingdoms, with applicatien to the Arts. For beginners. Beautifully and copiously illustrated.

ZOOLOGY.

Chambers' Elements of Zoology,

A complete and comprehensive system of Zoology, adapted for academic instruction, presenting a systematic view of the Animal Kingdom as a portion of external Nature.

Steele's Fourteen Weeks Course,

Notable for its superb and entertaining illustrations, which include every animal named; blackboard tables of classification and tabular review of the whole animal kingdom; interesting and characteristic facts and anecdotes; directions for collecting and preserving specimens, etc., etc. (See p. 34.)

Jarvis' Physiology and Laws of Health.

TESTIMONIALS.

From SAMUEL B. MCLANE, *Superintendent Public Schools, Keokuk, Iowa.*

I am glad to see a really good text-book on this much neglected branch. This is clear, concise, accurate, and eminently adapted to the *class-room.*

From WILLIAM F. WYERS, *Principal of Academy, West Chester, Pennsylvania.*

A thorough examination has satisfied me of its superior claims as a text-book to the attention of teacher and taught. I shall introduce it at once.

From H. R. SANFORD, *Principal of East Genesee Conference Seminary, N. Y.*

"Jarvis' Physiology" is received, and fully met our expectations. We immediately adopted it.

From ISAAC T. GOODNOW, *State Superintendent of Kansas—published in connection with the "School Law."*

"Jarvis' Physiology," a common-sense, practical work, with just enough of anatomy to understand the physiological portions. The last six pages, on Man's Responsibility for his own health, are worth the price of the book.

From D. W. STEVENS, *Superintendent Public Schools, Fall River, Mass.*

I have examined Jarvis' "Physiology and Laws of Health," which you had the kindness to send to me a short time ago. In my judgment it is far the best work of the kind within my knowledge. It has been adopted as a text-book in our public schools.

From HENRY G. DENNY, *Chairman Book Committee, Boston, Mass.*

The very excellent "Physiology" of Dr. Jarvis I had introduced into our High School, where the study had been temporarily dropped, believing it to be by far the best work of the kind that had come under my observation; indeed, the reintroduction of the study was delayed for some months, because Dr. Jarvis' book could not be had, and we were unwilling to take any other.

From PROF. A. P. PEABODY, D.D., LL.D., *Harvard University.*

* * I have been in the habit of examining school-books with great care, and I hesitate not to say that, of all the text-books on Physiology which have been given to the public, Dr. Jarvis' deserves the first place on the score of accuracy, thoroughness, method, simplicity of statement, and constant reference to topics of practical interest and utility.

From JAMES N. TOWNSEND, *Superintendent Public Schools, Hudson, N. Y.*

Every human being is appointed to take charge of his own body; and of all books written upon this subject, I know of none which will so well prepare one to do this as "Jarvis' Physiology"—that is, in so small a compass of matter. It considers the pure, simple *laws of health* paramount to science; and though the work is thoroughly scientific, it is divested of all cumbrous technicalities, and presents the subject of physical life in a manner and style really charming. It is unquestionably the best text-book on physiology I have ever seen. It is giving great satisfaction in the schools of this city, where it has been adopted as the standard.

From L. J. SANFORD, M.D., *Prof. Anatomy and Physiology in Yale College*

Books on human physiology, designed for the use of schools, are more generally a failure perhaps than are school-books on most other subjects.

The great want in this department is met, we think, in the well-written treatise of Dr. Jarvis, entitled "Physiology and Laws of Health." * * The work is not too detailed nor too expansive in any department, and is clear and concise in all. It is not burdened with an excess of anatomical description, nor rendered discursive by many zoological references. Anatomical statements are made to the extent of qualifying the student to attend, understandingly, to an exposition of those functional processes which, collectively, make up health; thus the laws of health are enunciated, and many suggestions are given which, if heeded, will tend to its preservation.

☞ For further testimony of similar character, see current numbers of the Illustrated Educational Bulletin.

NATURAL SCIENCE.

"FOURTEEN WEEKS" IN EACH BRANCH.

By J. DORMAN STEELE, A. M.

Steele's 14 Weeks Course in Chemistry (New Ed.)
Steele's 14 Weeks Course in Astronomy
Steele's 14 Weeks Course in Philosophy
Steele's 14 Weeks Course in Geology
Steele's 14 Weeks Course in Physiology
Steele's 14 Weeks Course in Zoology

Our Text-Books in these studies are, as a general thing, dull and uninteresting. They contain from 400 to 600 pages of dry facts and unconnected details. They abound in that which the student cannot learn, much less remember. The pupil commences the study, is confused by the fine print and coarse print, and neither knowing exactly what to learn nor what to hasten over, is crowded through the single term generally assigned to each branch, and frequently comes to the close without a definite and exact idea of a single scientific principle.

Steele's Fourteen Weeks Courses contain only that which every well-informed person should know, while all that which concerns only the professional scientist is omitted. The language is clear, simple, and interesting, and the illustrations bring the subject within the range of home life and daily experience. They give such of the general principles and the prominent facts as a pupil can make familiar as household words within a single term. The type is large and open; there is no fine print to annoy; the cuts are copies of genuine experiments or natural phenomena, and are of fine execution.

In fine, by a system of condensation peculiarly his own, the author reduces each branch to the limits of a single term of study, while sacrificing nothing that is essential, and nothing that is usually retained from the study of the larger manuals in common use. Thus the student has rare opportunity to *economize his time*, or rather to employ that which he has to the best advantage.

A notable feature is the author's charming "style," fortified by an enthusiasm over his subject in which the student will not fail to partake. Believing that Natural Science is full of fascination, he has moulded it into a form that attracts the attention and kindles the enthusiasm of the pupil.

The recent editions contain the author's "Practical Questions" on a plan never before attempted in scientific text-books. These are questions as to the nature and cause of common phenomena, and are not directly answered in the text, the design being to test and promote an intelligent use of the student's knowledge of the foregoing principles.

Steele's General Key to his Works.

This work is mainly composed of Answers to the Practical Questions and Solutions of the Problems in the author's celebrated "Fourteen Weeks Courses" in the several sciences, with many hints to teachers, minor Tables, &c. Should be on every teacher's desk.

Steele's 14 Weeks in each Science.

TESTIMONIALS.

From L. A. BIKLE, *President N. C. College.*

I have not been disappointed. Shall take pleasure in introducing this series.

From J. F. COX, *Prest. Southern Female College, Ga.*

I am much pleased with these books, and expect to introduce them.

From J. R. BRANHAM, *Prin. Brownsville Female College, Tenn.*

They are capital little books, and are now in use in our institution.

From W. H. GOODALE, *Professor Readville Seminary, La.*

We are using your 14 Weeks Course, and are much pleased with them.

From W. A. BOLES, *Supt. Shelbyville Graded School, Ind.*

They are as entertaining as a story book, and much more improving to the mind.

From S. A. SNOW, *Principal of High School, Uxbridge, Mass.*

Steele's 14 Weeks Courses in the Sciences are a perfect success.

From JOHN W. DOUGHTY, *Newburg Free Academy, N. Y.*

I was prepared to find Prof. Steele's Course both attractive and instructive. My highest expectations have been fully realized.

From J. S. BLACKWELL, *Prest. Ghent College, Ky.*

Prof. Steele's unexampled success in providing for the wants of academic classes, has led me to look forward with high anticipations to his forthcoming issue.

From J. F. COOK, *Prest. La Grange College, Mo.*

I am pleased with the neatness of these books and the delightful diction. I have been teaching for years, and have never seen a lovelier little volume than the Astronomy.

From M. W. SMITH, *Prin. of High School, Morrison, Ill.*

They seem to me to be admirably adapted to the wants of a public school, containing, as they do, a sufficiently comprehensive arrangement of elementary principles to excite a healthy thirst for a more thorough knowledge of those sciences.

From J. D. BARTLEY, *Prin. of High School, Concord, N. H.*

They are just such books as I have looked for, viz., those of interesting style, not cumbersome and filled up with things to be omitted by the pupil, and yet sufficiently full of facts for the purpose of most scholars in these sciences in our high schools; there is nothing but what a pupil of average ability can thoroughly master.

From ALONZO NORTON LEWIS, *Principal of Parker Academy, Conn.*

I consider Steele's Fourteen Weeks Courses in Philosophy, Chemistry, &c., the *best* school-books that have been issued in this country.

As an introduction to the various branches of which they treat, and especially for that numerous class of pupils who have not the time for a more extended course, I consider them *invaluable.*

From EDWARD BROOKS, *Prin. State Normal School, Millersville, Pa.*

At the meeting of Normal School Principals, I presented the following resolution, which was unanimously adopted: "*Resolved,* That Steele's 14 Weeks Courses in Natural Philosophy and Astronomy, or an amount equivalent to what is contained in them, be adopted for use in the State Normal Schools of Pennsylvania." The works themselves will be adopted by at least three of the schools, and, I presume, by them all.

LITERATURE.

Gilman's First Steps in English Literature,

The character and plan of this exquisite little text-book may be best understood from an analysis of its contents:

INTRODUCTION. Chapter I, Historical; II, Definition of Terms; III, Languages of Europe, with Chart.

PERIOD OF IMMATURE ENGLISH, with Chart. Chapter IV, Original English; V, Broken English; VI, Dead English; VII, Reviving English.

PERIOD OF MATURE ENGLISH, with Chart. Chapter VIII, The Italian Influence; IX, Puritan Influence; X, French Influence; XI, Age of Pope; XII, Age of Johnson; XIII, Age of Poetical Romance; XIV, Age of Prose Romance.

The volume concludes with a Chart of Bible Translations, a Bibliography or Guide to General Reading, and other aids to the student.

Cleveland's Compendiums,

ENGLISH LITERATURE. AMERICAN LITERATURE.
ENGLISH LITERATURE OF THE XIXTH CENTURY.

In these volumes are gathered the cream of the literature of the English-speaking people for the school-room and the general reader. Their reputation is national. More than 125,000 copies have been sold.

Boyd's English Classics,

MILTON'S PARADISE LOST. THOMSON'S SEASONS.
YOUNG'S NIGHT THOUGHTS. POLLOK'S COURSE OF TIME.
COWPER'S TASK, TABLE TALK, &c. LORD BACON'S ESSAYS.

This series of annotated editions of great English writers, in prose and poetry, is designed for critical reading and parsing in schools. Prof. J. R. Boyd proves himself an editor of high capacity, and the works themselves need no encomium. As auxiliary to the study of Belles Lettres, etc., these works have no equal.

Pope's Essay on Man,

Pope's Homer's Iliad,

The metrical translation of the great poet of antiquity, and the matchless "Essay on the Nature and State of Man," by ALEXANDER POPE, afford superior exercise in literature and parsing.

ÆSTHETICS.

Huntington's Manual of the Fine Arts,

A view of the rise and progress of Art in different countries, a brief account of the most eminent masters of Art, and an analysis of the principles of Art. It is complete in itself, or may precede to advantage the critical work of Lord Kames.

Boyd's Kames' Elements of Criticism,

The best edition of this standard work; without the study of which none may be considered proficient in the science of the Perceptions. No other study can be pursued with so marked an effect upon the taste and refinement of the pupil.

CLEVELAND'S COMPENDIUMS.

TESTIMONIALS.

From the New Englander.

This is the very best book of the kind we have ever examined.

From GEORGE B. EMERSON, Esq., *Boston.*

The Biographical Sketches are just and discriminating; the selections are admirable, and I have adopted the work as a text-book for my first class.

From PROF. MOSES COIT TYLER, *of the Michigan University.*

I have given your book a thorough examination, and am greatly delighted with it; and shall have great pleasure in directing the attention of my classes to a work which affords so admirable a bird's-eye view of recent "English Literature."

From the Saturday Review.

It acquaints the reader with the characteristic method, tone, and quality of all the chief notabilities of the period, and will give the careful student a better idea of the recent history of English Literature than nine educated Englishmen in ten possess.

From the Methodist Quarterly Review, New York.

This work is a transcript of the best American mind; a vehicle of the noblest American spirit. No parent who would introduce his child to a knowledge of our country's literature, and at the same time indoctrinate his heart in the purest principles, need fear to put this manual in the youthful hand.

From REV. C. PEIRCE, *Principal, West Newton, Mass.*

I do not believe the work is to be found from which, within the same limits, so much interesting and valuable information in regard to English writers and English literature of every age, can be obtained; and it deserves to find a place in all our high schools and academies, as well as in every private library.

From the Independent.

The work of selection and compilation—requiring a perfect familiarity with the whole range of English literature, a judgment clear and impartial, a taste at once delicate and severe, and a most sensitive regard to purity of thought or feeling—has been better accomplished in this than in any kindred volume with which we are acquainted.

POLITICAL ECONOMY.

Champlin's Lessons on Political Economy,

An improvement on previous treatises, being shorter, yet containing everything essential, with a view of recent questions in finance, etc., which is not elsewhere found.

From J. L. BOTHWELL, *Prin. Public School No. 14, Albany, N. Y.*

I have examined Champlin's Political Economy with much pleasure, and shall be pleased to put it into the hands of my pupils. In quantity and quality I think it superior to anything that I have examined.

From PRES. N. E. COBLEIGH, *East Tennessee Wesleyan University.*

An examination of Champlin's Political Economy has satisfied me that it is the book I want. For brevity and compactness, division of the subject, and clear statement, and for appropriateness of treatment, I consider it a better text-book than any other in the market.

From the Evening Mail, New York.

A new interest has been imparted to the science of political economy since we have been necessitated to raise such vast sums of money for the support of the government. The time, therefore, is favorable for the introduction of works like the above. This little volume of two hundred pages is intended for beginners, for the common school and academy. It is intended as a basis upon which to rear a more elaborate superstructure. There is nothing in the principles of political economy above the comprehension of average scholars, when they are clearly set forth. This seems to have been done by President Champlin in an easy and graceful manner.

ELOCUTION.

Thwing's Vocal Culture.

A Drill-Book for voice and gesture, by Rev. Prof. Thwing, of Brooklyn Tabernacle Lay College. Price 50 cts.

Taverner Graham's Reasonable Elocution,

Based upon the belief that true Elocution is the right interpretation of THOUGHT, and guiding the student to an intelligent appreciation, instead of a merely mechanical knowledge, of its rules.

Zachos' Analytic Elocution.

All departments of elocution—such as the analysis of the voice and the sentence, phonology, rhythm, expression, gesture, etc.—are here arranged for instruction in classes, illustrated by copious examples.

Sherwood's Self Culture.

Self-culture in reading, speaking, and conversatlon—a very valuable treatise to those who would perfect themselves in these accomplishments.

SPEAKERS.

Northend's Little Orator—Child's Speaker.

Two little works of the same grade but different selections, containing simple and attractive pieces for children under twelve years of age.

Northend's Young Declaimer.

Northend's National Orator.

Two volumes of Prose, Poetry, and Dialogue, adapted to intermediate and grammar classes respectively.

Northend's Entertaining Dialogues.

Extracts eminently adapted to cultivate the dramatic faculties, as well as entertain an audience.

Swett's Common School Speaker.

Selections from recent literature.

Raymond's Patriotic Speaker,

A superb compilation of modern eloquence and poetry, with original dramatic exercises. Nearly every eminent *living* orator is represented, without distinction of place or party.

COMPOSITION AND RHETORIC.

Brookfield's First Book in Composition,

Making the cultivation of this important art feasible for the smallest child. By a new method, to induce and stimulate thought.

Boyd's Composition and Rhetoric.

This work furnishes all the aid that is needful or can be desired in the various departments and styles of composition, both in prose and verse.

Day's Art of Rhetoric,

Noted for exactness of definition, clear limitation, and philosophical development of subject; the large share of attention given to Invention, as a branch of Rhetoric, and the unequalled analysis of style.

MIND AND MORALS.

Mahan's Intellectual Philosophy

The subject exhaustively considered. The author has evinced learning, candor, and independent thinking.

Mahan's Science of Logic

A profound analysis of the laws of thought. The system possesses the merit being intelligible and self consistent. In addition to the author's carefully elaborated views, it embraces results attained by the ablest minds of Great Britain, Germany, and France, in this department.

Boyd's Elements of Logic

A systematic and philosophic condensation of the subject, fortified with additions from Watts, Abercrombie, Whately, &c.

Watts on the Mind

The Improvement of the Mind, by Isaac Watts, is designed as a guide for the attainment of useful knowledge. As a text-book it is unparalleled; and the discipline it affords cannot be too highly esteemed by the educator.

Peabody's Moral Philosophy

A short course; by the Professor of Christian Morals, Harvard University—for the Freshman Class and for High Schools.

Fletcher's Practical Ethics

A topical analysis of each of the Virtues and Graces, furnishing outlines for the pupil to illustrate from his own experience or reading.

Alden's Text-Book of Ethics

For young pupils. To aid in systematizing the ethical teachings of the Bible, and point out the coincidences between the instructions of the sacred volume and the sound conclusions of reason.

Willard's Morals for the Young

Lessons in conversational style to indicate the elements of moral philosophy. The study is made attractive by narratives and engravings.

GOVERNMENT.

Howe's Young Citizen's Catechism

Explaining the duties of District, Town, City, County, State, and United States Officers, with rules for parliamentary and commercial business.

Young's Lessons in Civil Government

A comprehensive view of Government, and abstract of the laws showing the rights, duties, and responsibilities of citizens.

Mansfield's Political Manual.

This is a complete view of the theory and practice of the General and State Governments, designed as a text-book. The author is an esteemed and able professor of constitutional law, widely known for his sagacious utterances in the public press.

Martin's Civil Government

Emanating from Massachusetts State Normal School. Historical and statistical. Each chapter summarized by a succinct statement of underlying principles on which good government is based.

MODERN LANGUAGE.

Illustrated Language Primers,

FRENCH AND ENGLISH. GERMAN AND ENGLISH.
SPANISH AND ENGLISH.

The names of common objects properly illustrated and arranged in easy lessons.

Ledru's French Fables,

Ledru's French Grammar,

Ledru's French Reader,

The author's long experience has enabled him to present the most thoroughly practical text-books extant, in this branch. The system of pronunciation (by phonetic illustration) is original with this author, and will commend itself to all American teachers, as it enables their pupils to secure an absolutely correct pronunciation without the assistance of a native master. This feature is peculiarly valuable also to "self-taught" students. The directions for ascertaining the gender of French nouns—also a great stumbling-block—are peculiar to this work, and will be found remarkably competent to the end proposed. The criticism of teachers and the test of the school-room is invited to this excellent series, with confidence.

Worman's French Echo,

To teach conversational French by actual practice, on an entirely new plan, which recognizes the importance of the student learning *to think* in the language which he speaks. It furnishes an extensive vocabulary of words and expressions in common use, and suffices to free the learner from the embarrassments which the peculiarities of his own tongue are likely to be to him, and to make him thoroughly familiar with the use of proper idioms.

Worman's German Echo,

On the same plan. See Worman's German Series, page 42.

Pujol's Complete French Class-Book,

Offers, in one volume, methodically arranged, a complete French course—usually embraced in series of from five to twelve books, including the bulky and expensive Lexicon. Here are Grammar, Conversation, and choice Literature—selected from the best French authors. Each branch is thoroughly handled; and the student, having diligently completed the course as prescribed, may consider himself, without further application, *au fait* in the most polite and elegant language of modern times.

Pujol's French Grammar, Exercises, Reader,

These volumes contain Part I, Parts II and III, and Part IV of the Complete Class-Book respectively, for the convenience of scholars and teachers. The Lexicon is bound with each part.

Maurice-Poitevin's Grammaire Francaise,

American schools are at last supplied with an American edition of this famous text-book. Many of our best institutions have for years been procuring it from abroad rather than forego the advantages it offers. The policy of putting students who have acquired some proficiency from the ordinary text-books, into a Grammar written in the vernacular, cannot be too highly commended. It affords an opportunity for finish and review at once; while embodying abundant practice of its own rules.

Joynes' French Pronunciation,

Willard's Historia de los Estados Unidos,

The History of the United States, translated by Professors TOLON and DE TORNOS, will be found a valuable, instructive, and entertaining reading-book for Spanish classes.

Pujol's Complete French Class-Book.

TESTIMONIALS.

From PROF. ELIAS PEISSNER, *Union College.*

I take great pleasure in recommending Pujol and Van Norman's French Class-Book, as there is no French grammar or class-book which can be compared with it in completeness, system, clearness, and general utility.

From EDWARD NORTH, *President of Hamilton College.*

I have carefully examined Pujol and Van Norman's French Class-Book, and am satisfied of its superiority, for college purposes, over any other heretofore used. We shall not fail to use it with our next class in French.

From A. CURTIS, *Pres't of Cincinnati Literary and Scientific Institute.*

I am confident that it may be made an instrument in conveying to the student, in from six months to a year, the art of speaking and writing the French with almost native fluency and propriety.

From HIRAM ORCUTT, A. M., *Prin. Glenwood and Tilden Ladies' Seminaries.*

I have used Pujol's French Grammar in my two seminaries, exclusively, for more than a year, and have no hesitation in saying that I regard it the best text-book in this department extant. And my opinion is confirmed by the testimony of Prof. F. De Launay and Mademoiselle Marindin. They assure me that the book is eminently accurate and practical, as tested in the school-room.

From PROF. THEO. F. DE FUMAT, *Hebrew Educational Institute, Memphis, Tenn.*

M. Pujol's French Grammar is one of the best and most practical works. The French language is chosen and elegant in style—modern and easy. It is far superior to the other French class-books in this country. The selection of the conversational part is very good, and will interest pupils; and being all completed in only one volume, it is especially desirable to have it introduced in our schools.

From PROF. JAMES H. WORMAN, *Bordentown Female College, N. J.*

The work is upon the same plan as the text-books for the study of French and English published in Berlin, for the study of those who have not the aid of a teacher, and these books are considered, by the first authorities, the best books. In most of our institutions, Americans teach the modern languages, and heretofore the trouble has been to give them a text-book that would dispose of the difficulties of the French pronunciation. This difficulty is successfully removed by P. and Van N., and I have every reason to believe it will soon make its way into most of our best schools.

From PROF. CHARLES S. DOD, *Ann Smith Academy, Lexington, Va.*

I cannot do better than to recommend "Pujol and Van Norman." For comprehensive and systematic arrangement, progressive and thorough development of all grammatical principles and idioms, with a due admixture of theoretical knowledge and practical exercise, I regard it as superior to any (other) book of the kind.

From A. A. FORSTER, *Prin. Pinehurst School, Toronto, C. W.*

I have great satisfaction in bearing testimony to M. Pujol's System of French Instruction, as given in his complete class-book. For clearness and comprehensiveness, adapted for all classes of pupils, I have found it superior to any other work of the kind, and have now used it for some years in my establishment with great success.

From PROF. OTTO FEDDER, *Maplewood Institute, Pittsfield, Mass.*

The conversational exercises will prove an immense saving of the hardest kind of labor to teachers. There is scarcely any thing more trying in the way of teaching language, than to rack your brain for short and easily intelligible bits of conversation, and to repeat them time and again with no better result than extorting at long intervals a doubting "oui," or a hesitating " non, monsieur "

☞ For further testimony of a similar character, see special circular, and current numbers of the Educational Bulletin.

GERMAN.

A COMPLETE COURSE IN THE GERMAN.

By JAMES H. WORMAN, A. M.

Worman's Elementary German Grammar
Worman's Complete German Grammar

These volumes are designed for intermediate and advanced classes respectively. Though following the same general method with "Otto" (that of 'Gaspey'), our author differs essentially in its application. He is more practical, more systematic, more accurate, and besides introduces a number of invaluable features which have never before been combined in a German grammar.

Among other things, it may be claimed for Prof. Worman that he has been *the first* to introduce in an American text-book for learning German, a system of analogy and comparison with other languages. Our best teachers are also enthusiastic about his methods of inculcating the art of speaking, of understanding the spoken language, of correct pronunciation; the sensible and convenient original classification of nouns (in four declensions), and of irregular verbs, also deserves much praise. We also note the use of heavy type to indicate etymological changes in the paradigms and, in the exercises, the parts which specially illustrate preceding rules.

Worman's Elementary German Reader
Worman's Collegiate German Reader

The finest and most judicious compilation of classical and standard German Literature. These works embrace, progressively arranged, selections from the masterpieces of Goethe, Schiller, Korner, Seume, Uhland, Freiligrath, Heine, Schlegel, Holty, Lenau, Wieland, Herder, Lessing, Kant, Fichte, Schelling, Winkelmann, Humboldt, Ranke, Raumer, Menzel, Gervinus, &c., and contains complete Goethe's "Iphigenie," Schiller's "Jungfrau;" also, for instruction in modern conversational German, Benedix's "Eigensinn."

There are besides, Biographical Sketches of each author contributing, Notes, explanatory and philological (after the text), Grammatical References to all leading grammars, as well as the editor's own, and an adequate Vocabulary.

Worman's German Echo

Consists of exercises in colloquial style entirely in the German, with an adequate vocabulary, not only of words but of idioms. The object of the system developed in this work (and its companion volume in the French) is to break up the laborious and tedious habit of *translating the thoughts*, which is the student's most effectual bar to fluent conversation, and to lead him to *think in the language in which he speaks*. As the exercises illustrate scenes in actual life, a considerable knowledge of the manners and customs of the German people is also acquired from the use of this manual.

Worman's German Copy-Books, 3 Numbers,

On the same plan as the most approved systems for English penmanship, with progressive copies.

Worman's German Grammars.

TESTIMONIALS.

From Prof. R. W. JONES, *Petersburg Female College, Va.*

From what I have seen of the work it is almost certain *I shall introduce it* into this institution.

From Prof. G. CAMPBELL, *University of Minnesota.*

A valuable addition to our school-books, and will find many friends, and do great good.

From Prof. O. H P. CORPREW, *Mary Military Inst*, *Md.*

I am better pleased with them than any I have ever taught. I have already ordered through our booksellers.

From Prof. R. S. KENDALL, *Vernon Academy, Conn.*

I at once put the Elementary Grammar into the hands of a class of beginners, and have used it *with great satisfaction.*

From Prof. D. E. HOLMES, *Berlin Academy, Wis.*

Worman's German works are *superior.* I shall use them hereafter in my German classes.

From Prof. MAGNUS BUCHHOLTZ, *Hiram College, Ohio.*

I have examined the Complete Grammar, and find it *excellent.* You may rely that it will be used here.

From Prin. THOS. W. TOBEY, *Paducah Female Seminary, Ky.*

The Complete German Grammar is worthy of an extensive circulation. It is *admirably adapted* to the class-room. I shall use it.

From Prof. ALEX. ROSENSPITZ, *Houston Academy, Texas.*

Bearer will take and pay for 3 dozen copies. Mr. Worman deserves the approbation and esteem of the teacher and the thanks of the student.

From Prof. G. MALMENE, *Augusta Seminary, Maine.*

The Complete Grammar cannot fail to *give great satisfaction* by the simplicity of its arrangement, and by its completeness.

From Prin. OVAL PIRKEY, *Christian University, Mo.*

Just such a series as is positively necessary. I do hope the author will succeed as well in the French, &c., as he has in the German.

From Prof. S. D. HILLMAN, *Dickinson College, Pa.*

The class have lately commenced, and my examination thus far warrants me in saying that I regard it as *the best* grammar for instruction in the German.

From Prin. SILAS LIVERMORE, *Bloomfield Seminary, Mo.*

I have found a classically and scientifically educated Prussian gentleman whom I propose to make German instructor. I have shown him both your German grammars. He has expressed *his approbation* of them generally.

From Prof. Z. TEST, *Howland School for Young Ladies, N. Y.*

I shall introduce the books. From a cursory examination I have no hesitation in pronouncing the Complete Grammar *a decided improvement* on the text-books at present in use in this country.

From Prof. LEWIS KISTLER, *Northwestern University, Ill.*

Having looked through the Complete Grammar with some care I must say that you have produced *a good book;* you may be awarded with this gratification—that your grammar promotes the facility of learning the German language, and of becoming acquainted with its rich literature.

From Pres. J. P. ROUS, *Stockwell Collegiate Inst., Ind.*

I supplied a class with the Elementary Grammar, and it gives *complete satisfaction.* The conversational and reading exercises are well calculated to illustrate the principles, and lead the student on an easy yet thorough course. I think the Complete Grammar equally attractive.

THE CLASSICS.

LATIN.

Silber's Latin Course,

The book contains an Epitome of Latin Grammar, followed by Reading Exercises, with explanatory Notes and copious References to the leading Latin Grammars, and also to the Epitome which precedes the work. Then follow a Latin-English Vocabulary and Exercises in Latin Prose Composition, being thus complete in itself, and a very suitable work to put in the hands of one about to study the language.

Searing's Virgil's Æneid,

It contains only the first six books of the Æneid. 2. A very carefully constructed Dictionary. 3. Sufficiently copious Notes. 4. Grammatical references to four leading Grammars. 5. Numerous Illustrations of the highest order, 6. A superb Map of the Mediterranean and adjacent countries. 7. Dr. S. H. Taylor's "Questions on the Æneid." 8. A Metrical Index, and an Essay on the Poetical Style. 9. A photographic *fac simile* of an early Latin M.S. 10. The text according to Jahn, but paragraphed according to Ladewig. 11. Superior mechanical execution.

"Have examined it with great pleasure and can safely say it is the best edition of Virgil with which I am acquainted."—PROF. LESLIE WAGGENER, *Bethel College, Ky.*

"Am *very* much pleased. In following points think it surpasses: instructive illustrations, pointed and sensible notes where they are convenient to use, and a vocabulary that gives the *derivation of Latin words.*"—PRIN. E. L. RICHARDSON, *Addison Union School, N. Y.*

"A fine specimen of art, and edited in a *masterly manner.*"—SUPT. W. C. ROTE, *Lawrence Public Schools, Kansas.*

"Of Searing's Virgil I cannot speak in too high terms. While as a text-book it contains as many excellences as any I have ever seen, the fineness of the paper and the beauty of typography and exceeding neatness make it an ornament for the centre-table."—PRIN. E. C. SPALDING, *Nunda Academy, N. Y.*

☞ *For further testimonials, see page 45.*

Blair's Latin Pronunciation,

An inquiry into the proper sounds of the Language during the Classical Period. By Prof. Blair, of Hampden Sidney College, Va.

GREEK.

Crosby's Greek Grammar,
Crosby's Xenophon's Anabasis,

MYTHOLOGY.

Dwight's Grecian and Roman Mythology.

School edition, University edition,

A knowledge of the fables of antiquity, thus presented in a systematic form, is as indispensable to the student of general literature as to him who would peruse intelligently the classical authors. The mythological allusions so frequent in literature are readily understood with such a Key as this.

SEARING'S VIRGIL.

SPECIMEN FRAGMENTS OF LETTERS.

"I adopt it gladly."—PRIN. V. DABNEY, *Loudoun School, Va.*

"I like Searing's Virgil."—PROF. BRISTOL, *Ripon College, Wis.*

"Meets my desires very thoroughly."—PROF. CLARK, *Berea College, Ohio.*

"Superior to any other edition of Virgil."—PRES. HALL, *Macon College, Mo.*

"Shall adopt it at once."—PRIN. B. P. BAKER, *Searcy Female Institute. Ark.*

"Your Virgil is a *beauty*."—PROF. W. H. DE MOTTE, *Illinois Female College.*

"After use, I regard it the best."—PRIN. G. H. BARTON, *Rome Academy, N. Y.*

"We like it better every day."—PRIN. R. K. BUEHRLE, *Allentown Academy, Pa.*

"I am delighted with your Virgil."—PRIN. W. T. LEONARD, *Pierce Academy, Mass.*

"Stands well the test of class-room."—PRIN. F. A. CHASE, *Lyons Col. Inst., Iowa.*

"I do not see how it can be improved."—PRIN. N. F. D. BROWNE, *Charl. Hall, Md.*

"The most complete that I have seen."—PRIN. A. BROWN, *Columbus High School, Ohio.*

"Our Professor of Language very highly approves."—SUPT. J. G. JAMES, *Texas Military Institute.*

"It responds to a want long felt by teachers. It is beautiful and complete."—PROF. BROOKS, *University of Minnesota.*

"The ideal edition. We want a few more classics of the same sort."—PRIN. C. F. P. BANCROFT, *Lookout Mountain Institute, Tenn.*

"I certainly have never seen an edition so complete with important requisites for a student, nor with such fine text and general mechanical execution."—PRES. J. R. PARK, *University of Deseret, Utah.*

"It is charming both in its design and execution. And, on the whole, I think it is the best thing of the kind that I have seen."—PROF. J. DE F. RICHARDS, *Pres. pro tem. of University of Alabama.*

"In beauty of execution, in judicious notes, and in an adequate vocabulary, it merits all praise. I shall recommend its introduction."—PRES. J. K. PATTERSON, *Kentucky Agricultural and Mechanical College.*

"Containing a good vocabulary and judicious notes, it will enable the industrious student to acquire an accurate knowledge of the most interesting part of Virgil's works."—PROF. J. T. DUNKLIN, *East Alabama College.*

"It wants no element of completeness. It is by far the best classical text-book with which I am acquainted. The notes are just right. They help the student when he most needs help."—PRIN. C. A. BUNKER, *Caledonia Grammar School, Vt.*

"I have examined Searing's Virgil with interest, and find that it more nearly meets the wants of students than that of any other edition with which I am acquainted. I am able to introduce it to some extent at once."—PRIN. J. EASTER, *East Genesee Conference Seminary.*

"I have been wishing to get a sight of it, and it exceeds my expectations. It is a beautiful book in every respect, and bears evidence of careful and critical study. The engravings add instruction as well as interest to the work. I shall recommend it to my classes."—PRIN. CHAS. H. CHANDLER, *Glenwood Ladies' Seminary.*

"A. S. Barnes & Co. have published an edition of the first six books of Virgil's Æneid, which is superior to its predecessors in several respects. The publishers have done a good service to the cause of classical education, and the book deserves a large circulation."—PROF. GEORGE W. COLLORD, *Brooklyn Polytechnic, N. Y.*

"My attention was called to Searing's Virgil by the fact of its containing a vocabulary which would obviate the necessity of procuring a lexicon. But use in the class-room has impressed me most favorably with the accuracy and just proportion of its notes, and the general excellence of its grammatical suggestions. The general character of the book in its paper, its typography, and its engravings is highly commendable, and the fac-simile manuscript is a valuable feature. I take great pleasure in commending the book to all who do not wish a complete edition of Virgil. It suits our short school courses admirably."—HENRY L. BOLTWOOD, *Master of Princeton High School, Ill.*

RECORDS.

Cole's Self-Reporting Class-Book,

For saving the Teacher's labor in averaging. At each opening are a full set of Tables showing any scholar's standing at a glance and entirely obviating the necessity of computation.

Tracy's School-Record, Pocket edition,

For keeping a simple but exact record of Attendance, Deportment, and Scholarship. The larger edition contains also a Calendar, an extensive list of Topics for Compositions and Colloquies, Themes for Short Lectures, Suggestions to Young Teachers, etc.

Brooks' Teacher's Register,

Presents at one view a record of Attendance, Recitations, and Deportment for the whole term.

Carter's Record and Roll-Book,

This is the most complete and convenient Record offered to the public. Besides the usual spaces for General Scholarship, Deportment, Attendance, etc., for each name and day, there is a space in red lines enclosing six minor spaces in blue for recording Recitations.

National School Diary,

A little book of blank forms for weekly report of the standing of each scholar, from teacher to parent. A great convenience.

REWARDS.

National School Currency,

A little box containing certificates in the form of Money. The most entertaining and stimulating system of school rewards.. The scholar is paid for his merits and fined for his shortcomings. Of course the most faithful are the most successful in business. In this way the use and value of money and the method of keeping accounts are also taught. One box of Currency will supply a school of fifty pupils.

TACTICS.

The Boy Soldier,

Complete Infantry Tactics for Schools, with illustrations, for the use of those who would introduce this pleasing relaxation from the confining duties of the desk.

CHARTS.

McKenzie's Elocutionary Chart,

Baade's Reading Case,

This remarkable piece of school-room furniture is a receptacle containing a number of primary cards. By an arrangement of slides on the front, one sentence at a time is shown to the class. Twenty-eight thousand transpositions may be made, affording a variety of progressive exercises which no other piece of apparatus offers. One of its best features is, that it is so exceedingly simple as not to get out of order, while it may be operated with one finger.

Marcy's Eureka Tablet,

A new system for the Alphabet, by which it may be taught without fail in nine lessons.

Scofield's School Tablets,

On Five Cards, exhibiting Ten Surfaces. These Tablets teach Orthography, Reading, Object-Lessons, Color, Form, etc.

Watson's Phonetic Tablets,

Four Cards, and Eight Surfaces; teaching Pronunciation and Elocution phonetically—for class exercises.

Page's Normal Chart,

The whole science of Elementary Sounds tabulated. By the author of Page's Theory and Practice of Teaching.

Clark's Grammatical Chart,

Exhibits the whole Science of Language in one comprehensive diagram.

Davies' Mathematical Chart,

Mathematics made simple to the eye.

Monteith's Reference Maps, School series, Grand series,

Eight Numbers. Mounted on Rollers. Names all laid down in small type, so that to the pupil at a short distance they are Outline Maps, while they serve as *their own key* to the teacher.

Willard's Chronographers,

Historical. Four Numbers. Ancient Chronographer; English Chronographer; American Chronographer; Temple of Time (general). Dates and Events represented to the eye.

APPARATUS.

Harrington's Geometrical Blocks.

These patented blocks are *hinged*, so that each form can be dissected.

Harrington's Fractional Blocks,

Steele's Chemical Apparatus,

Steele's Philosophical Apparatus, (see p.28)

Steele's Geological Cabinet, (see p.28)

Wood's Botanical Apparatus, (see p.30)

Bock's Physiological Apparatus,

MUSIC.

The National School Singer,

Bright, new music for the day school, embracing Song Lessons, Exercise Songs, Songs of Study, Order, Promptness and Obedience, of Industry and Nature, Patriotic and Temperance Songs, Opening and Closing Songs ; in fact, everything needed in the school-room. By an eminent Musician and Composer.

Jepson's Music Readers. 3 vols.

These are not books from which children simply learn songs, parrot-like, but teach the subject progressively—the scholar learning to read music by methods similar to those employed in teaching him to read printed language. Any teacher, however ignorant of music, provided he can, upon trial, simply sound the scale, may teach it without assistance, and will end by being a good singer himself. The "Elementary Music Reader," or first volume, fully develops the system. The two companion volumes carry the same method into the higher grades, but their use is not essential.

The First Reader is also published in three parts, at 30 cents each, for those who prefer them in that form.

Bartley's School Hymn and Tune Book.

A selection of appropriate Hymns, of an unsectarian character, carefully classified and set to popular and "singable" Tunes, for opening and closing exercises. The National, Anniversary, and Parting Hymns form a valuable feature.

Nash & Bristow's Cantara,

The first volume is a complete musical text-book for schools of every grade. No. 2 is a choice selection of Solos and Part Songs. The authors are Directors of Music in the public schools of New York City, in which these books are the standard of instruction.

The Polytechnic

Collection of Part Songs for High and Normal Schools and Clubs. This work contains a quantity of exceedingly valuable material, heretofore accessible only in sheet form or scattered in numerous and costly works. The collection of "College Songs" is a very attractive feature.

Curtis' Little Singer,—School Vocalist,

Kingsley's School-Room Choir,—Young Ladies' Harp,

Hager's Echo (A Cantata).

DEVOTION.

Brooks' School Manual of Devotion,

This volume contains daily devotional exercises, consisting of a hymn, selections of Scripture for alternate reading by teacher and pupils, and a prayer. Its value for opening and closing school is apparent.

Brooks' School Harmonist,

Contains appropriate *tunes* for each hymn in the "Manual of Devotion" described above.

A. S. BARNES & CO.'S CATALOGUE.

DEPARTMENT OF GENERAL LITERATURE.

PRICES INCLUDING POSTAGE.

THE TEACHERS' LIBRARY.

Object Lessons—Welch, - - - - - - $1 00

This is a complete exposition of the popular modern system of "object-teaching," for teachers of primary classes.

Theory and Practice of Teaching—Page, - - 1 50

This volume has, without doubt, been read by two hundred thousand teachers, and its popularity remains undiminished—large editions being exhausted yearly. It was the pioneer, as it is now the patriarch, of professional works for teachers.

The Graded School—Wells, - - - - - - 1 25

The proper way to organize graded schools is here illustrated. The author has availed himself of the best elements of the several systems prevalent in Boston, New York, Philadelphia, Cincinnati, St. Louis, and other cities.

The Normal—Holbrook, - - - - - - 1 50

Carries a working school on its visit to teachers, showing the most approved methods of teaching all the common branches, including the technicalities, explanations, demonstrations, and definitions introductory and peculiar to each branch.

School Management—Holbrook, - - - - - 1 50

Treating of the Teacher's Qualifications; How to overcome Difficulties in Self and Others; Organization; Discipline; Methods of inciting Diligence and Order; Strategy in Management; Object Teaching.

The Teachers' Institute—Fowle, - - - - - 1 25

This is a volume of suggestions inspired by the author's experience at institutes, in the instruction of young teachers. A thousand points of interest to this class are most satisfactorily dealt with.

Schools and Schoolmasters—Dickens, - - - 1 25

Appropriate selections from the writings of the great novelist.

The Metric System—Davies, - - - - - 1 50

Considered with reference to its general introduction, and embracing the views of John Quincy Adams and Sir John Herschel.

The Student; The Educator—Phelps, - - each, 1 50

The Discipline of Life—Phelps, - - - - 1 75

The authoress of these works is one of the most distinguished writers on education; and they cannot fail to prove a valuable addition to the School and Teachers' Libraries, being in a high degree both interesting and instructive.

A Scientific Basis of Education—Hecker, - - 2 50

Adaptation of study and classification by temperaments.

Teachers' Hand-Book — Phelps - - - - - $1 50

By WM. F. PHELPS, Principal of Minnesota State Normal School. Embracing the objects, history, organization and management of Teachers' Institutes, followed by Methods of Teaching, in detail, for all the fundamental branches. Every young teacher, every practical teacher, every experienced teacher even, needs this book.

From the New York Tribune.

"The discipline of the school should prepare the child for the discipline of life. The country schoolmaster, accordingly, holds a position of vital interest to the destiny of the republic, and should neglect no means for the wise and efficient discharge of his significant functions. This is the key-note of the present excellent volume. In view of the supreme importance of the teacher's calling, Mr. Phelps has presented an elaborate system of instruction in the elements of learning, with a complete detail of methods and processes, illustrated with an abundance of practical examples and enforced by judicious counsels, which may serve as an aid to the teacher in the performance of his arduous duties, and in the attainment of the highest excellence in his profession. The author's directions may not always be accepted without challenge by experienced instructors, who, however, are encouraged to think for themselves; but they are always suggestive, and cannot fail to be of signal value to those who are just entering upon their profession and beginning to comprehend its difficulties, as well as to discover its secrets."

American Education — Mansfield - - - - - 1 50

A treatise on the principles and elements of education, as practised in this country, with ideas towards distinctive republican and Christian education.

American Institutions — De Tocqueville - - - - 1 50

A valuable index to the genius of our Government.

Universal Education — Mayhew - - - - - 1 75

The subject is approached with the clear, keen perception of one who has observed its necessity, and realized its feasibility and expediency alike. The redeeming and elevating power of improved common schools constitutes the inspiration of the volume.

Higher Christian Education — Dwight - - - - 1 50

A treatise on the principles and spirit, the modes, directions and results of all true teaching; showing that right education should appeal to every element of enthusiasm in the teacher's nature.

Oral Training Lessons — Barnard - - - - - 1 00

The object of this very useful work is to furnish material for instructors to impart orally to their classes, in branches not usually taught in common schools, embracing all departments of Natural Science and much general knowledge.

Lectures on Natural History — Chadbourne - - 75

Affording many themes for oral instruction in this interesting science—especially in schools where it is not pursued as a class exercise.

Outlines of Mathematical Science — Davies - - 1 00

A manual suggesting the best methods of presenting mathematical instruction on the part of the teacher, with that comprehensive view of the whole which is necessary to the intelligent treatment of a part, in science.

Nature and Utility of Mathematics — Davies - - 1 50

An elaborate and lucid exposition of the principles which lie at the foundation of pure mathematics, with a highly ingenious application of their results to the development of the essential idea of the different branches of the science.

Mathematical Dictionary — Davies and Peck - - 5 00

This cyclopædia of mathematical science defines, with completeness, precision, and accuracy, every technical term; thus constituting a popular treatise on each branch, and a general view of the whole subject.

Liberal Education of Women—Orton . . *$1 50

Treats of "the demand and the method;" being a compilation of the best and most advanced thought on this subject, by the leading writers and educators in England and America. Edited by a Professor in Vassar College.

Education Abroad—Northrop *1 50

A thorough discussion of the advantages and disadvantages of sending American children to Europe to be educated; also, Papers on Legal Prevention of Illiteracy, Study and Health, Labor as an Educator, and other kindred subjects. By the Hon. Secretary of Education for Connecticut.

The Teacher and the Parent—Northend . . *1 50

A treatise upon common-school education, designed to lead teachers to view their calling in its true light, and to stimulate them to fidelity.

The Teachers' Assistant—Northend *1 50

A natural continuation of the author's previous work, more directly calculated for daily use in the administration of school discipline and instruction.

School Government—Jewell *1 50

Full of advanced ideas on the subject which its title indicates. The criticisms upon current theories of punishment and schemes of administration have excited general attention and comment.

Grammatical Diagrams—Jewell *1 00

The diagram system of teaching grammar explained, defended, and improved. The curious in literature, the searcher for truth, those interested in new inventions, as well as the disciples of Prof. Clark, who would see their favorite theory fairly treated, all want this book. There are many who would like to be made familiar with this system before risking its use in a class. The opportunity is here afforded.

The Complete Examiner—Stone *1 25

Consists of a series of questions on every English branch of school and academic instruction, with reference to a given page or article of leading text-books where the answer may be found in full. Prepared to aid teachers in securing certificates, pupils in preparing for promotion, and teachers in selecting review questions.

School Amusements—Root *1 50

To assist teachers in making the school interesting, with hints upon the management of the school-room. Rules for military and gymnastic exercises are included. Illustrated by diagrams.

Institute Lectures—Bates *1 50

These lectures, originally delivered before institutes, are based upon various topics in the departments of mental and moral culture. The volume is calculated to prepare the will, awaken the inquiry, and stimulate the thought of the zealous teacher.

Method of Teachers' Institutes—Bates . . . *75

Sets forth the best method of conducting institutes, with a detailed account of the object, organization, plan of instruction, and true theory of education on which such instruction should be based.

History and Progress of Education *1 50

The systems of education prevailing in all nations and ages, the gradual advance to the present time, and the bearing of the past upon the present in this regard, are worthy of the careful investigation of all concerned in education.

THE SCHOOL LIBRARY.

The two elements of instruction and entertainment were never more happily combined than in this collection of standard books. Children and adults alike will here find ample food for the mind, of the sort that is easily *digested*, while not degenerating to the level of modern romance.

LIBRARY OF LITERATURE.

Milton's Paradise Lost. Boyd's Illustrated Ed., $1 60

Young's Night Thoughts . . . . do. . . 1 60

Cowper's Task, Table Talk, &c. .. do. . . 1 60

Thomson's Seasons . . . . do. . . 1 60

Pollok's Course of Time . . . . do. . . 1 60

These works, models of the best and purest literature, are beautifully illustrated, and notes explain all doubtful meanings.

Lord Bacon's Essays (Boyd's Edition) . . . 1 60

Another grand English classic, affording the highest example of purity in language and style.

The Iliad of Homer. Translated by POPE. . . 80

Those who are unable to read this greatest of ancient writers in the original, should not fail to avail themselves of this metrical version.

Compendium of Eng. Literature—Cleveland, 2 25

English Literature of XIXth Century do. 2 25

Compendium of American Literature do. 2 25

Nearly one hundred and fifty thousand volumes of Prof. CLEVELAND's inimitable compendiums have been sold. Taken together they present a complete view of literature. To the man who can afford but a few books these will supply the place of an extensive library. From commendations of the very highest authorities the following extracts will give some idea of the enthusiasm with which the works are regarded by scholars:

With the Bible and your volumes one might leave libraries without very painful regret.—The work cannot be found from which in the same limits so much interesting and valuable information may be obtained.—Good taste, fine scholarship, familiar acquaintance with literature, unwearied industry, tact acquired by practice, an interest in the culture of the young, and regard for truth, purity, philanthropy and religion are united in Mr. Cleveland.—A judgment clear and impartial, a taste at once delicate and severe.—The biographies are just and discriminating.—An admirable bird's-eye view.—Acquaints the reader with the characteristic method, tone, and quality of each writer.—Succinct, carefully written, and wonderfully comprehensive in detail, etc., etc.

Milton's Poetical Works—CLEVELAND . . . 2 25

This is the very best edition of the great Poet. It includes a life of the author, notes, dissertations on each poem, a faultless text, and is *the only* edition of Milton with a complete verbal Index.

LIBRARY OF HISTORY.

Seven Historic Ages—Gilman, - - - - $1 00

Or, Talks about Kings, Queens, and Barbarians. These delightful sketches of notable events stir the imagination of the young reader, and give him a taste for further historical reading. Illustrated.

Outlines of General History—Gilman, - - - 1 25

The number of facts which the author has compressed into these outline sketches is really surprising; the chapters on the Middle Ages and Feudalism afford striking examples of his power of succinct but comprehensive statement. In his choice of representative periods and events in the histories of Nations he shows very sound judgment, and his characterization of conspicuous historical figures is accurate and impartial.

Great Events of History—Collier, - - - - - 1 50

This celebrated work, edited for American readers by Prof. O. R. Willis, gives, in a series of pictures, a pleasantly readable and easily remembered view of the Christian era. Each chapter is headed by its central point of interest to afford association for the mind. Delineations of life and manners at different periods are interwoven. A geographical appendix of great value is added.

History of England—Lancaster, - - - - - 1 50

An arrangement of the essential facts of English History in the briefest manner consistent with clearness. With a fine Map.

History of Liberty—Aiken, - - - - - - 1 00

Explaining the growth of the "fair consummate flower" of freedom in America as the result of centuries of trial and experience in the Old World.

Critical History of the Civil War—Mahan, - - 3 00

A logical analysis of campaigns and battles, and the causes of victory and defeat. By Dr. Asa Mahan, first President of Oberlin College. Dr. Mahan never forgets that history is "philosophy teaching by examples," and his work should be a text-book for American youth.

History of Europe—Alison, - - - - - - 2 50

A reliable and standard work, which covers with clear, connected, and complete narrative the eventful occurrences of the years A. D. 1789 to 1815, being mainly a history of the career of Napoleon Bonaparte.

History of Rome—Ricord, - - - - - - 1 75

An entertaining narrative for the young. Illustrated. Embracing successively, The Kings; The Republic; The Empire.

Ecclesiastical History—Marsh, - - - - - - 2 00

A history of the Church in all ages, with a comprehensive review of all forms of religion from the creation of the world. No other source affords, in the same compass, the information here conveyed.

History of the Ancient Hebrews—Mills, - - - 1 75

The record of "God's people" from the call of Abraham to the destruction of Jerusalem; gathered from sources sacred and profane.

The Mexican War—Mansfield, - - - - - 1 50

A history of its origin, and a detailed account of its victories; with official despatches, the treaty of peace, and valuable tables. Illustrated.

Early History of Michigan—Sheldon, - - - 2 50

A work of value and deep interest to the people of the West. Compiled under the supervision of Hon. Lewis Cass. Portraits.

History of Texas—Baker, - - - - - - 1 25

A pithy and interesting resumé. Copiously illustrated. The State constitution and extracts from the speeches and writings of eminent Texans are appended.

NEW LIBRARY OF HISTORY.

Barnes' Centenary History, - - - - - - *$6 00

"*One Hundred Years of American Independence.*" This superbly illustrated work, by the author of "Barnes' Brief Histories" (for schools), is appropriately issued in the "centennial year" (1876). An extended Introduction brings down the history from the earliest times. The leading idea is to make American History *popular* for the masses, and especially with the young. The style is therefore life-like and vivid, carrying the reader along by the sweep of the story as in a novel, so that when he begins an account of an important event he cannot very well lay down the book until he finishes.

☞ *Sold only by subscription.*

Lamb's History of New York City.

One of the most important works ever issued. It opens with a brief outline of the condition of the old world prior to the settlement of the new, and proceeds to give a careful analysis of the two great Dutch Commercial Corporations to which New York owes its origin. It sketches the rise and growth of the little colony on Manhattan Island; describes the Indian Wars with which it was afflicted; gives color and life to its Dutch rulers; paints its subjugation by the English, its after vicissitudes, the Revolution of 1689; in short, it leads the reader through one continuous chain of events down to the American Revolution. Then, gathering up the threads, the author gives an artistic and comprehensive account of the progress of the City, in extent, education, culture, literature, art, and political and commercial importance, during the last century. Prominent persons are introduced in all the different periods, with choice bits of family history, and glimpses of social life. The work contains maps of the City in the different decades, and several rare portraits from original paintings, which have never before been engraved. The illustrations, about 250 in number, are all of an interesting and highly artistic character.

The work is now being published, by subscription only, in about 30 parts, at 50 cents each.

Carrington's Battles of the Revolution, - - - - $6 00

A careful description and analysis of every engagement of the War for Independence, with topographical charts prepared from personal surveys by the author, a veteran officer of the U. S. Army, and Professor of Military Science in Wabash College.

Baker's Texas Scrap-Book, - - - - - - $5 00

Comprising the History, Biography, Literature, and Miscellany of Texas and its people. A valuable collection of material, anecdotical and statistical, which is not to be found in any other form. The work is handsomely illustrated. (Sheep, $6.00.)

LIBRARY OF REFERENCE.

Home Cyclopædia of Literature and Fine Arts, - $3 00

A complete index to all terms employed in belles lettres, philosophy, theology, law, mythology, painting, music, sculpture, architecture, and all kindred arts.

The Rhyming Dictionary—Walker, - - - - 1 25

A serviceable manual to composers, being a complete index of allowable rhymes.

The Topical Lexicon—Williams, - - - - - 1 75

The useful terms of the English language *classified by subjects* and arranged according to their affinities of meaning, with etymologies, definitions, and illustrations. A very entertaining and instructive work.

Mathematical Dictionary—Davies and Peck, - - 5 00

A thorough compendium of the science, with illustrations and definitions.

LIBRARY OF BIOGRAPHY.

Autobiography of President Finney, - - - $2 00

The "Memoirs of Rev. Charles G. Finney, written by himself," with Portrait on steel. The work presents the experience, labors, and thoughts of the eminent Evangelist, Preacher, and Teacher. It gives the history of the great revivals in which he labored, and also his work in connection with Oberlin College.

The book is full of personal incidents illustrating the power of the Gospel upon the hearts and lives of men, and of practical suggestions for the promotion of revivals. It is also rich in its exhibition of personal religious experience, and of the nature and the efficacy of prayer.

Life of P. P. Bliss—Whittle, Moody & Sankey, - - 2 00

The memorials of the lamented singer and evangelist which have here been gathered by the hands of loving friends will commend themselves to a great multitude of interested readers. Ten thousand copies of the book were sold within thirty days after publication. It contains steel-plate engravings of the Bliss family, and a number of new songs with music not before published.

Life of Dr. Sam Johnson—Boswell, - - - 2 25

This work has been before the public for seventy years, with increasing approbation. Boswell is known as "the prince of biographers."

Henry Clay's Life and Speeches—Mallory. 2 vols., 4 50

This great American statesman commands the admiration, and his character and deeds solicit the study of every patriot.

Life and Services of General Scott—Mansfield, - 1 75

The hero of the Mexican war, who was for many years the most prominent figure in American military circles, should not be forgotten in the whirl of more recent events than those by which he signalized himself. Illustrated.

Garibaldi's Autobiography, - - - - - - 1 50

The Italian patriot's record of his own life, translated and edited by his friend and admirer. A thrilling narrative of a romantic career. With portrait.

Lives of the Signers—Dwight, . - - - 1 50

The memory of the noble men who declared our country free at the peril of their own "lives, fortunes, and sacred honor," should be embalmed in every American's heart.

Life of Sir Joshua Reynolds—Cunningham, - - 1 50

A candid, truthful, and appreciative memoir of the great painter, with a compilation of his discourses. The volume is a text-book for artists, as well as those who would acquire the rudiments of art. With a portrait.

Prison Life, - - - - - - - - - 75

Interesting biographies of celebrated prisoners and martyrs, designed especially for the instruction and cultivation of youth.

LIBRARY OF TRAVEL.

Life in the Sandwich Islands—Cheever . .$1 50

The "heart of the Pacific, as it was and is," shows most vividly the contrast between the depth of degradation and barbarism, and the light and liberty of civilization, so rapidly realized in these islands under the humanizing influence of the Christian religion. Illustrated.

The Republic of Liberia—Stockwell . . . 1 25

This volume treats of the geography, climate, soil, and productions of this interesting country on the coast of Africa, with a History of its early settlement. Our colored citizens especially, from whom the founders of the new State went forth, should read Mr. Stockwell's account of it. It is so arranged as to be available for a School Reader, and in colored schools is peculiarly appropriate as an instrument of education for the young. Liberia is likely to bear an important part in the future of their race.

Ancient Monasteries of the East—Curzon . 1 50

The exploration of these ancient seats of learning has thrown much light upon the researches of the historian, the philologist, and the theologian, as well as the general student of antiquity. Illustrated.

Discoveries in Babylon & Nineveh—Layard 1 75

Valuable alike for the information imparted with regard to these most interesting ruins, and the pleasant adventures and observations of the author in regions that to most men seem like Fairyland. Illustrated.

A Run Through Europe—Benedict, ... 2 00

A work replete with instruction and interest—an admirable guide-book.

St. Petersburgh—Jermann 1 00

Americans are less familiar with the history and social customs of the Russian people than those of any other modern civilized nation. Opportunities such as this book affords are not, therefore, to be neglected.

The Polar Regions—Osborn 1 25

A thrilling and intensely interesting narrative of one of the famous expeditions in search of Sir John Franklin—unsuccessful in its main object, but adding many facts to the repertoire of science.

Thirteen Months in the Confederate Army 75

The author, a northern man conscripted into the Confederate service, and rising from the ranks by soldierly conduct to positions of responsibility, had remarkable opportunities for the acquisition of facts respecting the conduct of the Southern armies, and the policy and deeds of their leaders. He participated in many engagements, and his book is one of the most exciting narratives of adventure ever published. Mr. Stevenson takes no ground as a partizan, but views the whole subject as with the eye of a neutral—only interested in subserving the ends of history by the contribution of impartial facts. Illustrated.

RELIGIOUS LIBRARY.

Abbott's Commentaries—MATTHEW AND MARK, $2 50

With Notes, Comments, Maps, and Illustrations; also, an Introduction to the study of the New Testament, a condensed Life of Christ, and a Tabular Harmony of the Gospels. Trade edition, $2.50; subscription edition, royal 8vo, $3.50.

ACTS OF THE APOSTLES, $1 75

With Notes, etc., as above; also, an Introduction to its study, a Gazetteer, Chronological Table, etc.

Ray Palmer's Poetical Works, ... 4 00

An exquisite edition of the complete hymns and other poetical writings of the most eminent of American sacred poets—author of "My faith looks up to Thee."

Dale on the Atonement, ... 2 00

The theory and fact of Christ's atonement profoundly considered.

The Service of Song—Stacy 1 50

A treatise on Singing, in public and private devotion. Its history, office, and importance considered.

True Success in Life—Palmer 1 50

Earnest words for the young who are just about to meet the responsibilities and temptations of mature life.

"Remember Me"—Palmer 1 50

Preparation for the Holy Communion.

Chrysostom, or the Mouth of Gold—Johnson 1 00

An entertaining dramatic sketch, by Rev. Edwin Johnson, illustrating the life and times of St. Chrysostom.

The Memorial Pulpit—Robinson. 2 vols., each 1 50

A series of wide-awake sermons by the popular pastor of the Memorial Presbyterian Church, New York.

Responsive Worship—Budington 60

An argument in favor of alternate Scripture reading by Pastor and Congregation.

Lady Willoughby 1 00

The diary of a wife and mother. An historical romance of the seventeenth century. At once beautiful and pathetic, entertaining and instructive.

Favorite Hymns Restored—Gage 1 25

Most of the standard hymns have undergone modification or abridgment by compilers, but this volume contains them exactly as written by the authors.

Poets' Gift of Consolation 1 50

A beautiful selection of poems referring to the death of children.

The Mosaic Account of Creation 1 50

The Miracle of To-day; or New Witnesses of the Oneness of Genesis and Science. With Essays on the Cause and Epoch of the present Inclination of the Earth's Axis, and on Cosmology. By Charles B. Warring.

VALUABLE LIBRARY BOOKS.

Principles and Acts of the Revolution, . . 3 00

Compiled from "Niles's Register." Being "a collection of Speeches, Orations, and Proceedings, with Sketches and Remarks on Men and Things." This work has long been standard, though for many years out of print, and the eager demand for its republication induces the publishers to offer this new edition.

American Institutions—De Tocqueville . . 1 50

Democracy in America—De Tocqueville . . 2 50

The views of this distinguished foreigner on the genius of our political institutions are of unquestionable value, as proceeding from a standpoint whence we seldom have an opportunity to hear.

Constitutions of the United States 2 25

Contains the Constitution of the General Government, and of the several State Governments, the Declaration of Independence, and other important documents relating to American history. Indispensable as a work of reference.

Public Economy of the United States . . . 2 25

A full discussion of the relations of the United States with other nations, especially the feasibility of a free-trade policy.

Grecian and Roman Mythology—Dwight . 3 00

The presentation, in a systematic form, of the Fables of Antiquity, affords most entertaining reading, and is valuable to all as an index to the mythological allusions so frequent in literature, as well as to students of the classics who would peruse intelligently the classical authors. Illustrated.

General View of the Fine Arts—Huntington 1 75

The preparation of this work was suggested by the interested inquiries of a group of young people concerning the productions and styles of the great masters of art, whose names only were familiar. This statement is sufficient index of its character.

The Poets of Connecticut—Everest 1 75

With the biographical sketches, this volume forms a complete history of the poetical literature of the State.

The Son of a Genius—Hofland 75

A juvenile classic which never wears out, and finds many interested readers in every generation of youth.

Sunny Hours of Childhood 75

Interesting and moral stories for children.

Morals for the Young—Willard 75

A series of moral stories, by one of the most experienced of American educators. Illustrated.

Improvement of the Mind—Isaac Watts . . 50

A classical standard. No young person should grow up without having perused it.

PUBLIC WORSHIP.

Songs for the Sanctuary, ... $2 25

By Rev. S. C. Robinson. 1344 Hymns, with Tunes. The most successful modern hymn and tune book, for congregations and choirs. More than 200,000 copies have been sold. Separate editions for Presbyterian, Congregational, and Baptist Churches. Editions without Tunes, $1.75; in large type, $2.50. Abridged edition ("Songs for Christian Worship"), 859 Hymns, with Tunes, $1.50. Chapel edition, 607 Hymns, with Tunes, $1.40.

Psalms and Hymns and Spiritual Songs, . 2 25

Also by Dr. Robinson. Differs from "Songs for the Sanctuary" in having *all the hymns* set to music, for pure congregational singing. 1294 Psalms and Hymns, with Tunes. Cheap edition, $1.75; edition without Tunes, 75 cents.

Baptist Praise Book, ... 2 50

By Rev. Drs. Fuller, Levy, Phelps, Fish, Armitage, Winkler, Evarts, Lorimer and Manly, and J. P. Holbrook, Esq. 1311 Hymns, with Tunes. Edition without Tunes, $1.75. Chapel edition, 550 Hymns, with Tunes, $1.25.

Plymouth Collection, ... 2 00

(Congregational.) By Rev. Henry Ward Beecher. 1374 Hymns, with Tunes. Separate edition for Baptist Churches. Editions without Tunes, $1.25 and $1.75.

Hymns of the Church, ... 2 25

(Undenominational.) By Rev. Drs. Thompson, Vermilye, and Eddy. 1007 Hymns, with Tunes. The use of this book is required in all congregations of the Reformed Church in America. Edition without Tunes, $1.75. Chapel edition ("Hymns of Prayer and Praise"), 320 Hymns, with Tunes, 75 cts.

Episcopal Common Praise, ... 2 25

The Service set to appropriate Music, with Tunes for all the Hymns in the Book of Common Prayer.

Hymnal, with Tunes, ... 1 25

(Episcopal.) By Hall & Whiteley. The new Hymnal, set to Music. Edition with Chants, $1.50. Edition of Hymns only ("Companion" Hymnal), 60 cts.

Metrical Tune Book. By Philip Phillips. 1 00

Quartet and Chorus Choir. By J. P. Holbrook. . 2 50

Containing Music for the Unadapted Hymns in Songs for the Sanctuary.

Pilgrim Melodies. By J. E. Sweetser. 1 25

Christian Melodies. By Geo. B. Cheever. Hymns and Tunes. 1 00

Mount Zion Collection. By T. E. Perkins. For the Choir. 1 25

Selah. By Thos. Hastings. For the Choir. 1 25

Public Worship (Partly Responsive) 1 00

Containing complete services (not Episcopal) for five Sabbaths; for use in schools, public institutions, summer resorts, churches without a settled pastor; in short, wherever Christians desire to worship—no clergyman being present.

The Union Prayer Book, ... 2 50

A Manual for Public and Private Worship. With those features which are objectionable to other denominations of Christians than Episcopal eliminated or modified. Contains a Service for Sunday Schools and Family Prayers.

The Psalter, ... 16mo, 60 cts.; 8vo, 90

Selections from the Psalms, for responsive reading.

IMPORTANT LIBRARY BOOKS.

Student's Common-Place Book—Fox, - - - $4 50

The result of over thirty years effective reading by a clergyman and teacher, forming a Cyclopedia of Illustration and Fact. Interleaved for Additions by the owner; thus combining a printed Manual of Literature with the Blanks of an Index Rerum. Its double value will make it the favorite book of the library.

Biographical and Critical Essays—Atlas Series, - - 1 50

Choice articles from the International Review on Macaulay, Ticknor, Ernst Curtius, Hamerton, Longfellow, Bryant, Poe, Chas. Tennyson, Freeman, Sumner, John Stuart Mill. By Edward A. Freeman, and other eminent writers.

Formation of Religious Opinions—Palmer, - - 1 25

Hints for the benefit of young people who have found themselves disturbed by inward questionings or doubts concerning the Christian faith.

Outlines of English Literature—Gilman, - - - 1 00

Gives, within the compass of two hundred pages, a suggestive outline sketch of the history of English Literature, grouping authors in accordance with the development of the language and literature.

PERIODICALS.

The International Review, - - - - - - $5 00

As its title indicates, presents "the ripest and best thought of the age" in all countries. Its contributors are the leading thinkers and writers of both Continents. Published bi-monthly, $5.00 per year. Bound volumes for 1874 and succeeding years, each, $6.00.

Magazine of American History, - - - - - 5 00

For the collection and preservation of all material relating to our country. Edited by John Austin Stevens, Librarian of the New York Historical Society. Monthly, $5.00 per year.

FURNITURE.

(SUPPLIED BY THE NATIONAL SCHOOL FURNITURE CO.)

PEARD'S PATENT FOLDING DESK AND SETTEE.

This great improvement for the school-room has come already into such astonishing demand as to tax the utmost resources of the company's two factories to supply it. By a simple movement the desk-lid is folded away over the back of the settee attached in front, making a false back, and at once converting the school-room into a lecture or assembly-room. When the seat also is folded, the whole occupies *only ten inches of space*, leaving room for gymnastic exercises, marching, etc., or for the janitor to clean the room effectively.

NATIONAL STUDY DESK AND SETTEE.

When not in use for writing, the desk-lid slides back vertically into a chamber, leaving in front an "easel," with clamps, upon which the student places his book and studies in an erect posture. As a folding-desk this offers many of the same advantages as the "Peard."

THE GEM' DESK AND SETTEE.

Fixed top, and folding seat. This is the *neatest* pattern of the Standard School Desk, and the *strongest* in use.

THE ECONOMIC DESK AND SETTEE.

This is the *cheapest* good desk, with stationary lid and folding seat.

All descriptions of

HIGH SCHOOL DESKS,	**SCHOOL SETTEES,**
TEACHERS' DESKS,	**CHURCH SETTEES,**
BLACKBOARDS,	**PEW ENDS,**
CHAIRS,	**LECTERNS, Etc.**

Also,

TAYLOR'S PATENT

CLASS AND LECTURE CHAIR.

The difficulty of reconciling furniture appropriate for the Lecture-room or Church with that convenient for the Sunday-school is an old one. This article effectually remedies it. It consists simply of a plan by which chairs of a somewhat peculiar shape are connected with a coupling. The rows of chairs thus adjusted may at pleasure and with ease be spread out straight in one line, forming pews or benches; or they may be bent in an instant into a semi-circular form to accomodate classes of any size to receive instruction from teachers seated in their midst.

For further particulars, consult catalogues of the National School Furniture Co. and the Taylor Patent Chair Co., which may be obtained of A. S. Barnes & Co.

The Peabody Correspondence.

New York, April 29, 1867.

To the Board of Trustees of the Peabody Educational Fund:

Gentlemen—Having been for many years intimately connected with the educational interests of the South, we are desirous of expressing our appreciation of the noble charity which you represent. The Peabody Fund, to encourage and aid common schools in these war-desolated States, cannot fail of accomplishing a great and good work, the beneficent results of which, as they will be exhibited in the future, not only of the stricken population of the South, but of the nation at large, seem almost incalculable.

It is probable that the use of meritorious text-books will prove a most effective agency toward the thorough accomplishment of Mr. Peabody's benevolent design. As we publish many which are considered such, we have selected from our list some of the most valuable, and ask the privilege of placing them in your hands for gratuitous distribution in connection with the fund of which you have charge, among the teachers and in the schools of the destitute South.

Observing that the training of teachers (through the agency of Normal Schools and otherwise) is to be a prominent feature of your undertaking, we offer you for this purpose 5,000 volumes of the " Teacher's Library "—a series of professional works designed for the efficient self-education of those who are in their turn to teach others—as follows:—

500 Page's Theory and Practice of Teaching.
500 Welch's Manual of Object-Lessons.
500 Davies' Outlines of Mathematical Science.
250 Holbrook's Normal Methods of Teaching.
250 Wells on Graded Schools.
250 Jewell on School Government.
250 Fowle's Teachers' Institute.
250 Bates' Method of Teachers' Institutes
250 De Tocqueville's American Instit'ns.
250 Dwight's Higher Christian Educat'n.
250 History of Education.
250 Mansfield on American Education.
250 Mayhew on Universal Education.
250 Northend's Teacher's Assistant.
250 Northend's Teacher and Parent.
250 Root on School Amusement.
250 Stone's Teachers' Examiner.

In addition to these we also ask that you will accept 25,000 volumes of school books for intermediate classes, embracing—

5,000 The National Second Reader.
5,000 Davies' Written Arithmetic.
5,000 Monteith's Second Book in Geography.
3,000 Monteith's United States History.
5,000 Beers' Penmanship.
500 First Book of Science.
500 Jarvis' Physiology and Health.
500 Peck's Ganot's Natural Philosophy.
500 Smith & Martin's Book-keeping.

Should your Board consent to undertake the distribution of these volumes, we shall hold ourselves in readiness to pack and ship the same in such quantities and to such points as you may designate.

We further propose that, should you find it advisable to use a greater quantity of our publications in the prosecution of your plans, we will donate, for the benefit of this cause, *twenty-five per cent.* of the usual wholesale price of the books needed.

Hoping that our request will meet with your approval, and that we may have the pleasure of contributing in this way to wants with which we deeply sympathize, we are, gentlemen, very respectfully yours, A. S. BARNES & CO.

Boston, May 7, 1867.

Messrs. A. S. Barnes & Co., Publishers, New York:

Gentlemen—Your communication of the 29th ult., addressed to the Trustees of the Peabody Education Fund, has been handed to me by our general agent, the Rev. Dr. Sears. I shall take the greatest pleasure in laying it before the board at their earliest meeting. I am unwilling, however, to postpone its acknowledgment so long, and hasten to assure you of the high value which I place upon your gift. Five thousand volumes of your " Teachers' Library," and twenty-five thousand volumes of " School-books for intermediate classes," make up a most munificent contribution to the cause of Southern education in which we are engaged. Dr. Sears is well acquainted with the books you have so generously offered us, and unites with me in the highest appreciation of the gift. You will be glad to know, too, that your letter reached us in season to be communicated to Mr. Peabody, before he embarked for England on the 1st inst., and that he expressed the greatest gratification and gratitude on hearing what you had offered.

Believe me, gentlemen, with the highest respect and regard, your obliged and obedient servant, ROBT. C. WINTHROP, Chairman.

www.ingramcontent.com/pod-product-compliance
Lightning Source LLC
LaVergne TN
LVHW010247110826
845151LV00004B/1409

* 9 7 8 1 4 2 5 5 2 3 1 2 1 *